Verbivore's
FEAST

A BANQUET OF
WORD & PHRASE
ORIGINS

from
Chrysti the Wordsmith

FARCOUNTRY
PRESS
Helena, Montana

For more information on our books write Farcountry Press,
P.O. Box 5630, Helena, MT 59604; call (800) 821-3874;
or visit www.farcountrypress.com.

Created, produced, and designed in the United States.
Printed in Canada.

08 07 06 05 04   1 2 3 4 5

Library of Congress Cataloging-in-Publication Data

Chrysti, the Wordsmith.
  Verbivore's feast : a banquet of word and phrase origins / from Chrysti
the Wordsmith.
       p. cm.
  Includes bibliographical references and index.
  ISBN 1-56037-267-2 (softbound) -- ISBN 1-56037-265-6 (hardbound)
  1. English language--Etymology. 2. English language--Terms and
phrases. I. Title.
  PE1571.C48 2004
  422--dc22
                                  2004004390

To Steven B. Mueller
(1961–1997)

Preface

I was twenty-one when I became officially wordstruck. Listening to the radio in my apartment one spring morning, I heard poet/etymologist John Ciardi (host of National Public Radio's *A Word in Your Ear*) discuss the development of the word *jazz*. For three minutes he parsed the term, contemplating its age, intoning its various pronunciations, and calling to life the players involved in its development.

I was transfixed. By the time Ciardi signed off, I wanted everything: the radio, Ciardi's voice, his brain, his books. I wanted to devour the paper he had typed on and read from. But most of all I coveted the word *jazz,* everything it stood for, the people who shaped it, and all the places it had lived.

Though I had been a casual dictionary reader for several years, occasionally memorizing terms and their definitions, on that spring morning I dedicated myself to words with the zeal of a convert. Renouncing my lukewarm reading habits and substandard dictionary, I began agitating the pages of the *Oxford English Dictionary* for more *jazz*-like stories.

I found them. *Dyspepsia,* Greek for "bad digestion." *Guillotine,* from Joseph Guillotine, French physician who advocated use of the device during the French Revolution. *Muslin,* after Mosul, Iraq, where the cloth was manufactured. *Chicago,* Algonquin for "garlic field."—*O mirabile dictu!* (Latin, "wonderful to relate!")

Though these word histories were indeed wonderful for me to relate, I found few people with the patience to listen to my clumsy storytelling. Never very vocally articulate, I usually puzzled my audience before I managed to tie the ends of the word-tale together. Frozen smiles hinted that my narrative skills were, at best, embryonic.

So I took a hiatus from telling word histories and concentrated on the geeky business of dictionary collecting. First there were the antiques snatched up for a dollar or two at yard sales and thrift stores. Then there came the language pundit's tomes: *I Always Look up the Word Egregious* by Maxwell Nurnberg, *What's the Good Word?* by William Safire, *Word Origins and Their Romantic Stories* by Wilfred Funk. Words prowled around my house, snuffled at my door, stared through the window. By the dozens, nay, the hundreds, I took them in and bid them welcome, embracing them as my own. Soon, they wanted *out*.

And then—*mirabile dictu!*—along came KGLT. Housed on the campus of Montana State University in Bozeman (where I had enrolled as an anthropology student in 1989), KGLT is a classic free-form university radio station. Staffed by students and community volunteers, KGLT offers live DJ programming twenty-four hours a day and is refreshingly unsullied by corporate or commercial concerns.

KGLT may be one of the few remaining venues where a dictionary lover and verbivore with no radio experience could, say, launch an audio series about the stories behind words. It was a scheme I nervously incubated for weeks before approaching the station's general manager, Phil Charles. Charles approved of the idea and generously took a chance on turning me loose in the studio to record a series of essays and stories about words and dictionaries.

I called the show *Chrysti the Wordsmith* after (and bloody

cleverly, I thought) my name, Chrysti Smith. The two-minute daily series was launched in 1990, my sophomore year at MSU–Bozeman. Serendipitously, I was paired with experienced radio engineer/producer Barrett Golding, who for five years mentored me in the crafts of radio writing and microphone wrangling.

Hosting the series addressed many issues at once. It provided the escape valve for all the words cramming every convolution of my brain. Because I carefully wrote and narrated every installment, my improvisational storytelling impulses began to lie politely, mercifully dormant. Writing and recording on deadlines taught me much about words, dictionaries, and general linguistic principles.

My quest for information and ideas for the show led me to individuals with inspirational knowledge and enthusiasm. Tom Roll, my academic advisor, guided me to the answers to many cultural and anthropological questions. Chris and Carolyn Pinet cheerfully helped with French and Spanish terms. Alanna Brown gave constant encouragement. Many early radio scripts were edited by Marjorie Smith. Gwyn Ganjeau and Nancy Kessler gave me some smashing words and lively conversations about them. The late educator and wordsmith Gerald Sullivan was an inspiration.

My thanks go to many: Phil Charles and KGLT for taking the chance. Barrett Golding, more than words can say. Marvin Granger and his staff at Yellowstone Public Radio in Billings, who have been so supportive since first carrying the series in 1991. Stuart Weber, preeminent Montana guitarist, who provides the theme music for the *Chrysti the Wordsmith* series, from his *Hired Man's Dream* on Bridger Records. The many friends and acquaintences who've suggested intriguing words for the series.

Producer Karen Gaulke, script editor Phil Gaines, and studio engineer Nous are indispensable to the success of the radio series.

Tim Crawford of Pheasant Farms and Hal and Cristina Berg of Rocky Mountain Roasting Company in Bozeman keep *Chrysti the Wordsmith* on the air with their generous corporate sponsorship.

My family, Carol Smith and Rhonda Smith, unfailingly cheer me on. My late father, Bud, a maverick wordsmith, lit the flame. Thanks to Rusty for steady companionship. Awesome Polka Babes Tana, Cynthia, Mary, Marjorie, and Nyla have been there through it all.

Thanks to all at Farcountry Press who not only took on this project but also made it a pleasant experience. All errors and omissions in the text belong to me, and with trepidation do I claim them.

All the stories in this book have previously been broadcast on KGLT-FM in Bozeman and Yellowstone Public Radio (KEMC-FM) in Billings. The edited, printed collection is called *Verbivore's Feast*. Bon apetit!

Aardvark, Aardwolf

Most of us are acquainted with the word *aardvark,* not from safari sightings nor zoo-viewings, but from its conspicuous double-*a* place on the first pages of dictionaries and encyclopedias. And the first illustration in these books is generally of an aardvark, too—an odd, humped-up creature with a tubular snout and rabbity ears.

This African mammal is also equipped with powerful claws for excavating termite mounds in search of its favorite food. When it locates a rich vein of termites, the aardvark laps them up with its sticky, 18-inch tongue.

Aardvarks are protected against termite attacks by the ability to seal their nostrils, which are further buttressed by a fringe of stiff bristles. Shy and nocturnal, aardvarks spend the daylight hours in underground dens.

The name of this creature comes to English from Afrikaans, a language spoken in South Africa by the descendants of 17th century Dutch immigrants. The animal's subterranean habits, coupled with its swinelike appearance, suggested the name *aardvark,* Afrikaans for "earth-pig."

The aardwolf, another denizen of southern Africa, is a hyena-like creature that also raids termite mounds for food. Like the aardvark, this animal is nocturnal and burrow-dwelling, earning for itself the Afrikaaner name *aardwolf,* "earth-wolf."

ACADEMY

The word *academy* has a lofty denotation. Who would have thought that its roots are found in the passions leading to the infamous Trojan War? That conflict was ignited when the handsome Paris of Troy seduced and kidnapped Helen, the beautiful queen of Sparta. This was Helen's most famous abduction, but it was not her first.

Helen was still a child when the Greek hero Theseus kidnapped and hid her in the city of Athens for safekeeping until she was nubile. Helen's twin brothers, Castor and Pollux, rushed to their little sister's rescue. The brothers threatened war against the city when the Athenians refused to disclose Helen's whereabouts.

Bloodshed was averted when a farmer named Akademos led Castor and Pollux to their captive sister, who was then safely returned to her family in Sparta. In gratitude, the Spartans bought an olive grove near Athens and gave it to the courageous farmer. It was to be called the Grove of Akademos.

Hundreds of years later, in 387 B.C., the philosopher Plato established a school in that very grove and instructed his students there for forty years. After the philosopher's death, Plato's followers continued to study in the Grove of Akademos.

Our language is enriched by this ancient tale because it's from the name of the Athenian farmer, and through Plato and his school, that we derive our modern English word *academy,* a place of learning.

Edmund Hoyle was a British barrister by vocation, but his passion, apparently, was parlor games. In 1742, at the age of 70, Hoyle published *A Short Treatise on the Game of Whist,* a handbook of systematized rules for that card game.

Hoyle followed that publication with a treatise on backgammon and another on chess. His signature work, however, was *Hoyle's Standard Games,* a compilation of rules for several parlor pastimes. It was reprinted hundreds of times and is still available in paperback.

Even after Hoyle's death in 1769, at age 97, his name was printed generically on many types of game rule publications, though the games themselves did not exist in Hoyle's day.

We invoke his name whenever we employ the cliché *according to Hoyle.* His authoritative treatises on parlor games gave us this expression referring to accuracy of game rules. In an extended meaning, *according to Hoyle* is a general idiom for conformity to social rules and correctness in general.

ACHILLES' HEEL

According to Greek mythology, the river Styx, flowing through the Underworld of Hades, made invincible anyone who bathed in its waters. So when a sea nymph named Thetis gave birth to a son, she submerged him in the Styx so he might never know defeat in battle. Grasping her infant tightly by the heel, Thetis plunged him headfirst into the magical waters.

The boy, Achilles, grew to become one the most fearsome warriors of the ancient world. Convinced by his mother of his immortality, Achilles was dauntless on the battlefield, fighting bravely for the Greeks during the Trojan War.

According to one legend, even the sound of his voice sent Troy's army running. The Trojan warriors, led by the mighty Paris, became obsessed with vanquishing the seemingly invincible Achilles.

Finally, the god Apollo revealed to Paris that Achilles was indeed vulnerable to the weapons of war, but only if shot through the heel that Thetis had held above the waters of the Styx. A poisoned arrow from the quiver of Paris ended Achilles' life.

From this ancient story comes the modern expression *Achilles' heel,* a fatal weakness or flaw rendering one vulnerable to failure.

ACRONYMS

An *acronym* is a word formed by joining the first letters of a series of words. The pages of newspapers and magazines are peppered with acronyms: NATO, AIDS, OSHA, MADD, UNICEF. Economical and easy to pronounce, acronyms are indispensable to our written and spoken communication.

The tradition of abbreviation of written text is centuries old. Manuscripts from the Middle Ages and the Renaissance contain countless examples of abbreviations. But during the two world wars, a specialized type of abbreviation, the acronym, arose in response to the coinage of hundreds of war-related terms. The First World War produced the acronym ANZAC, short for Australian and New Zealand Army Corps, the name of the military force that landed on Gallipoli in April 1915.

Coined in 1935, RADAR is the acronym of "radio detection and ranging." A system for detecting underwater objects is SONAR ("sound navigation and ranging"), an acronym first recorded in 1945. The women's branch of the U.S. Navy was the WAVES (Women Appointed for Volunteer Emergency Service).

The word *acronym* itself is a clever hybrid of two Greek terms: *akros,* "tip," and *onyma,* "name." Etymologically, an acronym is a "name" formed from the "tips" or first letters of a string of words. The word appears to have been invented by a Bell Laboratories researcher working on war projects in the early 1940s.

AEGIS

The ancients regarded Zeus as the mightiest god in the Greek pantheon. Dispenser of justice and guardian of order, Zeus had no peer on Mount Olympus. He also controlled the elements. When he rattled his shield, the heavens darkened and thunder pealed from cloud to cloud. Below, mortals trembled with dread.

Zeus' shield, with the power to stir meteorological havoc, was also his refuge. Called the *aegis,* this shield was constructed of goatskin (*aegis* is derived from *aix,* the Greek word for goat) and imbued with protective powers. When the king of the gods battled the terrifying race of giants, the Titans, the aegis protected him. Zeus loaned the shield to his daughter Athena, who often carried it with her into battle.

The glory of the Olympian immortals is now a bit tattered, but the term *aegis* lives on in our vocabulary. No longer referring to Zeus' goatskin shield, the word is now used to figuratively describe a protective influence or authoritative license.

The late word lover and poet John Ciardi said, "Under the aegis of the Medici, Galileo developed the telescope safe from papal interference." In Ciardi's example, the Medici represent an agency of authority and protection—a metaphorical reflection of the aegis of Zeus.

Every word has a secret life hiding behind its dictionary definition. *Aftermath* has a particularly intriguing history, one that takes us to the fragrant hay meadows of ancient Britain.

Aftermath means consequences, results, after-effects. The *math* in this term has nothing to do with numbers. It comes from the 15th century Old English term *mæth,* which meant "a mowing." An aftermath etymologically refers to the cutting of a second hay crop following the harvest of the first and best growth.

By the mid-17th century, the word was used figuratively to mean "resulting condition" or "that which follows an event." It often bears the negative connotations implied in the expressions *aftermath of battle,* or *aftermath of a hurricane.* Warfare and storm suggest a "cutting down" of life and property, just as aftermath is a cutting of hay.

The harvest and preservation of dried grass for livestock has always been an important activity. Hay-reapers of earlier centuries were so valued that they acquired the occupational surname Mather and its variants Mathur and Meder. Harvard president Increase Mather (1639-1723) and the minister Cotton Mather (1663-1728) were descendants of earlier European hay-harvesters.

ALABAMA

The area in the southeastern United States now known as Alabama has been continuously occupied by humans for at least the past 8,000 years. Prehistoric home of the Choctaw, Chickasaw, Creek and Cherokee, the Alabama area had an estimated population of 50,000 before European contact. By 1814, the Spanish, French, and Americans had decimated or displaced most of these native inhabitants. Alabama was declared an American territory in 1817, a state in 1819.

Yet the original inhabitants of the area left many of their words on the Alabama map: *Tuskaloosa, Tuskeegee, Sipsey, Talahatta, Tombigbee,* and even *Alabama* itelf. These are terms of the Muskhogean linguistic family to which all of the native groups belonged.

Tuscaloosa, a city and county in west central Alabama, was named after a Choctaw leader who battled the Spanish explorer Hernando de Soto in 1540. The *Sipsey* River in western Alabama was named after the Choctaw word for cottonwood. *Alabama* is a Choctaw word that has been translated as "plant reapers." Robert Hendrickson, in his *Facts on File Encyclopedia of Word and Phrase Origins,* suggests that the word originally meant something like "I am the one who works the land and harvests food from it."

ALASKA

If you superimpose the outline of Alaska on a map of the United States, Barrow, Alaska's northernmost settlement, is situated near Lake of the Woods, Minnesota. The southernmost Alaskan city, Ketchikan, lies atop Charleston, South Carolina. From east to west, the superimposed state touches both the Atlantic and Pacific coasts of the Lower forty-eight.

"Cut our state in two and make yours third in size" is what Alaskans say to muzzle-bragging Texans. With the highest North American mountain, three million lakes, and 33,000 miles of coastline, this state towers over its 49 siblings.

It was called "Seward's Folly" and "Icebergia" when Secretary of State William Seward arranged to buy Alaska from the Russians in 1867. Most 19th century Americans considered the territory cold, dark, barren, and simply too wild to govern, but the abundance of mineral and natural resources since discovered in "Icebergia" has made Seward appear visionary.

The Tlingit, Haida, Tsimshian, and Athapaskan natives and their ancestors have inhabited the area for 20,000 years. From the speakers of a boreal language called Aleut (and whom the Aleutian Islands were named after) came the word *alakshack,* which the Russians converted to *Alaska.* The original Aleut word means something like "mainland, great land."

The Latin word *albus,* meaning "white," is the progenitor of the modern English words *albino, album, Albuquerque, albumen,* and *Albion.*

Creatures, human and otherwise, lacking the pigment melanin exhibit the pink skin and white hair of *albinism.*

In classical Rome, an *album* was a white tablet upon which public notices were inscribed. Later, in England, an *album* became a collection of white or blank pages reserved for ledgers, diaries, or signatures. The phrase *phonograph album* comes from the days when phonograph recordings came in a booklike binder, similar to the white ledger albums of England.

The Latin-based name *Albuquerque* means "white oak." The name of the North American city of Albuquerque was taken from the name of a city in Spain.

Another etymological relative is *albumen,* which refers to the white of an egg.

Albion is an old poetic name for England. Some etymologists believe this word was fashioned from the Latin *albus,* in reference to the white cliffs of Dover.

The century-old *Universal Dictionary of the English Language* says the phrase *album Graecum,* literally "Greek white," describes dog excrement when it turns white as chalk. *Album Graecum* is not an entry in most contemporary dictionaries. It seems extinction has claimed this phrase.

ALL BALLED UP

While sometimes exhilarating, winter horseback riding can also be dangerous. If the temperature is above freezing, the soft and sticky snow on the ground can cling to your mount's hooves. The snow accumulates until it forms hard platforms of ice on the horse's feet. These can stack so tall that your horse becomes clumsy and you're forced to dismount and literally chip the snowballs away.

This was a serious, sometimes lethal complication in the era of horse-powered travel. Imagine a team of two or more horses coursing through a winter landscape, sledge in tow. One of the lead animals, with two inches of icepack on her hooves, looses her footing and falls. The other horses, attached to her by harness, trip and stumble. The sledge collides with the fallen mass of horseflesh, and all is chaos.

Most American etymologists believe this situation gave rise to the expression *all balled up,* meaning to be confused, tangled, and exasperated. The *ball* in this phrase is the pernicious balls of ice on the horse's feet.

ALMA MATER

We call the college or university from which we've graduated our *alma mater,* Latin for "nourishing mother."

This title was originally bestowed by the Romans on the goddesses responsible for abundance. Ceres, the deity in charge of grains and the harvest, was an early alma mater, a "mother" who sustained her mortal children with ample crops.

As universities proliferated throughout Europe, the title was applied to an individual's school, with the notion that the institution was the "mother" or source of intellectual and spiritual nourishment for the student. Alexander Pope, the English poet and satirist, was the first to use the term *alma mater* in this sense, in 1718. A former pupil of an alma mater is an *alumnus,* "he who is nourished." The feminine form, *alumna,* was recorded in the 1880s.

Alma mater is related to the thorny word *alimony*, which originally meant simply "sustenance." We've specialized this word in recent centuries; now it designates "sustenance in the form of money for an ex-spouse." Another etymological relative is *aliment,* "food, nutriment." The *alimentary canal* is the tubular canal that functions in the digestion and absorption of food.

ALZHEIMER'S DISEASE

An eponym is a proper name that has become a common word. The medical field has many eponyms that acknowlege the individual who first described a syndrome, disease, or body organ. Alois Alzheimer is the eponym of a brain disease afflicting millions.

Dr. Alzheimer was a German physician working in an asylum in the early years of the 20th century. Amongst his many patients was a relatively young woman, age 51, whose problems were unusual. The woman appeared healthy, with normal reflexes and coordination. Yet she roamed the halls of the asylum, unable to find her way back to her room. She had difficulty comprehending the speech of others and was often frustrated in her attempts to communicate verbally.

Dr. Alzheimer's unusual patient died after having suffered gradual, inexorable mental deterioration. An autopsy revealed her brain was smaller than might be expected in a woman her age. The physician noted a reduced number of brain cells and abnormally dilated ventricles in the brain. It seemed to Dr. Alzheimer that his patient's brain had shrunk and atrophied.

As the seminal investigator of this type of malady, the German physician loaned his name to Alzheimer's disease.

Anatomical Euphemisms

All cultures linguistically surround their anxieties in a cloud of euphemisms, or indirect expressions replacing those considered offensive or embarrassing. Victorian-era euphemists invented dozens of "acceptable" synonyms for body parts and the clothing covering them. Their obsession with fig-leafing every aspect of the human anatomy is puzzling to 21st century moderns.

In the 1830s, for example, it was considered vulgar to utter the word *leg* in mixed company. *Limb* was the preferred euphemism, with the most refined saying "limb of a table" or "limb of a piano." *Bender* was the proper term for a woman's knee in the mid-19th century, and *extremities* euphemised both *legs* and *arms*. Even the word *body* was questionable; *physique* was the safer choice.

A gentleman's trousers were modestly called *continuations* because they "continued" his waistcoat in a direction too delicate to mention. Men wore *nether garments* and *subtrousers* under their continuations.

The subject of women's underwear was sanitized with legions of euphemisms including *unspeakables, inexpressibles,* and *conveniences*. There were *dainties, frillies, upper unmentionables, lower unmentionables,* and the all-purpose *foundations,* which referred to anything a woman might don under her dress. The whispered *it's snowing down south* meant a slip was visible, as did the confidential *pettycoat's peeping,* which was then sub-euphemised with the initials *P. P.*

Greek and Latin are the languages of anatomy and physiology. Though scholarly sounding, words such as *phalanges, patella,* and *solar plexus* are made of colorful stories.

For example, the word *muscle* comes from the Latin *musculus,* which means "little mouse." To early physicians, the rolling motion of muscles resembled little mice running back and forth under the skin.

The bones of the toes and fingers are called *phalanges.* This is the plural of the Greek term *phalanx,* meaning "soldiers in close order." The fingers and toes, working cooperatively, brought to the Greek mind a vision of a body of well-trained soldiers.

Molars are the thick flat grinding teeth in the back of the mouth. They were so named after the Latin word *mola,* which means millstone.

The technical name of the kneecap is *patella.* This is a Latin word meaning "little plate."

The solar plexus is the area of the belly below the sternum. *Solar* comes from the Latin term for "sun," and *plexus* means "something woven." This name reflects the notion that the network of nerves in this area radiates like the rays of the sun.

Humans and animals have coexisted on this planet for millions of years. Willingly or not, animals have served humans in countless ways over the millennia as sources of food, clothing, traction, sport, and companionship. They also provide metaphor for our daily discourse. Animals and their appearances and behaviors are represented in hundreds of common English expressions.

To *play possum* is to pretend innocence or unawareness. This cliché alludes to the possum behavior of feigning death when caught or threatened.

A *snake in the grass* is a treacherous individual. The expression echoes the durable, ancient loathing humans have for snakes. The reptiles seem vile and sneaky to us as they wind their ways, nearly invisibly, through the underbrush.

A person who out of spite hoardes something that someone else needs is a *dog in the manger*. This is a reference to the Aesop's fable of a snarling dog that prevented oxen from eating their hay, though a meal of dried grass was worthless to the canine.

To *live high on the hog* is to prosper. Cheaper, less flavorful cuts of meat are taken from the feet and legs of the hog, while the choicest selections come from the sides and back of the animal, or "high" on the hog.

Aphrodisiac

Aphrodite was the sensual and mysterious goddess of love. When Greek poets told of her birth, they recounted the tale of the ancient ruler of the sky, Uranus, who was vanquished in a terrible battle between the gods. The conquered Uranus was castrated and his genitals thrown into the sea. From the waves at that very spot arose the goddess Aphrodite, fully grown and beautiful.

Aphrodite was married to the fire god, Hephaestus, but had many lovers. One affair engendered Eros, the god of love, from whom comes the term *erotic*.

Aphrodite was a powerful goddess who inspired awe and fear in the hearts of the ancients. Her sensuality is reflected in *aphrodisiac,* a word derived from her name.

Since the 18th century, many things were thought to have inspired sexual or aphrodisiac passion: truffles, mushrooms, tomatoes, the powdered horns of bulls and rhinos. Former secretary of state Henry Kissinger once said, "Power is the ultimate aphrodisiac."

The English language has a generous vocabulary. With over half a million words at their disposal, English speakers can express the subtle distinctions between *nice* and *pleasant, weather* and *climate, discover* and *invent.*

Our language serves us well when we need words to describe gradations of religious faith. Consider the terms *atheist, agnostic,* and *infidel.* What sets them apart from one another?

An agnostic questions any religious tenet requiring belief in the supernatural as well as the existence of a divine being, heaven, or hell. Agnostics contend that, since these matters can't be scientifically proven, their reality can neither be affirmed nor denied. The biologist Thomas Huxley coined the word *agnostic* in 1870; it derives from the Greek "unknown."

An atheist denies the existence of supernatural beings and rejects all religious practices. Greek in origin, *atheist* is a blend of the prefix *a-,* "without," and *theos,* "God." The *theos* element in *atheist* also occurs in the name *Theodore,* "gift of God," and *theology,* the study of godly things.

The infidel is etymologically "unfaithful." Infidels may embrace religious beliefs but reject creeds of the prevailing religion. A non-Muslim amongst Islamic adherents may be branded with this epithet. This Latin-based term is related to *fidelity, confide,* and the classic dog name *Fido,* which means "I am faithful."

ATLAS

Eons ago, when the earth was young and humans had not yet been born, Gaia the Earth-Mother and Uranus the Sky-Father ruled the planet and the heavens. The pair had many children and grandchildren who, over the years, divided into factions and battled for dominion over the earth.

Atlas, a grandson of Gaia and Uranus, fought his cousin Zeus in a fierce contest for supremacy. Zeus ultimately conquered his rival and sentenced Atlas forever to bear the weight of the heavens on his shoulders. For ages, the vanquished Atlas held the earth and sky apart until he finally turned to stone.

The Atlas Mountains, running east–west across the northern tier of Africa, were once said to be the petrified body of the ancient Greek god. The ocean immediately west of the Atlas Mountains, the Atlantic, was also named for the ill-starred grandson of Gaia and Uranus.

Why is a collection of maps called an *atlas*? The 16th century Flemish cartographer Gerhardus Mercator established the tradition by publishing an image of the globe-bearing Atlas on the frontispiece of his map collection. Succeeding cartographers perpetuated this tradition, until the maps themselves became known as atlases.

The first cervical vertebra below the skull is also called the *atlas,* bearing as it does the weight of the head just as the ancient god sustained the burden of the sky.

Automobile Words

The invention and proliferation of the automobile in the early 20th century required scores of new and retrofitted terms to denominate the technology. As the automobile drove its way through the heart of our country, the words it inspired were on the lips of every American.

Motel is a word that owes its popularity to the invention of the auto. This word made its linguistic debut in 1925 in San Luis Obispo, California, where separate cottages with attached garages were offered to overnight motor guests. This California establishment was the first to be called a motel, the word being a blend of *motor* and *hotel*.

Jaywalk is another term inspired by the automobile culture. A jaywalker crosses busy streets disregarding traffic regulations. This term was inspired by the blue jay, a bird often associated with rural living. *Jay* is an early term for a rustic or hick. Ignorant of the traffic patterns of busy streets, the visiting country folk, or jays, wandered across thoroughfares, imperiling themselves and motorists.

The term *dashboard,* referring to the panel mounted beneath the windshield of a car, was originally a plank mounted on the front of a horse-drawn carriage to prevent mud from being "dashed" up from the horse's hooves into the vehicle. The evolution of the term *dashboard* is an example of an old word accommodating new technology.

BALLOT

The ballot voting method is used in all democratic countries to enable each citizen to cast a secret vote, and to protect against reprisal and coersion in the exercising of his or her vote.

Voting by ballot is traditional in the western world. The ancient Greeks voted secretly by dropping stones, shells, or balls into jars. An approving vote was represented by a white stone or ball; a black ball represented a negative vote for the candidate. The vote of a white stone by an Athenian juror indicated acquittal, and a black stone signified condemnation.

Ballot, from the Italian *ballota,* "little ball," referred to the small objects used by the ancients for casting votes. Early Americans often voted for or against their candidates with beans and corn kernels. Though paper tickets have been used to record votes since the 19th century, when we *cast a ballot* on election day we still etymologically "throw a little ball."

The term *blackball*—to exclude someone from an organization or club by voting against his application—is a linguistic echo of the tradition of a black ball representing a negative vote.

Banana

A full century after the signing of the Declaration of Independence, Americans tasted bananas for the first time. At the Philadelphia Centennial Exhibition of 1876, foil-wrapped bananas were sold for ten cents apiece.

Though the banana was a novel addition to the American diet in the late 19th century, people around the world had been eating them for hundreds of years. The earliest written evidence of the banana comes out of India in writings from the 5th century B.C. The plant was carried and cultivated throughout the tropics by traders, missionaries, and settlers. Bananas were brought to the Western Hemisphere in 1516; they were subsequently established on plantations throughout the islands of the Caribbean and Central America.

The common name *banana* most likely originated in the coastal West African languages of Wolof and Malinke. Swedish botanist Carolus Linnaeus created the plant's genus name, *Musa,* possibly from the Arabic word for banana, *mouz* or *moz.* Other sources claim that *Musa* is a commemoration of Antonius Musa (63-14 B.C.), the physician to the Roman emperor Octavius Augustus.

The word *banana* made its way into the American English slang vocabulary throughout the 20th century, appearing in such expressions as the vaudeville *top banana* and his straight man, the *second banana*. There was also *banana belt, banana nose, banana oil, banana republic,* and the phrase *go bananas.*

Since the 1920s, *banana oil* has meant "idle talk, insincere flattery." This expression is probably a quirky elaboration of the word *oil,* long used as a synonym for unctuous compliments.

Banana republic generally refers to a small country economically dependent on fruit exports and paralyzed by the power of a despotic ruler. This term appeared in print in 1904.

Top banana, second banana, and *go bananas* are theatre terms. The second banana was always the lesser performer on the vaudeville totem pole, while the top banana delivered the best lines. Although the reason for this nomenclature has been lost, the *Dictionary of American Slang* speculates that it was reinforced by the soft, water- or air-filled banana-shaped bladder club carried as a standard item by comedians, which they usually used to hit other comedians over the head, akin to the phallic symbols carried by the comedians on the ancient Greek stage. To *go bananas,* meaning to go crazy or wild with joy, may have been influenced by the lunacy perpetrated on vaudeville stages by the top and second bananas.

Banjo

There is some dispute surrounding the origin of the term *banjo*. Some sources, such as the *Oxford Dictionary of English Etymology*, claim *banjo* is simply an alteration of the Spanish term *bandore*, a 16th century lute-like instrument.

In her book *That Half-Barbaric Twang, the Banjo in American Popular Culture*, ethnomusicologist Karen Linn contends that the word and the instrument are certainly of African origin. She writes, "The North American banjo developed from an African prototype. [It] was made from a gourd with a slice taken out of it, covered with a skin head, fitted with a neck and strung with several strings."

African slaves in both the West Indies and North America, says Linn, called this instrument *banjo, banjul, banza, banjer,* and *banshaw*. Sources citing an African origin of *banjo* say it is a form of *mbanza,* the name of a stringed instrument in the Kimbundu language of northern Angola.

If the African origin theory of *banjo* is valid, that word then falls into kinship with other words on loan from the languages of that continent. *Boogie-woogie, chigger, goober, jazz, jukebox, tote, voodoo, yam,* and *zombie* come from the various tongues of Africa.

BARBIE DOLL

In the late 1940s, toymakers Ruth and Elliot Handler were enjoying the successful sales of their homemade wooden dollhouse furniture. Encouraged by the popularity of their inventions, the Handlers designed and marketed a line of increasingly sophisticated toys: a children's ukulele, a cap gun, a hand-crank music box.

The Handlers were inspired, in part, by the toys their own children preferred. Observing her young daughter at play, Ruth Handler noted that the child consistantly chose to dress and undress her adult-looking paper dolls, while her baby dolls lay toybox-bound. Mrs. Handler designed for her daughter a three-dimensional teenaged doll complete with adult curves and trendy wardrobe.

Marketed through the Handlers' fledgling toy company, Mattel, the splashy doll made her debut at the 1959 American Toy Fair in New York City. Mrs. Handler called the doll "Barbie," the pet name of her own daughter, Barbara. Barbie's "boyfriend," Ken, named for the Handlers' son, appeared on the shelves in 1961.

Barbie has been criticized by feminists and others who contend that she represents an unattainable ideal of beauty. Impossibly proportioned, a life-sized Barbie would measure 39-21-33. The moniker *Barbie* is often applied to a trendy blonde with more style than substance, *Barbie and Ken* to a young couple whose combined appearance seems to be their finest asset.

A person mentally impaired by grief, nervousness, or fear is sometimes saddled with the moniker *basket case*. The title implies that one so afflicted is temporarily distracted and needs care and attention from those around him. This term has been so used in America since the late 1940s.

In recent decades the phrase has been applied to entities beyond the individual, such as in this passage from *Time* magazine of August 1981: "The suburbs...sucked the blood out of the central cities and left behind some of the urban basket cases we see today."

A less common use of the term appears in automobile and mechanical jargon. Here, a *basket case* is an abandoned vehicle or piece of equipment stripped of its useful parts.

Though today we employ this phrase casually or even jokingly, its origin is grim. During the First World War, stories circulated about quadruple amputees, soldiers so injured that they were literally carried about in baskets. In 1919 the U.S. Army Surgeon General denied the existence of any so-called basket cases, but military rumors held that there were hundreds of these casualties housed in secluded hospital wings. The idea was kept in circulation through a novel about a basket case that was published in 1939 called *Johnny Got His Gun,* by Dalton Trumbo.

Bee

A remarkable early American tradition was the seasonal gathering of neighbors for such tasks as crop harvesting and quilt making. These communal events were called *bees,* and they were an integral part of American farm and frontier life from the 17th century through the turn of the 20th.

The tradition was probably sparked on the eastern seaboard with cornhusking bees, first mentioned in print in 1693. Spinning bees soon followed as did road-building, wood-chopping, candy-making, knitting, shingling, and house-cleaning bees. When innundated with vermin, property owners organized rattlesnake, pigeon, and squirrel bees.

The spelling bee, a New England tradition, became popular after the Civil War. Still a thriving institution, this spelling contest is one of the very few communal events still known as a *bee.* The word seems to be falling out of favor with American English speakers.

We haven't attached this notion to our 21st century activities; for example, there are no wine-tasting or Scrabble bees, no basketball bees, no more harvesting bees.

Before this term disappears from the collective memory, let's look at its origin, which is surprisingly elusive. Some word watchers contend the term arose from the notion of highly organized and efficient bee societies. Other etymological evidence indicates that *bee* comes from *bean,* a dialectal word from Yorkshire, England, that refers to a day set aside for a special activity such as barn building or harvest.

Just as the Stetson hat is named after its inventor, John Batterson Stetson, Alexander Graham Bell and a cartoon character named Fritz have also loaned their names to the English language as eponyms.

Alexander Graham Bell was born in Scotland in 1847. In 1870 he moved to America, where he began a series of his famous electrical experiments. Bell established a school of vocal physiology in Boston and is best known for inventing the telephone. He's linguistically memorialized in the words *bel* and *decibel*. A bel is a unit of measurement for the loudness of electrical signals, and a decibel is simply one-tenth of a bel.

When things go *on the Fritz,* who are we blaming? While some lexicographers are unsure about the source of this phrase, others believe it comes from the Fritz of the "Katzenjammer Kids," a cartoon strip created by Rudolph Dirks in 1897. Twins Fritz and Hans of this series were merry pranksters who played endless tricks on their parents and the town police. We say that an unreliable clock or a car that won't start is *on the Fritz,* as though it were sabotaged by that naughty trickster Fritz Katzenjammer.

BENCHMARK, HALLMARK

Is there a bench in *benchmark*? A hall in *hallmark*? Yes, and yes.

Originally a surveyor's term recorded circa 1842, *benchmark* refers to a mark on a permanent object (a rock or wall, for example) indicating elevation. It is so called because of the use of the mark as a place to insert an angle iron that serves as a support—a "bench"—for a leveling rod. In general usage, it represents a standard of excellence or achievement. A benchmark in digital parlance is a type of test used to measure hardware or software performance.

The hall in *hallmark* is began life as a literal one—a building in London. As early as 1300, the Goldsmith's Company of London assayed all gold and silver products used in trade. By order of Edward I, all such items were to be marked with an official stamp attesting to their purity. Because the stamping was carried out in Goldsmith's Hall in London, the imprint became known as the *hall-mark*. The first citation of the word appears in the 18th century.

Modern English speakers know this word best in its figurative sense as a distinguishing trait or feature. Thus, fluid and effortless movement is the hallmark of a ballet dancer; or, as Wilfred Funk writes in his *Word Origins and Their Romantic Stories,* "courtesy is the hallmark of a gentleman."

Beyond the Pale

The expression *beyond the pale* means "unacceptable, outside the rules of society." The *pale* in this phrase comes from the Latin word *palum,* meaning "stake, or fence made of stakes." From the time of the Roman colonization of Europe, *pale fences,* or *palings,* were used to demarcate territory belonging to a certain district. *English Pale* was the name given to the portion of Ireland under English domination.

Originally meaning "outside the limits designated by a fence" or "past the boundary of one's country," *beyond the pale* was eventually used as a metaphor for the behavior of someone refusing to conform to societal customs and principles. Such offenders are figuratively assigned to the margins of civilization.

The expression was used by Susan Caba in the *Seattle Times* on September 3, 1997, when she quoted comments about photographs taken of the site at which Princess Diana died in an automobile accident: "'To my mind, there's blood on those photographs,' Bill Buncon, editor in chief of the tabloid *Star* magazine, said yesterday, explaining his refusal to buy the pictures. 'The person that took those photographs contributed to the accident,' he said. 'It was beyond the pale.'"

Related terms are *palisade,* "wall of stakes used for defense," and *impale,* "pierce with a stake."

BIKINI

On July 1, 1946, a twenty-kiloton atomic bomb exploded over a chain of tiny islands in the Pacific Ocean. This detonation was part of a series of tests called "Operation Crossroads" conducted by a U.S. Army–Navy joint task force. The team planted a fleet of seventy-five unmanned Japanese and American sailing vessels, designed to monitor the destructive capacity of the detonation, in the lagoon formed by these small islands. The damage to the ships was extensive, and the radiation level at the blast site was reported to have been lethal to humans.

The Operation Crossroads explosion, similar to those that destroyed Hiroshima and Nagasaki only a year earlier, dominated the world media.

Concurrently, a bomb of another type was about to detonate in the fashion world. Parisian designer Louis Reard was concocting a new style of swimwear consisting of about a yard of material designed to barely conceal the parts of a woman which distinguish her from a man. Its debut was scheduled for July 6, 1946, only five days after the atomic explosion in the Pacific.

Reard took advantage of the media opportunity offered by Operation Crossroads. He called his skimpy two-piece swimsuit the *bikini,* the name of the Pacific island that had "hosted" the atomic bomb only days earlier.

BIMBO

In the 21st century, the word *bimbo* is an epithet applied to females. A century ago, however, *bimbo* was a generic reference to a male, usually a "tough guy," "one of the boys," or in its most insulting incarnation a fellow whose combined belt and hat size approximated his IQ.

The word became associated with females in the 1920s. In that decade, a *bimbo,* or *bim,* was simply a man's date or girlfriend. Then, in a turn for the pejorative, the bimbo of the '30s and '40s became a young woman considered attractive but simple, and perhaps promiscuous; she became cousin to the *floozy.* In the early 1980s the moniker *bimbette* emerged; etymologically this is a "little bimbo."

Most likely the term is a form of the Italian *bambino,* "baby, child." The editors of the magnificent 1960 *Dictionary of American Slang,* Harold Wentworth and Stuart B. Flexner, wrote, "Although this meaning is usually said to be derived from 'bimbo' = baby as a term of endearment, it was used in jocular disrespect and…now implies a certain moral cynicism on the part of the speaker."

The color black provides a metaphor for evil in the term *black-hearted*. *Black market* points to a venue for exchanging illegal goods. The brother we don't talk about is the *black sheep* of the family.

One curious linguistic member of this color family is *blackmail,* the extortion of money under threat. This "black" word, however, is not what it appears to be. The *mail* in this word is not delivered in the post office box, nor is the *black* meant to suggest the color of evil.

The *mail* of *blackmail* comes from a Scottish word referring to the rent a tenant or farmer paid a 16th century absentee British landlord. If the sum was offered in silver coin, it was *white mail*. When tenants had no coin to give, they paid rent in *black mail*—produce or livestock from the farm. *Blackmail* earned its pejorative meaning when landlords charged their cash-poor tenants more in livestock than they would have surrendered in coin.

Farmers and landholders living near the border of Scotland and northern England lived in fear of border thieves who demanded grain for their horses and meat for their own bellies. If they were sufficiently supplied by the farmer, the freebooters agreed to not plunder any of his property. This "protection fee" was also known as *black mail,* edible goods extorted from a cashless landowner.

BLIMP

In 1250 the English philosopher Roger Bacon considered the possibility of a lighter-than-air craft. He wrote, "Such a machine must be a hollow globe of copper... wrought extremely thin. It must then be filled with ethereal air or liquid fire and launched from some elevated point...when it will float like a vessel on water." Roger Bacon's imaginings were realized in the development of the zeppelin and the blimp, airships classified as *dirigibles,* a word derived from a Latin term meaning "to steer or guide."

The *zeppelin,* a type of dirigible with a rigid structure, is the namesake of its inventor, the German Count Ferdinand von Zeppelin. Von Zeppelin, a general in the German army, was inspired to experiment with airships after a balloon ascent he made in Minnesota in the late 19th century.

No one is certain of the origin of the word *blimp,* the name of a "nonrigid" dirigible manufactured by the Goodyear Company in the early 20th century. One etymological theory makes the word *blimp* an onomatopoeia. Inspecting one of the aircraft in 1915, a Lieutenant Cunningham of the British Royal Navy Air Service flicked his finger on the taut fabric of the craft. The story goes that when Cunningham vocally imitated the sound of his finger against the bag, he said "Blimp!" and the name was born.

Blizzard

In the northern tier of the United States, winter snow-storms can howl nine months out of the year. These white shrieking tempests kill livestock, leave country dwellers snowbound for days, and blind motorists with blasts of vertical snow. The term designating this type of wintry monster, *blizzard,* is uniquely American and etymologically elusive.

The word *blizzard* turns up twice in David Crockett's diary from the 1830s, when he used it first to refer to a shot-gun blast, then later to a blast of words. During the Civil War, a volley of musketry was called a *blizzard*.

In 1870 the Midwest was pounded by a savage spring storm. An Estherville, Iowa, newspaper editor, O. C. Bates, wrote about this "blizard" in the *Northern Vindicator.* In 1880 another ferocious winter gale hit the Midwest, and the word *blizzard* appeared in many newspapers during that storm season. An 1881 publication of the *New York Nation* said, "The hard weather has called into use a word which promises to become a national Americanism, namely blizzard. It designates a storm (of snow and wind) which we cannot resist away from shelter."

Although most sources say this word is of unknown origin, others suggest that the ultimate ancestor of the term is the German *Blitz,* "lightning."

BLOCKBUSTER

A *blockbuster* in modern American English is a runaway movie hit or perhaps a lavish Broadway production. The term implies success, or at least spectacle, on a colossal scale. But what do spectacular performances or productions have to do with busting blocks?

Blockbuster probably arose in Britain during the Second World War. The Royal Air Force employed aerial bombs large enough to destroy significant building complexes, which they called *blocks*. The power of these so-called blockbuster bombs was so stunning that the style of assault was quickly transferred to a metaphorical arena, wherein something large or important had *blockbuster* force.

The expression surfaced in a nonmilitary sense in the early 1940s and is now an important component of our American slang vocabulary.

The term *blockbuster* influenced the real estate expression *blockbusting,* the practice of inducing homeowners to sell their properties at a low price, especially by exploiting fears that minority families will move into the area. Here, unscrupulous brokers have the power to "bust up" blocks of established neighborhoods.

BLOOMERS

Born in Homer, New York, in 1818, Amelia Jenks Bloomer seemed destined to defy convention. She caused a sensation in 1849 when she published the first copy of *The Lily,* America's first magazine for women. As its editor, she championed the rather shocking notions of education for girls, female suffrage, and the reform of marriage laws.

Bloomer further shattered the mold of 19th century femininity when she established a career as deputy postmaster of Seneca Falls, New York, declaring she wanted to give a "practical demonstration of a woman's right to fill any place for which she has capacity."

Addressing the needs of the total woman, Amelia Bloomer championed female dress reform as well. Women of her day were obliged to wear voluminous hoop skirts, too wide for doorways and too long for muddy streets.

Bloomer and other feminists proposed a more rational outfit for women: an ensemble consisting of Turkish pantaloons covered by a kneelength skirt. She was harshly ridiculed for her proposal, and the style became forever associated with her surname, Bloomer. From the mid-19th century and throughout the 20th, the word *bloomers* referred generally to women's undergarments or any type of loose fitting legwear.

BLUE EXPRESSIONS

Color words are loaded with symbolic significance. Green represents money and envy, red symbolizes anger, and black is the traditional color of death and mourning.

Blue is perhaps the most versatile color in the spectrum of symbolism. It represents royalty and faithfulness, it is the color of depression, and it is emblematic of the middle-class trade worker. But it also symbolizes excellence in the expression *blue ribbon*.

True blue indicates faithfulness, steadfastness. This phrase comes from the color of a fabric manufactured during the Middle Ages at Coventry, England. The cloth was prized for its durable blue dye, which, unlike others of the day, resisted fading.

Blue blood is said to course through the veins of aristocrats. This term is a direct translation of the Spanish *sangre azul,* coined by the Spanish nobles of Castile whose fair skin revealed the blue veins underneath, while the darker skin of their neighbors, the Moors, did not.

Blue collar workers, conversely, make no claim to royalty. This moniker was coined in the America of the 1950s, associating the millions of factory and trade workers with their blue work shirts.

Lexically speaking, *the blues* have been with us for centuries. Slang-slingers of 18th century London said they were *blue* with depression and melancholy. The American *blues* style of music tells tales of misery and hard luck.

On the other hand, the *blue* in *blue ribbon* bespeaks excellence. The original blue ribbon was one worn below the left knee of a 14th century British knight who was admitted into the Most Noble Order of the Garter, a coveted title.

BLURB

A blurb is a short endorsement written on the jacket of a book: *"Absolutely goose-pimpling! This is horror writing at its finest!! A masterfully rendered saga of Britain's colonial expansion!!!"* Everyone knows blurbs are essential components in book marketing, but how many know the story behind the origin of this strange little term?

This word was invented by a 20th century American humorist, Gelette Burgess. The author of several popular books at the time, Burgess was a guest of honor at the 1907 American Booksellers Association annual dinner, where he gave away copies of his most recent publication.

He waggishly devised a self-promoting jacket for his own book. Mocking the advertising style of the era, he adorned the front of his volume with the portrait of what he called a "sickly sweet young woman," the kind regularly featured on boxes of dental preparations and medicinal elixirs. Burgess dubbed his model "Miss Belinda Blurb." Next to her "sickly sweet" visage, the author inserted several self-congratulatory comments about his book.

Burgess thereafter referred to all pithy book endorsements as *blurbs.* The word must have filled a linguistic vacuum, for within a short twenty years of its coinage it had found a permanent place in the American English vocabulary.

BOB

The brief word *bob* packs a mighty punch in American English. Consider its significance in such terms as *bobsled, bobcat, bobbie pin, bob tail,* and *bobby socks.* What is the role of this little term in our lexicon?

This word meant "knob or cluster" early in its career. The *Oxford English Dictionary* supplies a quotation from 1483 that refers to "a Bob of grapys"; another citation from 1570 speaks of "a bob of flowers." In 1752 a *bob* was also a weight (or *knob*) at the end of a pendulum. In that same century, a *bobbed* horse was one with a short, knoblike tail.

Bob-periwigs and *bob-perukes* were 17th century wigs with the bottom locks turned up into "bobs," or short curls. In 19th century America, young fashionable women did not don perukes; instead they *bobbed* their own hair into bobs— short, straight, and even all around. The style was held in place with *bob pins,* or *bobbie pins.*

Bob became an American catch-all term for anything short. The *bobcat* was named for its abbreviated tail. A *bobsled* is one with short runners. *Bobby socks,* worn by teenage girls in the 1940s, were the brief version of long cotton or wool stockings.

The source of this handy term with its variety of applications is ultimately unknown. The *Oxford English Dictionary* suggests that the Irish word *baban,* meaning "tassel or cluster," is in *bob's* linguistic lineage.

BOISE

Boise is the capital and largest city of the state of Idaho. Situated on a river by the same name, Boise is home to over 200,000 people.

In 1811, French fur trappers entered and named the fertile Boise Valley. Fifty years later, a military fort was established on the modern city site. The post straddled the Oregon Trail, while the valley had abundant water and grass, as well as wood and stone for building. A townsite was soon laid out near the new fort, and by 1869 Boise had four hundred buildings and a thousand inhabitants. Those thousand relied on gold mining for their livelihood but, as the population grew, agriculture became vital to the local economy.

Though isolated, Boise adopted a sophisticated persona early on. An elaborate natatorium with a 125-foot-long warm, spring-fed pool was erected there in 1892. The elegant Egyptian Theatre, built in 1927, still stands in Boise as a monument to the "Egyptomania" that captured the nation after the discovery of Tutankhamen's Tomb in 1922.

Boise, a western city of culture, was named after a natural feature. When early fur traders overlooked the valley in which Boise now sits, they were impressed by its woods. The French term *boise* means "wooded."

BOONDOGGLE

The noun *boondoggle* is a task of little practical value; the verb *to boondoggle* is to waste time and money on unnecessary work. No one has been able to trace the history of this word with certainty. Several theories on its origin have evolved since it began appearing in American publications in the 1920s and '30s.

One account says a *boondoggle* in Scotland is a marble one receives without having to work for it. Another source speculates that the word is related to *boondocks,* a term from the Tagalog language spoken in the Philippines. A third offering has *boondoggle* coming from iron-smelting lingo, where it designates a failed attempt to produce iron from slag.

Many etymological sources associate the term with a Rochester, New York, Scoutmaster named Robert H. Link. In 1929, Link applied this term to the lanyards that Boy Scouts braided as a craft item, thus inspiring the meaning of any small task to keep someone busy, or a trinket produced from that task.

During the New Deal of the Great Depression, the unemployed were given make-work assignments so unproductive that they were called *boondoggles,* after the Boy Scout lanyards. By the mid-1930s, the word had become a part of the lingo of the American working class, as in this October 4, 1935, example from the *Chicago Tribune:* "To the cowboy, [boondoggling] meant the making of saddle trappings out of the odds and ends of leather, and they 'boondoggled' when there was nothing else to do on the ranch."

BRAILLE

The Braille system, a method of embossed writing interpreted by touch, has enabled legions of the blind to read and write. Musical and mathematical notations have also been transcribed into the Braille system.

A young Frenchman is responsible for this method of reading and writing, and for placing the word *braille* on countless tongues.

Louis Braille was born in 1809 in a village outside Paris. When he was three, he accidentally drove an awl through his left eye while playing in his father's workshop. Though blindness eventually claimed both of Louis's eyes, he nevertheless attended the village school with all his peers, learning the alphabet by feeling twigs shaped into letters.

Louis's father sent him to the National Institution for the Young Blind in Paris, where the boy learned to read from a collection of three enormous books, weighing hundreds of pounds apiece, engraved with embossed letters of the alphabet.

By happy coincidence, the French army was then developing a system of communication called "night writing," an arrangement of dots and dashes embossed on a thin cardboard by which sentinels could send messages in the dark. Revising the night writing system to suit the blind, Louis Braille developed an alphabet, musical notations, and mathematical signs.

The Braille system, eponymously named for its talented inventor, was officially adopted by the Institution for the Blind in 1854, two years after the death of Louis Braille.

Bread Words

Nobody knows where bread-baking was invented, but it is a practice of considerable antiquity. The Egyptians were baking loaves in ovens of Nile clay 5,000 years ago. Bread has sustained countless generations of humans in the Near East, Europe, and more recently the New World. The significance of bread as the underpinning of any diet is reflected in the Old Testament reference to it as the staff of life and in the use of the words *bread* and *dough* as 20th century synonyms for money.

The English word *bread* comes from an ancient Germanic source. The modern German term for this staple, *Brot,* is similar to the English.

Bread in the Romance languages Spanish, French, and Italian is *pan, pain,* and *pane,* terms derived from the Latin *panis,* bread.

This Latin term is sandwiched in the common English word *companion.* Etymologically, a companion is one who shares your bread (*com,* "with"; *panis,* "bread"). This word reflects the bonding that occurs when people share food, or "break bread," together. A *company* of people etymologically eat bread at the same table; when we entertain *company,* we extend our hospitality. *Pantry,* "bread room," derives from the French *paneterie,* and a *pannier* is a "bread basket."

Bring Home the Bacon

To *bring home the bacon* means to win a prize, return home with something valuable, or support a family by working. The most likely source of this expression is the greased-pig contests at American county fairs—whoever captures the pig gets to keep it and bring home the "bacon." This "greased pig" sense of the phrase was first recorded in 1925.

Another suggestion—less likely but more colorful, and certainly more ancient—involves an annual custom initiated in 1111 in Dunmow, Essex County, England. The church officials in that town offered a whole side of bacon (called the *Dunmow flitch*) to any couple who could prove their marital felicity. The contenders were to kneel on two sharp stones beside the Dunmow church door and swear before God that they had neither quarreled nor wished themselves unmarried for a year.

The trick for the couples was convincing a mock jury of six bachelors and six maidens of the veracity of the claim. The names of the fortunate couples who *brought home the bacon* are recorded permanently in the church at Dunmow.

BUG, INSECT

It is unclear how the word *bug* came to refer to an insect or a thing small, leggy, and creepy-crawly. It possibly derives from a Celtic word, *bwg,* meaning "specter, hobgoblin." For centuries, *bwg* and related words *bugaboo, bugbear,* and *bogy* were associated with goblins, ghosts, and supernatural beings, such as the shadowy and terrifying *bogeyman.*

By the 1600s, the word *bug* was being used in reference to insects in general, especially the tiny bedbugs infesting every home, emerging at night to suck the blood of sleeping humans. The nocturnal habits of these pests may have suggested the activity of malevolent spirits. Some scholars contend that this is the etymological interface of *bwg,* the night goblin, and *bug,* the small, crawling creature.

Other sources speculate that *bug* is connected with the Old English term *budde,* "beetle."

But to entomologists, or insect specialists, *bug* has a specific meaning. Scientifically, this term indicates creatures of the insect order Hemiptera, which means "half-wing." These include bedbugs, waterbugs, squashbugs, stinkbugs, and boxelder bugs. The true bugs are characterized by sucking mouthparts and wings that are half membranous and half leathery. In contrast, the word *insect* comes from the Latin *animal insectum,* "creature divided up in segments," and refers to the head, thorax, and abdomen partitioning of the true insects.

BULL

The word *bull* has been pressed into a variety of meanings over the centuries. Originally designating males of certain species, such as cattle, moose, elk, and elephants, *bull* has been especially successful in the raucous vocabulary of slang.

In the 1811 *Dictionary of the Vulgar Tongue* originally printed in London, we find a colorful array of the slang uses of *bull*. A *bull calf* in 19th century England was a "great hulkey or clumsy fellow." A fat, chubby child was unkindly called a *bull chin*. A *bully*, then as now, was a "cowardly fellow who gives himself airs of great bravery." This word was coined from the bull's legendary aggressive nature.

But in 19th and 20th century America, the word began to have its way with the vocabulary in such formations as *bull artist,* a habitual liar or flatterer. *Bull butter* was a disparaging name for margarine in the late 19th century. To *bulldoze* is to intimidate or coerce with threats of violence.

Bull pen designates different kinds of confined spaces for holding men. In the 1800s, it was a small room for prisoners awaiting interrogation or punishment. By the 1920s, a bull pen was a holding area for baseball players waiting to be called into the game. The word was also used to designate men's bunkhouses at logging camps and men's college dormatories.

And of course, there are the euphemistically constucted phrases—*bull roar, bull dust, bull dinky, bull crap, bull pucky,* and *bull hockey*—designed to replace the stronger, scatological epithet that means lies, exaggeration, and tomfoolery.

Bum

The word *bum,* synonymous with tramp or hobo, has been a part of our linguistic landscape since the 1830s. Its progenitor is the German verb *bummeln,* meaning to stroll, loiter, or waste time. Jobless and footloose, bums are conspicuous against the backdrop of geographically fixed American workers. They are, as the Germans would say, *bummlers:* loafers, idlers.

As decades passed, we sliced and diced the word *bum,* adding it to America's slang stew. Ladled from this broth was the *bum* referring to an inferior boxer or racehorse, or an orphaned bottle-fed lamb.

Generally, though, a bum is a man with little money or status. In a 1957 film, Humphrey Bogart's screen wife asked why he was so anxious about money. Bogart replied, "All I know is, if you haven't got it, they call you a bum."

Early in the 20th century, the adjective form of this word appeared in print. *Bum leg* and *bum knee* refer to anatomical parts which, like a tramp, simply will not work.

In Britain, the word *bum* refers not to a tramp but to the buttocks and related nether regions. The term is so potentially offensive to the Brits that, when Al Jolson's 1933 film *Hallelujah, I'm a Bum* was shown in England, the title was euphemised to *Hallelujah, I'm a Tramp.*

BUM PHRASES

When *bum* fell into the whirligig of American slang, it picked up a few linguistic hitchhikers, giving us such concoctions as *crumb-bum, bum's rush, bummer.* It even became a verb: *to bum* means to borrow without repaying, a habit of people with no jobs and no money

The moniker *crumb-bum,* meaning a worthless and despicable person, was popular in the 1930s, '40s, and '50s and is fossilized in movie dialogues of that era. The *crumb* in this expression is not food fallout, but a synonym for lice or bedbugs, making a crumb-bum a truly filthy vagabond.

The *bum's rush* is the forcible ejection of a person from a public place at the speed of a tramp being removed from high tea.

Misleading information is a *bum steer. Steer* in this expression is not of the bovine variety; it's an early 20th century slang synonym for advice. A bum steer, much like a hobo, just doesn't work. The expression *bum trip,* coined in the mid-1960s, is of the same construction. It refers to an unpleasant or frightening drug experience—one, again, that "doesn't work." A spin-off of *bum trip* is *bummer,* anything difficult, unpleasant, tedious, or depressing.

BUTLER

Butlers walk a fine line between deference and power. This balancing act is nicely illustrated in a story of a butler in the employ of Lady Astor, the first woman elected to Parliament. When her manservant threatened to quit following a household dispute, Lady Astor replied, "In that case, tell me where you are going, because I am coming with you."

Nowadays, butlers are almost more common on screen and in print than in real life, with characters such as Inspector Clousseau's Cato, the Addams family's Lurch, Bertie Wooster's unflappable man Jeeves.

In England before the Second World War, there were more than 18,000 butlers; by 1970, fewer than 100.

Butlering traditions, however, have remained constant. For centuries, hallmarks of the trade have been discretion, diplomacy, and loyalty to employer. The traditional duties of a butler were directing the household staff and serving food. Many butlers today are employed by business people to handle payrolls, manage the household, plan parties, or book flights.

One of the more important duties of yesteryear's manservant was that of wine steward. This task is reflected in the etymology of the word *butler*. The term is the offspring of the Old French *bouteiller,* meaning "bottle bearer."

This word is also a surname. If you are of a Butler family, one of your male ancestors may well have tipped the bottle for an aristocratic European family.

BUXOM

A typical bride in 15th century England promised to be a *buxom* wife until the day she died. This was not a pledge to stay forever amply endowed; it was instead a vow of compliance and obedience.

Buxom comes to us from the Old English verb *bugan,* which means "yield, bend, or acquiesce." *Bow,* meaning to submit, also derives from this source.

From the sense of "compliance, agreeableness," *buxom* acquired the meanings "bright, lively, blithe" and was applied to both men and women. In Shakespeare's *Henry V,* the character Bardolph is described as "a soldier firm and sound of heart, and of buxom valor."

On the other hand, 18th century lexicographer Samuel Johnson defined the word as "wanton," implying that an obedient and blithe woman would yield easily to pleasure and be willing to accommodate in every way.

In the 19th century, a buxom or lively woman was seen as sturdily built and agreeably plump. She remains so today, although a bit more attention is focused on the ample breasts of the modern buxom woman.

Jane Mills, author of a dictionary called *Womanwords,* says, "Although not exactly pejorative, *buxom* is not exactly complimentary either. This may be because the large-breasted female runs counter to the fashionable, slim, boyish-looking female ideal of today."

CALIFORNIA

California was the thirty-first state to join the Union, on September 9, 1850. The statistics on the state of California comprise a roster of superlatives. California contains both the highest and the lowest points in the contiguous United States: Mount Whitney and Death Valley, respectively. The giant sequoia, believed to be the oldest living organism on earth, thrives within the borders of this state. Though superceded in size by Alaska and Texas, California ranks first in population among the fifty states.

There are no clear records documenting the christening of California. Some accounts indicate the word may come from a combination of the Latin terms *calida* and *forno,* "hot furnace."

The name most likely arose from a story by 16th century Spanish writer Ordonez de Montalvo. In this romantic tale, California was the name of a beautiful, mythical island near the Indies ruled by a queen named Calafia. When Spanish explorers came upon the peninsula south of present-day California, today's Baja California, they believed it to be an island and gave it the name of the mythical isle of de Montalvo's story. This poetic title was passed from explorer to explorer and settler to settler until it became the official state name in 1850.

CALLIOPE

Calliope was one of the nine Muses of ancient Greece. Like her eight sisters, Calliope was an Olympian immortal, one of the many daughters of Zeus. Each of the Muses presided over a branch of science or art, and Calliope was responsible for fostering eloquence and epic poetry.

Calliope means "beautiful voice" in the Greek language. The Muse was given the name in honor of her lovely poetic recitations, and possibly in reference to her singing, as song was a talent shared by all the Muses.

In the mid-19th century, an inventor from Massachusetts named William Stoddard created an elaborate pipe organ mounted on a wagon. The steam-powered pipes emitted piercing notes audible up to ten miles. This device, pulled down the street by a team of horses, was designed to lure townspeople to the spectacle of a traveling circus, so popular in the 19th century.

With a tip of the hat to the classical world, Stoddard named his shrieking contrivance the *calliope,* or "beautiful voice," after the Muse of epic poetry and eloquence.

CANARY

The Canary Islands lie in the Atlantic Ocean, 70 miles off the northwest shoulder of Africa. The seven islands in the Canary archipelago constitute two Spanish provinces. Volcanic in origin, the islands tower over the ocean waters. Mt. Tiede, at 12,162 feet, is the highest point in Spain.

The steep and rugged Canary Islands have long attracted passing mariners to their shores. Ancient Greeks and Phoenicians visited the Canaries; the Roman historian Pliny mentions an expedition to the islands in 40 B.C. Arabs, Normans, Portuguese, and Spanish all landed on or inhabited the Canaries.

By the middle of the 16th century, European explorers were capturing and exporting a small songbird native to the islands. This creature became wildly popular throughout Europe as a cage bird and was named *canary* after its homeland.

But centuries before the songbird was discovered on these islands, there were the dogs: large, wild creatures that thrived on the biggest island of the archipelago. The area's earliest explorers, noting the indigenous wild dogs, called the big island *Canaria,* "Island of Dogs," a name that eventually designated the entire group of volcanic islands. Ironically, the word we most often associate with the bright yellow songbird is the Latin-based name for a wild canine.

CANDIDATE

In ancient Rome, one who campaigned for public office customarily wore a toga rubbed white with chalk. Symbolic of the individual's purity, the color white was the visible representation of a spotless character. The Latin adjective *candidatus* meant "dressed in a white toga." This word came ultimately from the term *candidus,* or "white."

From the notion of the pure-hearted political hopeful in the spotless toga comes the term *candidate.* The white garment etymologically embedded in the word *candidate* has atrophied, giving us a modern term referring to any person, pure or not, aspiring to public office.

The Latin *candidus* has engendered a handsome handful of modern English terms, such as *candid,* meaning frank or honest. This word, like *candidate,* bears vestiges of the whiteness or purity of truth. *Candle* and *incandescent* are also members of this word group, as are the names *Candida* and *Candide.*

Canopy

The early Greek historian Herodotus, born circa 480 B.C., spent many of his sixty years traveling throughout the ancient world. Herodotus recorded the customs and mythologies of the Mediterranean peoples he encountered. In his written collection *The History,* Herodotus describes a practice peculiar to the Egyptians of the 4th century B.C.

> In parts of Egypt above the marshes the inhabitants pass the night upon lofty towers, as the mosquitoes are unable to fly to any height on account of the winds. In the marshy country, where there are no towers, each man possesses a net. By day it serves him to catch fish, while at night he spreads it over the bed, and creeping in, goes to sleep underneath. The mosquitoes...do not so much as attempt to pass the net.

The scourge of countless mosquitoes spawned in the marshes of the Nile drove the Egyptians to invent what was possibly the world's first mosquito net or canopy.

The word *canopy* comes from the Greeks, who imported the invention from Egypt. They called the mosquito net *konopion,* after *konops,* their word for mosquito or gnat.

By the 14th century, the word arrived in the English language as *canopy,* the anglicized version of the Greek name for the mosquito.

CARDIGAN

Born in 1797 to a wealthy family, James Brudenell, later Lord Cardigan, possessed all the trappings of the English aristocracy: wealth, title, good looks, and a stable of fine riding horses.

Though amply outfitted for the gentrified life, Cardigan had from childhood aspired to military leadership. In 1826 he purchased the lieutenant colonelcy of the 11th Light Dragoons for 40,000 pounds. Because Cardigan prized appearance and military precision above all, he dressed and drilled his regiment to perfection. The men found him harsh, vain, and overbearing—qualities that rendered him a most unpopular commander and human being. Cardigan punished and jailed his men for any minor offense and became outraged when the regiment's horses turned up lame. When Cardigan ordered a soldier flogged on Easter Sunday for some peccadillo, outraged Londoners booed and hissed him at his every social appearance.

Lord Cardigan redeemed himself, albeit briefly, after leading the Light Brigade into the Battle of Balaclava during the Crimean War. Valiantly and foolishly, Cardigan charged straight into the teeth of the Russian cavalry and survived, though six hundred of his men perished.

England thereafter proclaimed Cardigan a hero. Queen Victoria honored him with an invitation to Windsor. The woolen military jacket he wore was copied by the thousands and sold across Britain as the *cardigan*. The modern version of this is a button-up sweater with a collarless neck, an adaptation of Lord Cardigan's original campaign jacket.

CARDINAL

The term *cardinal* is a hard-working English word. Consider the several definitions of the term: a bird, a brilliant red, and an official in the Roman Catholic church. It also designates something of primary importance, such as the cardinal numbers or directions.

Seemingly disparate, all *cardinals* are united directly or indirectly by a single etymological element. It comes from the Latin term *cardo,* meaning "hinge," the kind to which something important is attached.

For example, prudence, justice, temperance, and fortitude are the four *cardinal virtues* on which good conduct is hinged.

Catholic cardinals are so named because of their prominent office, eclipsed only by that of the pope. Important decisions "hinge" on a cardinal's judgment.

In Medieval Latin, *cardo* took on the sense of "chief or principle." So the cardinal directions (North, East, South, West) and the cardinal numbers (1, 2, 3, 4...) are "primary, principle."

And the little red songbird? Named, of course, after the Catholic cardinal's scarlet vestments. The moniker for this North American bird is by far the most modern sense of the word, having been recorded for the first time in 1802.

CARNATION

Generous of blossom, the fringe-petaled carnation has been a standard flower in corsages, boutonnieres, and table arrangements for decades. The pink carnation was selected in 1907 as the official floral symbol for Mother's Day.

This blossom is a native of the Mediterranean region. The Roman naturalist and historian Pliny, writing in the 1st century, reported that the Romans first encountered the flower in Spain, where the locals used it to spice their beverages.

The carnation may have been introduced to the British Isles during the Norman invasion, when the seeds of the flower were said to have clung to the stone the Normans imported for building. Reputedly, the wild plant still grows on the walls of the castle of William the Conquerer.

During the Elizabethan era, the English spiced their wine and ale with carnations. This practice inspired an alternative title for the flower, Sops-in-Wine.

The name of this famous blossom may come from *coronation* because the dented or toothed petals seemed to resemble "little crowns." More likely the word has its origins in the Latin *caro,* meaning "flesh." The pink blossoms of the carnation were thought to be the flesh color of light skin.

The word *carnation* has some unlikely etymological relatives in *carnivore,* "flesh-eater"; *carnival,* "farewell to flesh"; and *carnage,* the "flesh of battle."

Cat Words

Humans and cats have been close associates for the past 5,000 years. Domesticated by the Egyptians, cats were valued as hunters of mice and rats that plagued the immense state granaries. Egyptian cat owners so revered their animals that they embalmed them after death in preparation for their journey to the next life.

Cats slipped a few notches in popularity during Europe's Middle Ages, when they were associated with witchcraft and burned at the stake with their owners.

Cats inhabit our homes and our lexicon. A *catty* person, for example, is sneering and sarcastic; the adjective reflects the sharp claws and hisses of an offended feline.

The expression *cat's paw* recalls the fable of a clever monkey who tricks a cat into raking some chestnuts out of the fire with her paw. The monkey gets the chestnuts; the cat, nothing but burns from the fire. A cat's paw is a gullible person who may easily be used as a pawn.

The word *cat* has been slang for "prostitute" since the 14th century, and a *cathouse* was her place of employment. *Cat* is a lexical reference to the noisy lovemaking of amorous felines.

A *catcall* is a yell of scorn. In 17th century England, a catcall was a squeaky instrument played by music hall audiences to express disapproval. The *1811 Dictionary of the Vulgar Tongue* says, "It derives its name from...its sounds, which greatly resembles the modulation of an intriguing boar cat."

CATA-

The prefix *cata-* is the uniting element in words such as *catapult, catastrophe, cataract,* and *catadromous.* It is from the Greek and means "down."

The word *catapult* is a good place to start in illustrating this prefix. An ancient device designed to hurl missiles, a catapult launches weapons with fatal force. The etymology of the word reflects the action of the object: the *pult* in *catapult* comes from a Greek verb meaning "to hurl." Attach *cata-* and you have a word meaning "hurl down."

A *cataract* is a large, rushing waterfall. This word is a blend of *cata-* and the Greek verb *rattien,* "to dash." Cataracts literally (and etymologically) "dash down" the mountainside.

What about *catastrophe,* meaning a momentous, tragic event? With the *cata-* prefix attached to a verb meaning "to turn," we have a word that means, at heart, "a turning down or overturning," suggesting a violent inversion.

Finally, we have the intriguing adjective *catadromous.* A catadromous creature lives in fresh water and swims seaward to spawn. Eels are catadromous. The *dromous* portion of this word, again Greek in origin, means "to run." *Catadromous:* "running down" to the sea.

Other relatives in this word clan are *cataclysm, catatonic,* and *catalogue.* You can find the stories behind these *cata-* terms on the pages of any good dictionary.

CAUCASIAN

For centuries, philosophers, naturalists, and anthropologists have observed and tried to explain varieties of physical characteristics within human populations. Why, for instance, do certain groups of people have long slender body types while others are round and short? Why do some people have curly hair while others have straight? Why such variety in human skin color? Such inquiries have driven scientists to formulate elaborate analyses of human diversity.

In the late 18th and early 19th centuries, German naturalist Johann Blumenbach strove to answer these questions. Blumenbach asserted that the shape of the human skull was a significant racial trait, and, compelled by this belief, amassed a collection of crania from around the world. Based on various peoples' skull size and shape, as well as skin color, hair type, facial, and other physical characteristics, Blumenbach divided the people of the world into five races: American Indians, Mongolians, Ethiopians, Malayans, and Caucasians.

Blumenbach derived the word *Caucasian* from Caucasia, a region in southeastern Europe between the Black and Caspian seas. He had obtained a skull from this territory which he believed typified the Europeans, Hindus, Persians, Arabs, Hebrews, and North Africans—people whom Blumenbach included in the Caucasian race.

CHEAPSKATE

The English language has a generous vocabulary describing stingy people: *tightfisted, miser, tightwad, scrooge, penny-pincher.* While these are fairly self-explanatory epithets, one term in this category that resists ready explanation is the moniker *cheapskate. Cheap* is obvious, but where does *skate* fit in?

In the English language, *skate* is a homonym, meaning it has multiple unrelated definitions. It can be a shoe with a blade or wheels attached, or a marine creature similar to a manta ray. In American English slang, *skate* is a verb meaning to leave in a hurry, or to pass by rapidly.

The *Oxford English Dictionary* lists yet another definition of this term. It says a worn-out, inferior horse, a nag, is also called a *skate*. The American writer Ernest Hemingway used the term in this way in the 1925 collection *Two Stories.*

Yet we find none of these in the meaning of *cheapskate.* What we do find is the British slang word *skate,* rarely used on this side of the Atlantic, which means "chap" or "fellow." This apparently is an alteration of the Scottish term *skyte,* meaning "a contemptible person." This word, in turn, is derived from an even older term that means "excrement"; etymologically this word is "cheap shit."

A linguistic indictment of the miserly, *cheapskate* was first seen in print in the late 19th century.

Chinese Adoptees

English speakers are promiscuous collectors of foreign words and expressions. Thousands of our terms are adoptees from such languages as Basque, Tagalog, Italian, Hebrew, and Arabic. The various languages spoken in China have also contributed several words to modern English.

Kowtow—"show deference, to fawn"—was introduced to English speakers in the early 19th century. This word is the derivative of a Mandarin Chinese expression that means literally "knock the head," and that refers to the custom of touching the forehead to the ground as a gesture of respect.

The word *ketchup* is an anglicized pronunciation of a Chinese (Amoy dialect) word, spelled *ke-tsiap* in some 17th century documents. Originally a fish sauce, ketchup was introduced to Europe by Dutch and English merchants. English speakers adopted the word in the early 1700s. The sauce became the familiar red elixer in the 19th century when Americans began adding tomatoes to the mix.

The expression *gung-ho*, meaning "enthusiastic, eager, ready," is a relative newcomer from China. Lieutenant Col. Evans F. Carlson is responsible for adopting this phrase from the Chinese circa 1942. Carlson used *gung-ho* as a training slogan for his Rangers during the Second World War. It's the American pronunciation of a Chinese phrase that means "everybody work together."

Circum-

There are a host of words in our vocabulary beginning with the prefix *circum-*. This prefix is Latin-based; it's related to the words *circle* and *circus* and means "around, on all sides." *Circum-* shows up in words like *circumlocution, circumnavigate, circumspect,* and *circumstance.*

Circumnavigate means literally "sail completely around." Early explorers circumnavigated the globe in ocean-going vessels; modern travelers circumnavigate planet Earth in aircraft and spacecraft.

The *spect* in circumspect comes from a Latin verb meaning "to look" and is related to *spectator* and *spectacle.* So, *circumspect* literally means "looking around," or, in our usage, being prudent and mindful of potential consequences.

The prefix *circum-,* or "around," heads up the term *circumlocution,* the use of indirect locution or language. In other words, a circumlocutor "talks in circles."

A *circumstance* is an event or condition that etymologically "stands all around." Objects that encircle the sun are *circumsolar;* moon satellites are *circumlunar.*

CLICHÉS

Linguist David Crystal, author of many works on the English language, calls clichés "lexical zombies." They are zombies, Crystal says, because while clichés appear alive on the tongues of millions of English speakers, the vitality of these expressions has been sapped by repetition. Clichés such as *rule of thumb, take it or leave it, cool as a cucumber,* says Crystal, are moribund with overuse.

Critics, pundits, and teachers argue for the extermination of these dog-eared expressions. Clichés, opponents contend, rob our verbal and written communication of any novel expression.

Yet, perhaps clichés are not altogether useless. There are reasons they endure. We recruit them when conversation lags or while attempting to extend comfort at a funeral. When wit and charm fail us, a well-timed cliché can bestow a sort of lame grace upon an awkward situation.

Many of these expressions "sound good" to our ears. Hundreds of clichés owe their survival to the charm of alliteration: *bevy of beauties, lap of luxury, now or never.* The alliterative *rags to riches* is an American favorite and the theme of the 19th century Horatio Alger stories, wherein the hero rises from humble origins to pinnacles of great wealth and happiness.

Some clichés rhyme or repeat: *ants in his pants; lock, stock, and barrel; out and out; up and up; wine and dine.* Clichés reflect our love of wordplay, of rhyme and lexical rhythm.

And yet, opponents of these expressions disdain their use. They see them as living on in an eternal twilight: never fully animated, yet not diseased enough to expire. Viewed in this pallid light, clichés are lexical zombies indeed.

CLUE

We consider a clue a helpful bit of information in solving a puzzling situation. Sleuths are forever sniffing out clues to identify and nail culprits. If we put the word *clue* under the etymological magnifying glass, its astonishing history comes into focus. The sense of *clue* as a key to a mystery came from a Greek legend.

A young Athenian warrior named Theseus purposed to vanquish a bloodthirsty half-man, half-bull known as the Minotaur. This beast lived on the island of Crete in a complex underground maze from which no human had ever escaped. When Theseus entered the Minotaur's labyrinth, he took with him a ball of thread, which he unraveled as he moved throughout the maze. After killing the Minotaur, he followed the yarn back to the entrance.

Geoffrey Chaucer, retelling this tale in the 14th century, referred to the ball of yarn as a *clew*. It was an amusement throughout Europe to follow *clewes*, or balls of thread, out of garden mazes.

Clew (in Modern English *clue*) came to mean something that points the way out of the labyrinth of a mystery.

COCKTAIL

The word *cocktail* has an unsettled history. Though most word watchers agree it appeared in print in America in the early years of the 19th century, no one has been able to substantiate its origin. Even so, theories proliferate.

Perhaps it comes from the French word for an eggcup, *coqutier.* There is evidence of a New Orleans apothecary who sold tonics and bitters out of eggcups (the kind used to hold soft-boiled eggs) in the 1700s. The drink may eventually have acquired its name from its original container, *coquetier.*

Or the word may be a variant of the British term *cock-ale,* which was a mixture of chicken broth and ale. Another possibility comes from earlier British English, wherein the word *cocktailings* designated an admixture of the tailings of several liquor kegs.

A further speculation involves a fruit and rum drink concocted by a New England tavern owner during the Revolutionary War. According to this legend, French officers called this beverage *le coq's tail* because it purportedly was decorated with colorful rooster feathers. An interesting swizzle stick indeed!

Though the theories of the origin of *cocktail* are numerous, one thing remains consistent: every dictionary states "origin unknown" beside the entry of this word.

COFFEE

In a legend from Abyssinia (modern Ethiopia), a goatherd named Kaldi observed that his animals became unusually animated after eating the red berries of a certain tree growing wild in the mountains. The fabled berry of this Abyssinian legend is thought to be the wild progenitor of the modern cultivated coffee bean.

The coffee tree, indigenous to the highlands of Abyssinia, was cultivated for its berries as early as the 6th century. By the 15th century, the plant had been introduced to the Arabs, who roasted, ground, and then infused the beans in water to concoct a dark, stimulating beverage. In 1511 the world's first "coffee house" was established in Mecca.

Most etymologists believe *coffee* is a derivative of the Arabic term *qahwah,* "wine," from the early practice of making a fermented beverage from the ripe berries of the tree. Others, however, see the word coming from *Kaffa,* the name of a coffee-growing region of Ethiopia.

Whatever its source, the word has appeared around the world in various incarnations. English citations of the 17th century preserve the renderings *chaoua, cahve, caffe,* and *kauhi.* Turkish, German, Dutch, French, and Italian have *kaveh, Kaffee, koffie, cafe,* and *caffe.* Curiously, the local name for coffee in its native Ethiopia is *bun.*

CONESTOGA

Thanks to those instructive illustrations in our grade-school history books, we can all recall an image of the 18th century Conestoga wagon. A lumbering, canvas-covered vehicle, the Conestoga was designed to haul heavy freight with a six-horse team. The first of these wagons was built in about 1750 in the Conestoga Valley of Pennsylvania. Before the development of a railroad network into the interior of the continent, the Conestoga was the principle vehicle for inland commerce.

Some historians contend that the wagons, built with the brake on the left-hand side, compelled the teamsters to sit on the left side of the wagon. This in turn obliged them to drive on the right side of the trail for an unimpeded view of the road. It was this habit, apparently, which induced Americans to abandon the British custom of driving on the left.

This wagon was culturally momentous, but it is also sur-rounded by linguistic significance. *Conestoga,* or a word re-sembling it, was the name of a small but powerful East Coast Indian tribe. The valley in Pennsylvania was named after this group in the early 1700s. The wagon, in turn, was given the name of the valley in which it was first manufactured.

Later, the moniker of a small, inexpensive cigar—the *stoga* or *stogie*—was teased from the name Conestoga, as the smokes were a favorite of the Pennsylvania teamsters.

CONFLAGRATION

On Sunday evening, October 8, 1871, a fire started in Chicago at the home of the O'Leary family and nearly decimated the city. The blaze devoured over 17,000 buildings, claimed 250 lives and left 98,000 homeless before it was finally extinguished twenty-six hours later.

A fire of this magnitude is often called a *conflagration*. This term is a fusion of the prefix *con-*, "completely," and the Latin verb *flagrare*, "to blaze."

Flagrare also appears in the word *flagrant*. The notion of "burning" is also embedded in this term, *flagrant* meaning "flaming, glaring, notorious," and by extension "shocking." A flagrant criminal, for instance, commits misdeeds openly, in blazing contempt of propriety.

The Latin phrase *in flagrante delicto* is a first cousin to the words *conflagration* and *flagrant*. This expression means "caught red-handed" and is often used in the context of catching illicit lovers in the throes of passion. Carolyn Banks, in her review of Michael Korda's novel *The Fortune*, contributed this to the March 14, 1989, *Washington Post:* "This novel opens with the man who handles legal matters for the legendary Bannerman family traveling...to announce the death of Arthur Aldon Bannerman.... Bannerman, 65, died *in flagrante delicto* in an apartment inhabited by a ravishing 24-year-old woman." Literally translated, *in flagrante delicto* means "while the crime still blazes."

CONFUSABLE TERMS

The number of words in the English lexicon is unknown. The most authoritative compendium of the English language, the *Oxford English Dictionary,* boasting a half million entries, is incomplete. It can't possibly keep abreast of our rapidly morphing slang and technological terminologies.

With so many words at our command, it's not surprising that we confuse one word with another at times. For example, what is the difference between *meteoroid* and *meteorite? Bigamy* and *polygamy?* Our uncertainty about the subtle distinctions between such words can cause us to avoid them.

But in the case of the latter pair, a little word scrutiny clears confusion. *Bigamy* is the state of having two spouses. *Polygamy* indicates multiple marriage partners. The *gamy* portion in these words comes from the Greek word for marriage. The *bi-* in bigamy means "two" (this prefix is also in *bicycle* and *bisexual*). The *poly-* in *polygamy* means "many, multiple." *Bigamy* and *polygamy:* two and many marriages, respectively.

What of the *meteoroid/meteorite* dilemma? Interplanetary masses of metal and stone in flight are meteoroids. When they plunge through the earth's atmosphere and survive the flaming descent as solid chunks of matter, they're meteorites. Alas, unlike the previous pair of confusable terms, the difference between these two must simply be committed to memory.

Is it *modesty* or *prudery? Livid* or *vivid?* The English language is a maze of confusing pairs of words resembling each other in pronunciation or meaning or both. Most of us have violated the language by scrambling such word pairs as *fluid* and *liquid, successful* and *successive, stalagmite* and *stalactite.*

What is the difference between *modesty* and *prudery? Modesty,* a term of Latin derivation, suggests shyness, sobriety, freedom from vanity and pretension. Generally, it's a positive term. *Prudery,* on the other hand, is a pejorative or negative word. It implies self-conscious propriety. A *prude* is a slave to respectability, one who "masquerades" modesty. Interestingly, this word is an adaptation of the French *prudefemme,* meaning "excellent woman."

Livid and *vivid* are nearly twins in sound but unrelated in meaning. *Livid* is a ghastly blue-gray, as you might see on a corpse or a bodacious bruise. Latin by birth, *livid* comes from a verb meaning "to be blue" and may be etymological kin to *lavender. Vivid,* on the other hand, comes from a Latin verb meaning "to live." Related to *vivacious* and the exuberant cry "Viva!," *vivid* means lively, brilliant, or vigorous. It also can imply the production of sharp mental images, as in *vivid description.*

Other pairs of near synonyms to consider are *preface* and *foreword, presently* and *soon, sarcastic* and *sardonic, dock* and *pier.* The confusability of these terms is the curse or blessing of speaking a language containing a hyperabundance of words.

CONNOTATION, DENOTATION

Most of us learned the difference between *connotation* and *denotation* under the tutelage of a long-suffering English teacher. While understanding this difference is not essential for a long and prosperous life, musing on the concepts behind these words can foster an appreciation for the richness and beauty of our language.

The *denotation* of a term is its exact and literal meaning. Consider the word *home*. Its denotation, or precise meaning, is "residence or fixed dwelling place." The denotation of the word *city* is "center of population and commerce."

A word's *connotation,* on the other hand, consists of its emotive value. For example, connotations of the word *home* might be refuge, resting place, even predictable or boring habitation. The word *city* might connote place of excitement, energy, danger, or even sin.

Connotational meanings are almost symbolic, with the symbolism varying according to individual experience. This is how *home* can connote "sanctuary" to one and "dreary dwelling" to another. The connotations of *city* can move from cultural hub to human cesspool, depending on the opinions and memories of the person using the word.

Think of denotation as the dictionary definition of a word, using the *d* as a mnemonic device. A connotation is the subjective, personal, even poetic interpretation of a word.

CORNY, CHEESY

Every native speaker of American English understands the significance of this pair of slurs. In our slang vocabulary, *cheesy* is anything cheap, overripe, or second-rate, as in cheesy motel décor. *Corny* points to that which is sentimental, trite, or hopelessly out of date.

Corny appeared on the American slangscape sometime in the 1930s. Probably invented by jazz musicians, the term originally referred to country or old-time styles of music. Some sources claim the word comes from the farm corn that was raised and fed to stock animals. Others contend that *corny* arose from the homespun jokes and artwork sprinkled throughout the so-called corn catalogues advertising all types of seed to American farmers.

Cheesy predates *corny* by about fifty years. It shows up in print in the late 19th century and has been used consistently throughout the decades to describe things chintzy, gaudy, or shabby. The source of this term is cloudy. It may be the lexical offspring of the expression *big cheese,* self-important person, referring to the gaudy or obvious tastes of such a cheese. Or, *cheesy* may evoke the pungent, unpleasant odor of over-ripe or spoiled cheese—too much of a good thing.

Cosmos Words

Our word *cosmos* comes from Greek *kosmos,* a term that implies a well-ordered and harmonious physical world. This word is an important element in the terms *cosmopolitan, cosmonaut,* and *microcosm.*

As a title for a prominent women's magazine, *Cosmopolitan* suggests worldliness, style, and sophistication. But this term has a philosophic origin. The Stoic philosophers of the 4th and 3rd centuries B.C. believed that all humans shared the same mind and understanding. The Stoics saw a unity in humankind, and all could claim an equal place on the earth. In the Stoic philosophy, we are all *cosmopolitans.* This word means "citizen of the world," from *kosmos,* "world," and *politan,* meaning "dweller of a city, a citizen."

Soviet astronauts are *cosmonauts.* The *naut* in *cosmonaut* implies a sailor or adventurer; it's related to our English words *nautical* and *navy.* A cosmonaut is etymologically a "sailor of the world, an adventurer of the universe."

A *microcosm* is literally a "little world." Insects inhabit microcosms (relative to the size of our dwellings), little worlds in which these creatures live, procreate, and die.

CRANE

When spring returns to the northern states, so does the elegant and graceful sandhill crane. Flying in from their Texas and New Mexico winter feeding grounds, flocks of cranes announce their vernal arrival with wild, trumpeting cries. Pairs of birds establish nesting sites, perform elaborate courtship dances, mate, and raise their chicks.

The North American sandhill crane has cousins all over the world. The crowned crane is an African inhabitant; the common crane lives in Europe and Asia. In Japan, cranes are symbolic of long life, and in folklore they are reputed to live a thousand years. Crane courtship displays in Australia inspire the dances of aboriginal "corroborees," while the Ainu tribe of Japan has a dance honoring the indigenous Manchurian crane.

The English word *crane* comes from an ancient Germanic term meaning "to cry hoarsely." The scientific designation of this avian family is Gruidae, from the Latin word for crane, *grus,* also a syllabic representation of the bird's hoarse call. In modern French, the word for this bird is *grue.*

The French *pied du grue* became the English *pedigree.* It literally means "foot of the crane." How is a crane's foot related to the reckoning of genetic heritage? The notion behind the metaphor is that this bird's splayed footprint resembles the branching lines of the diagram of a family tree.

CRETIN

In past centuries, many babies born in the French Alps were profoundly disfigured and stunted both physically and mentally. Often these dwarfish children were deaf, mute, and afflicted with goiter.

These maladies were probably the result of a thyroid deficiency, now known as myxedema, caused by a lack of iodine in the diet. This phenomenon is common in Alpine regions, where iodine is washed from the soil by rain water.

A baby born with these defects was called, in the French Alpine dialect, *Chrétien*. Meaning "Christian," the title was given kindly, implying that though deformed, the child was not a beast. He possessed a Christian soul and, being of simple mind, was innocent of sin.

In the 18th century this word passed into standard French as *cretin,* without the benevolent connotation. In a turn for the worse, *cretin* came to mean "stupid, vulgar person." English speakers adopted this word in its pejorative sense in the late 1700s.

The word *cretinism* first appeared in print in 1801. A clinical designation, *cretinism* refers to the conditions of dwarfism and deformity manifest in a person with thyroid deficiency.

CRYPT

A *crypt* is a vault, an underground chamber, a grotto. We often associate the word *crypt* with bodies long deceased in creepy, drippy underground graves. Indeed, the remains of martyrs and saints are installed in subterranean crypts of some European cathedrals. This term comes to us ultimately from the Greek word *kruptos,* meaning "hidden." A crypt, whether grave or cave or chamber, is a secret, sequestered place.

The Greek *crypt* element manifests itself in a sizable etymological family. Consider *cryptic,* an adjective meaning mysterious, enigmatic, hidden. A *cryptogram* is a piece of writing in secret characters. *Cryptanalysis* is the deciphering of cryptograms.

A *cryptonym* is a secret name. *Cryptasthesia,* a term coined in 1923, refers to the talents of a clairvoyant or telepath and means "sensing that which is hidden."

A novel twist on this ancient word emerged in the 1940s with the moniker *cryptocommunist,* or simply *crypto,* for one who conceals his allegiance to that political philosophy.

CULINARY INSULTS

There are many edible and nutritious items that are not a part of the standard American diet. Our culture does not generally recognize worms, horses, or monkeys as edible, while others consider them quite palatable. On the other hand, we find that cow's milk, considered essential to our diet, is repugnant to a sizable percentage of the world's people.

Because food preferences vary so much across cultures, people often categorize others by what they eat. These classifications creep into vocabularies as so-called ethnic slurs based on culinary preference. Here are a few examples.

Because of their fondness for fermented cabbage, the Germans were called *Krauts.* The French were *Frogs,* an insult possibly generated by the English, who preferred beef over amphibian. The English in turn were called *Limeys* because of the lime juice taken by British sailors to prevent scurvy. A Scandinavian was a *Herring Choker.* The epithet *Garlic Snapper* was given to Italian immigrants; those of Mexican descent, *Beaner* or *Beano.*

This phenomenon appears not to be restricted to the European/American experience. The name *Eskimo* is an Algonquin term of derision meaning "eaters of raw flesh." The Eskimo, who call themselves *Inuit,* "the People," obviously do not categorize themselves by what they eat.

CUTE

We generally reserve the adjective *cute* to describe something pretty, small, or perhaps pertly attractive. Almost all creatures are cute in infancy: puppies, colts, bunnies. The adjective is also a term of approval for fashionable clothing— a cute blouse, coat, pair of shoes. We also apply the word to a charming boy or girl. Consider, though, that most adults, and certainly most men, are not considered "cute," at least not in the pertly attractive sense.

It may seem surprising that this term is the direct off-spring of the no-nonsense adjective *acute,* meaning sharp, clever, or keen-witted. By way of a linguistic process called aphesis, the unaccented vowel in the first syllable of *acute* was dropped, leaving its truncated form, *'cute.*

When this short form first appeared in print in the 1700s, it was identical in meaning to its parent. Quotations from the 18th and 19th centuries mention 'cute lawyers and 'cute businessmen. By the mid-1800s, *cute* began to acquire its current meaning of adorable, fine-featured, and attractive.

Why this bifurcation in meaning? Perhaps it arose from a notion that cleverness and attractiveness in humans are somehow associated. But feminist and writer Jane Mills, editor of a dictionary called *Womanwords,* asserts that when women and girls are perceived by men as attractive or cute, these alluring females then are also *acute,* slyly skillful and deftly coy.

DEAD AS A DOORNAIL, DEAD RINGER

Have you ever wondered what kinds of mortalities are involved in *dead as a doornail* and *dead ringer?* We get a lot of mileage out of these expressions without understanding what drives them. If you can't imagine why a doornail or ringer is deader than any other inanimate object, don't despair. No one else has a firm grasp on these concepts either. But here are the best conjectures.

The nail in *dead as a doornail* may have been a heavy stud against which a door knocker was struck. After many visitors had brutally percussed on the nail, it was said to have had the life knocked out of it. Appearing in 1350, the phrase is firmly established in our language. It probably owes its longevity to its catchy alliteration.

The expression *dead ringer* doesn't involve death at all. Instead, it refers to an excellent imitation of something. The *Henry Holt Encyclopedia of Word and Phrase Origins,* by Robert Hendrickson, reminds the reader that the term *ringer* was "once slang for counterfeit, derived from the sale of brass rings for gold at country fairs." The *dead* of *dead ringer* doesn't imply the cessation of life. Just as the expression *dead on* means "completely on target," a dead ringer is an absolutely convincing counterfeit or duplication.

DEADLINE

No matter our vocations or avocations, we all have them—deadlines: dates or times when we must deliver or face the consequences.

Our 21st century notion of *deadline* differs from the original meaning of this expression. Though today it's a temporal demarcation, during the Civil War, when it was established, a deadline was a physical border.

The word was first used in the notorious Confederate prison camp in Andersonville, Georgia. The prison was a stockade enclosing about 26 acres and designed to hold 10,000 captives. In August of 1864, Andersonville contained 33,000 Union soldiers, a third of which died of starvation, disease, or exposure.

Lining the entire inside of the stockade, standing 20 feet from the outer wall, was a fence about 4 feet high. Any prisoner attempting to cross this fenceline was considered an escapee and shot dead by guards. The fence was succinctly labeled the *dead line*.

In decades to follow, the expression was used metaphorically to delineate class or racial borders within towns. To breach this *dead line* was a social, but not a mortal, offense.

By 1920, journalists and editors had appropriated the term. A story or article breaching the temporal border was deemed dead to that particular edition; it had violated its *dead line*.

Death Euphemisms

Euphemisms are polite, agreeable words we substitute for unpleasant or embarrassing ones. We use euphemisms to avoid the unpleasantness of death, to steer clear of uttering sacrilegious oaths, and to mitigate some of the disturbing realities of life.

The discourse of the funeral industry is almost always euphemized. What used to be called a *deadhouse* in earlier centuries is now more comfortingly labeled a *funeral home,* and graveyards are now *memorial parks.*

People operating funeral homes were formerly *undertakers,* but in 1895 the euphemistic term *mortician* was coined in imitation of the prestigious-sounding *physician.* In the 21st century, undertakers and morticians are *funeral directors.*

Deceased and *departed* are funeral euphemisms for the dead. The deceased is no longer placed in a coffin but a *casket,* which is not buried but *interred.* And in the alternative disposition, it's not the ashes, it's the *cremains.*

Euphemism comforts us, linguistically at least, with such expressions as *she passed on, went home, passed away, went to her reward, gave up the struggle, crossed to the other side.*

Dec-

The Latin word for ten is *decem*. In Greek, ten is *deka*, which shows up in English as the prefix *deca-*. Together, these two "tens" are the progenitors of the modern English *December, decimal, decimate, decathlon, decade, decahedron,* and others.

December is the name of our twelfth and last month of the year. The ancient Roman calendar, however, consisted of only ten lunar cycles, beginning with March and closing with December, which is etymologically "month number ten," from the Latin *decem*. When Julius Caesar revised the ancient calendar by inserting months January and February, December was bumped from month ten to (the etymologically incorrect) month twelve.

Decem is also the precursor of the word *decimal*, "relating to ten or tenths." The *decimal system* is based on units of ten. To *decimate* is to etymologically "destroy by one-tenth." In a practice called *decimation,* one in ten Roman soldiers was chosen by lot to be executed for any corporate military crime such as mutiny or treason.

The Greek *deka* appears in *decade,* a period of ten years. A *decennial* is a tenth anniversary. A *decathlete* competes in a *decathlon,* a track and field contest of ten events. A *decahedron* is a solid figure with ten sides, and a *decagon* is a plane figure with ten sides and ten angles.

DECOY

For centuries, American hunters have used bird decoys to lure waterfowl into shotgun range. These waterbird doppelgangers are fashioned from a variety of buoyant materials: cork, reeds, canvas, and all types of wood.

The word *decoy* is not confined to the denomination of duck and goose lures. Over the centuries, it's been applied to human impostors who entice innocents into dangerous situations. During wartime, *decoy ships* are employed to deceive and distract enemy vessels. Federal officials set *decoy deer* to draw the illegal fire of poachers.

The original decoys were neither lures nor impostors, but cages set over water. A *decoy*, says the *Oxford English Dictionary* of the 17th century use of the word, is "a pond or pool out of which run narrow arms...covered with network or other contrivances into which wild ducks or other fowl may be allured and there caught." The "covering of network" was probably willow, tightly woven to prevent the escape of the trapped birds.

This technology was used by the Dutch, whose word for cage is *kooi*. *De kooi* means "the cage." When the British adopted the woven device and its name in the early 17th century, they retained the definite article *de* and grafted it to the noun, so that the Dutch *de kooi* became the English *decoy*. Eventually, this word came to indicate any device used to allure and entrap.

DELIRIOUS

A *delirious* person is afflicted by confusion, anxiety, disorientation, and in extreme cases hysteria and hallucinations. Delirium can be precipitated by the toxic effects of drugs, or by illness or disease.

Despite the alarming symptoms associated with delirium, the words *delirium* and *delirious* have rather lyrical origins. They were, in fact, inherited from the peaceful tradition of agriculture as practiced in the ancient Mediterranean world.

In the Latin language, the word *lira* refers to the orderly ridges of a plowed field. A willing traction animal and a strong farmer could turn over long, straight furrows and ridges for planting. A man beset with distraction, fatigue, or illness, however, might waver, upsetting the order of these productive and logical rows.

The word *delirium* reflects the adulteration of the systematic progression of planting. With *lira* referring to the ridges of a field, *delirium* means, then, a deviation from the straight ridges, with the *de-* prefix meaning "away from."

A delirious person metaphorically produces irregular ridges; his or her illness distracts from the logic of an ordered life.

DEMOCRACY

A *democracy* is government by the people. *Democracy* is Greek in origin and a blend of a pair of terms: *demos,* which means simply "the people," and *kratos,* meaning "power or authority."

Demos also appears in the term *demagogue,* which means "leader of the people." The original Greek demagogues were governers drawn from the corps of commoners. During the 17th century, however, the word *demagogue* became a pejorative, referring no longer simply to a popular leader but to an agitator who gains power by irresponsibly appealing to emotions and prejudices.

The Greek *demos* element appears in the terms *demography* and *demographics.* Demography is the study of the characteristics of groups of people or human populations. The literal translation of the term would be "writings about the people," with the *graphy* in the word coming from the Greek verb *graphein,* meaning "to write."

Demos is present but tucked away in the terms *epidemic* and *pandemic.* An *epidemic* is a disease etymologically "upon the people," with *epi-* meaning "upon." A *pandemic* is a plague affecting all of the people, with *pan-* as a prefix referring to "all or every."

DIALECTS

If you speak English, you have a dialect. Many Canadians, Australians, and Jamaicans are English speakers, but they communicate in different dialects. Linguists refer to dialects as mutually intelligible versions of the same basic language structure.

Every language has dialects. What causes these variations? One way that dialectal diversity can develop is when groups of people separate geographically. In A.D. 872, for example, wanderers left the land now known as Norway and sailed westward to settle on an island we now call Iceland. Both the mainlanders and the islanders originally spoke a language called Old Norse; but over the centuries, mutually intelligible versions, or *dialects,* of that language developed. The dialects have grown apart to such an extent that the Icelandic spoken on the island is now considered a language completely separate from, but related to, mainland Norwegian.

English, brought to the New World by colonists, has developed into several American dialects, including northern, midland, southern, western, southwestern, and Rocky Mountain as well as a handful of specific subvariations. All of these have been influenced by patterns of immigration and the development of geographical and political boundaries.

The study of dialects is complex and fascinating. Dialectologists devote their careers to tracking the distribution of language variations. These scholars produce remarkably detailed dictionaries and atlases from the data they gather. If this type of study interests you, go to your library and check out the *Dictionary of American Regional English (DARE),* edited by Frederic Cassidy, Joan Hall, and others.

Just as every American dictionary of quality is compiled with the aid of a panel of experts, so too was the *Dictionary of American Underworld Lingo*, published in 1950. But rather than a panel of sociologists, biologists, linguists, and other respected scholars, the linguistic advisors for this dictionary were Bad Bill (armed robber), Hal the Rebel (auto-theft gang boss, JoJo (terrorist), and the Colonel (purse snatcher).

In his introduction, editor-in-chief Hyman E. Goldin says the *Dictionary of American Underworld Lingo* is the product of twenty-five years of collaboration with these and other convicts. Together they divulged 5,000 words and phrases engendered by underground activities in the shadows of American streets and behind the bars of Sing Sing, San Quentin, and Columbus State Penitentiary in the 19th and early 20th centuries.

Some words and phrases in this lexicon are classic tough-guy gangster movie slang. You'll find the familiar *stool pigeon, rat, shake-down,* and *fink* on the pages of the *Dictionary of American Underworld Lingo.* But most entries are more obscure, such as the word *muggles,* early underworld for marijuana cigarettes. An evening of narcotics consumption was a *night on the rainbow. Ketchup dog* was another name for a bloodhound used to hunt escaped convicts. One who robs a drunk was a *lush diver.* In underworld lingo, a gun or pistol was called a *gat,* the abbreviation of Gatling machine gun.

A *gabo* was one who talked too much. A crudely made underworld bomb was a *guinea football.* To *kick the mooch around* was to smoke on an opium pipe. *Worm-workers* specialize in stealing silk. A *Mary Magdalene* was a reformed prostitute. An inmate of a mental institution was said to *play with the squirrels,* while a *crap merchant* was a liar or persuasive talker.

The *Dictionary of American Underworld Lingo* is divided into "Underworld–English" and "English–Underworld" sections for easy reference. The "Underworld–English" section lists such entries as *make a kisser:* to grimace an expression of distaste, contempt, or annoyance; *pack horse:* one who assumes criminal guilt to protect others. Entries from the "English–Underworld" section include die: *chalk out, check out, croak, slam off;* policeman: *door-shaker, mama bull, crapper dick, town clown, fuzz;* addiction to hypodermic narcotics: *be on the hype-stick, on the light artillery, shooting the pin;* handshake: *mitt-glom;* professional female criminal: *knock around broad, gun moll, racket broad, moll whiz.*

Unusual lexicons such as the *Dictionary of American Underworld Lingo* are windows to new worlds where language is pulled apart and recombined into contortions that somehow make sense. Specialized dictionaries teach us about our own patterns of speech and use of expressions and illustrate the elasticity of language and our utter delight in playing with words.

A Dictionary of Surnames

To most of us, a dictionary is a volume of standard English words and their definitions. But a closer inspection of the library or bookstore shelf reveals lexicons of all stripes: dictionaries of abbreviations, acronyms, sports and cowboy terms, theatrical terminology, clichés, literary terms, and political jargon.

A Dictionary of Surnames investigates the origins of last names. This 800-page treasure contains the origins and variations of European surnames from *Aaron,* Hebrew for "mountain of strength," to *Zwilling,* German for "twin."

Gorton, we discover, derives from the name of a town in Lancashire, England. In Old English, the name means "dirt settlement." The *-ton* in many English last names—Gorton, Stapleton, Stanton, Sutton—refers to a settlement or enclosure. *Sutton* means "southern settlement." *Stanton* is a "stone enclosure." *Stapleton* means "post enclosure."

The Czech surname *Novak* and the English *Newcomb* and *Newman* are triplets in meaning. These three designate a "newcomer" to a village or district. In a place and age of relatively little travel, new inhabitants were often marked by such monikers.

A Dictionary of Surnames was compiled by Patrick Hanks and Flavia Hodges and published in 1988 by Oxford University Press.

Diploma, Diplomat

These days a graduate gets a robe, a tassel, gifts from relieved parents, and, most important, a diploma. Diplomas have not, however, always been a student's reward. Before the mid-17th century, a *diploma* was an official state document, or a letter of recommendation. This word hails from the Greek term *diplous,* meaning "double, twofold," ultimately giving us a word that means "piece of paper folded over."

Officials traveling abroad on state business often carried with them such diplomas, or "folded documents." Such individuals were the first *diplomats,* making *diplomacy* the tact and discretion exercised by prudent officials bearing official documents to foreign leaders. *Diplomacy* was introduced to English speakers late in the 18th century by the British political theorist Edmund Burke in his *Letters on a Regicide Peace* (1795–1797).

A student's diploma is an official document conferring rights and privileges on the graduate. Scholastic diplomas may have once been "folded over" as the name suggests, but today diplomas are simply a single-page document inscribed with the appropriate academic incantations to graduate a student.

DISCOVER, INVENT, INNOVATE

The terms *discover, invent,* and *innovate* are not synonymous, yet the distinctions among them aren't always clear.

Discover says exactly what it means: to un-cover, to reveal something that exists but has heretofore been obscured. A star, a new species of insect, or a chemical element, for example, are all candidates for discovery.

To *invent,* on the other hand, involves the application of known principles or discoveries in creating a novel object or idea. The candle is an invention; it's an amalgam of fire (a discovered element), a wick, and tallow. Other tangible inventions are the plow, anesthesia, and the compass. Intangible inventions include geometry and democracy. The word *invent* comes ultimately from the Latin term *invenire,* "to come upon, find."

At the heart of the word *innovate* is the Latin *novus,* meaning "new." Siblings of *innovate* are *novel, novice,* and *nova.* To *innovate* is to make changes in something already established, to "re-new" an invention. For example, Henry Ford was not so much inventor as innovator. Ford didn't invent the car, but he made it more accessible through assembly line production—an innovation in the auto manufacturing process that enabled millions to purchase this four-wheeled invention.

DISGRUNTLE

The word *disgruntle* has been a part of the English lexicon since at least the 17th century. For over three hundred years, the definition of this term has remained remarkably stable, meaning "to chagrin, disgust, put into a sulky mood."

The adjective *disgruntled* means "peevish, ill-humored." In the late 20th and early 21st centuries, we see this adjective conjoined to all types of plural nouns: disgruntled employees, students, smokers, investors, sports fans, teachers. Most familiar is the disturbing *disgruntled postal worker,* a phrase frequently headlined as reports of armed assaults at Post Office sites surfaced across the nation. *Disgruntled* has become the adjective of choice to invoke the frustration and anger employees feel toward powerful corporate or government entities.

Despite its implied rage, the word has a relatively pacific etymological background. *Gruntle* is based on a Middle English verb meaning "complain." The related, modern word *grunt* originally suggested complaint as well.

Is *disgruntle,* then, the opposite of *gruntle?* To "uncomplain"? No. Confusingly, the *dis* in this word is a variant of the prefix *di-,* meaning "double," as in *dichromatic,* "two-colored," and *dichotomy,* "a separation into two." Etymologically, *disgruntle* is "double-gruntle," to grunt, grumble, or complain repeatedly.

DOGIE

In the traditional western tune "Get Along Little Dogie," the cowboy sings:

> Whoopee ti yi yo, git along little dogie,
> It's your misfortune and none of my own,
> Whoopee ti yi yo, git along little dogie,
> You know that Wyomin' will be your new home.

The *dogie* immortalized in this song is an orphaned calf, or in the colorful words of the cowboy, "a calf who has lost its mammy and whose daddy run off with another cow."

The origin of this word is obscure. It may have come from the Afro-Creole term *dogi,* meaning "small" or "short," in reference to the stunted stature of orphaned calves. Perhaps because the calves were malnourished and barely larger than dogs, cowboys may have called them doggies or dogies, again in reference to their diminutive size.

The most plausible explanation is given by Ramon Adams, editor of a cowboy dictionary called *Western Words.* He tells us that, forced to eat grass before they could efficiently digest it, the motherless calves developed distended, bloated bellies. To the cow man, it looked as though these orphans had a belly full of sourdough. The calves were called *dough-guts,* a word that later became *doughies* or *dogies.*

This term was printed for the first time in an 1888 edition of *Century* magazine.

Dog in the Manger

Aesop was an ancient Greek storyteller whose name has been attached to a number of fables featuring talking, moralizing animals. These tales have been repeated through the oral traditions of many cultures and have been retold in hundreds of printed collections. Aesop's fables have inspired dozens of English language expressions such as *sour grapes, cry wolf,* and *slow and steady wins the race.*

Dog in the manger is another cliché inspired by Aesop's beast fables. It labels someone who not only doesn't appreciate a certain thing or activity but also prevents others from enjoying it. As Aesop told it, a dog seeking a comfortable place to nap curled up on the hay in an ox's stable. At day's end, the hungry ox returned to his stable, looking for feed. Enraged because his nap had been interrupted, the dog snarled and snapped at the ox whenever he approached the hay.

The ox became exasperated. "Dog," he said, "I would share my dinner with you if you were inclined to eat hay. But you can't eat it yourself, nor will you let me enjoy it. Your behavior is selfish and irrational."

Aesop's moral or application of this tale is "Some begrudge others what they themselves cannot enjoy." Like the dog in the manger.

DOLLAR, CURRENCY, BUCK

The author Washington Irving, in a November 12, 1836, edition of the *Knickerbocker Magazine,* wrote, "the almighty dollar, that great object of universal devotion throughout our land." In this passage, Irving coined the expression *almighty dollar,* a phrase that reflects the status we've accorded to money.

The word *dollar* itself is a variation of the German word *Joachimsthaler,* a coin minted in 1519 in Joachimsthal, Bohemia. *Joachimsthaler* became *thaler,* which resulted in the pronunciation "dollar" in England in 1581. By 1683, Americans began calling their coins *dollars.* Thomas Jefferson, in 1784, suggested that the dollar, and not the English pound, be the basic unit of currency on this continent.

The word *currency,* referring to money in circulation, was so named because it refers to the "current," generally accepted medium of exchange.

Though *buck,* the American slang term for "dollar," has been fabulously successful, its origin is elusive. Some sources assert that it comes from *buckskin,* an important trade item on the American frontier. In the early 19th century, skins were classified as "bucks" and "does," with the former being larger and more valuable. According to this theory, the term *buck* gradually became synonymous with the money given for the skin.

DONNYBROOK

About three miles southeast of the city center in Dublin, Ireland, lies the residential district of Donnybrook. It is situated on the main road from Dublin to the seaside resorts of Bray and Greystones.

This relatively peaceful district has a wild and checkered past, which began in the year 1204, when the town was granted permission by King John to hold a two-week fair every August. The celebration attracted merchants, buyers, and sellers from all surrounding districts.

As the decades rolled by, the fair at Donnybrook became more and more animated. Fortified with *usquebaugh* (whiskey) and beer, inebriated revelers year after year cheerfully whacked each other's skulls with fist and *shillelagh* (club).

By the late 18th century, the Donnybrookers were making liquor from the corn and cane imported from the New World. The chummy Donnybrook carousal turned violent, and heads were split in earnest. The fair was abbreviated from two weeks to one, then was finally suppressed by the government in 1855.

An element of that annual brawl survives in our language. The term *donnybrook* means any loud, uncontrolled argument, in the spirit of the rowdy fairs of the old Irish district.

Doozy

The development of the automobile in the late 19th and early 20th centuries created a linguistic vacuum for new words to describe this invention and the culture it inspired. Our American slang word *doozy,* meaning fine or excellent, is an example of such a term.

The story of this word begins with the last name of engineer Frederick Duesenberg, a German who immigrated to Iowa in the late 19th century. As a young man, Frederick operated a bicycle shop. Frederick himself was a bicycle racer, and he became locally famous by winning contests with running horses.

Frederick's love for speed was later expressed in his most famous engineering creation, the Duesenberg, an early luxury automobile capable of cruising at 130 miles per hour. Duesenberg's 1921 Model A was the first automobile with a straight-eight engine and four-wheel hydraulic brakes. At least one of these opulent autos graced the driveways of the glamorous Greta Garbo, Clark Gable, and Mae West.

And the word inspired by this handsome automated carriage? *Doozy,* a word meaning fine or excellent on the scale of Frederick Duesenberg's sumptuous chariot. At times this word is turned on its head with sarcasm, as in "he pulled a real doozy," meaning someone committed a first-class blunder.

Doughboy

Although U.S. infantrymen were called *doughboys* for almost two centuries, the origin of this curious term is lost in the haze of history. There are as many propositions about the birthplace of *doughboy* as there are people who propose such things.

The celebrated lexicographer H. L. Mencken believed the first doughboys fought for the Continental Army. These soldiers reputedly applied white clay dust to the piping on their uniforms to keep them bright. The dust thickened in the rain, congealing into blobs of doughlike clay that clung to the soldiers' uniforms.

Another explanation involves dust as well, this time the powdery earth of southwest Texas. Foot soldiers traversing the Rio Grande were often begrimed with the dust of adobe soil. Mounted troops called the infantry soldiers *adobes,* then *dobies,* and finally *doughboys.*

George Armstrong Custer's wife, Libby, provides the next etymological possibility for this disputed term. In her 1888 memoir, *Tenting on the Plains,* she writes: "A doughboy is a small round doughnut served to sailors on shipboard, generally with hash. Early in the Civil War, the term was applied to the large globular brass buttons of the infantry uniform, from which it passed by natural transition to the infantrymen themselves."

DRAG

Carl Sandburg said, "Slang is a language that rolls up its sleeves, spits on its hands, and goes to work." One of the hardest working members of our slang vocabulary has to be the term *drag*.

In the 1700s, a *drag* was a cart or wagon "dragged" by horses. In the early years of the mechanized age, folks linguistically blurred the line between horses and horsepower by referring to automobiles as *drags*. The association between wheeled drags and the roads they traversed may have inspired the expressions *main drag* and *drag race*.

In the teen slang of the mid-20th century, a *drag* was a young woman who needed an escort to a dance, or one's girlfriend or sweetheart—someone to affectionately "drag along."

Then, of course, there's the *drag* on a cigarette that draws smoke into the lungs, and the human *drag* who's a disappointing bore.

To dress *in drag* is an expression galvanized by men assuming women's roles onstage during the 18th and 19th centuries. The long skirts dragging across the floor created a sensation antithetical to trousered locomotion. The phrase *dress in drag,* in all its novel implications, follows us boldly into the 21st century.

DRUNK

American English slang staggers with synonyms for the state of inebriation. Slang terms for *drunk* number in the thousands and have been a conspicuous part of our parlance for centuries.

For example, the word *boozy* turns up in written citations from the early 1500s; *soused* was a common term in the 1600s; and *lushy* appears circa 1811.

It seems as if English speakers have always enjoyed slinging the slang of drunkenness. Paradoxically, during the Prohibition years (1919–1932) drunk slang became an American linguistic obsession. Citizens could become *gassed, polluted, fried, blotto, canned, crocked,* and *swacked* on bootleg liquor.

Lexicographers Harold Wentworth and Stuart Berg Flexner, compilers of the excellent *Dictionary of American Slang* published in 1960, arrange drunk monikers into several categories. There are terms alluding to being high or happy, such as *jolly, feeling no pain, lit up, elevated, relaxed, rosy.* Other terms refer to being cooked, bottled, or contained, such as *canned, pickled, stewed, preserved, mulled.* Another of Wentworth and Flexner's drunk slang categories involves the concept of being bent or beaten: *hammered, clobbered, smashed, whipped, stunned.*

DUNCE

We've all seen images of the schoolroom dunce—the unfortunate child displayed on a high stool before the class, wearing the unmistakable conical cap. The title *dunce,* given unkindly to slow-witted pupils, comes, ironically, from the name of a 14th century European scholar.

John Duns Scotus, whose name means "John Duns from Scotland," was born in 1265. He joined the Franciscan order in 1291, after which he lectured at Oxford. He became regent master in theology in Paris early in the 14th century.

Scotus was a gifted philosopher and theologian. Clever in reasoning and methods of analysis, he was given the moniker "Subtle Doctor" by his colleagues. The Catholic Church formally embraced as dogma the doctrine of Immaculate Conception in part because Scotus so passionately defended it.

For two hundred years after his death in 1308, John Duns Scotus remained a great influence on European philosophy and theology. His adherents, the "Dunsmen," read and taught his doctrines in the most prestigious universities. But the Dunsmen despised and resisted change. The new thinkers of the Renaissance called the hidebound Dunsmen "old barking curs" and accused them of philosophic hair-splitting. The Dunsmen became the *dunces*—philosophical slaves, lacking powers of reasoning and argument.

DUTCH INSULTS

In the 17th century, the English and Dutch empires were both flexing their muscles. Rivals in international commerce, the two nations resented each economic toehold gained by the other.

The British vented their spleen by verbally skewering their rivals, inventing insulting epithets that endured into the 20th century. *Dutch treat* is probably the most familiar of these insults, a phrase that is an invitation to pay one's own bill.

Dutch defense meant a surrender; *Dutch steak,* a hamburger; *Dutch nightingale,* a frog.

The recipients of these nettles were justifiably insulted. In 1934, the Dutch eliminated the word *Dutch* from their official documents. They replaced it with various forms of the term *Netherland.* The British paid no attention. The barbs continued to fly. Among them we find these: *Dutch concert,* a barroom chorus; *Dutch leave,* to desert; *Dutch rose,* the hammer mark left on a piece of wood when a carpenter misses the nail; *Dutch cap,* a diaphragm; and *Dutch courage,* false bravado inspired by liquor.

Dys-

Two common words, *dyslexia* and *dysfunctional,* are headed up by the Greek prefix *dys-,* three little letters that always mean trouble. This prefix means "bad, abnormal, impaired, difficult."

Dystopia is a place in which the condition of life is grim, as from starvation or hardship. *Dystopia* lies opposite a place called *Utopia. Euphoria* is a state of elation or delirious happiness. The opposite of this agreeable sensation is *dysphoria,* a state of feeling unwell or unhappy.

The *dys-* prefix appears in many words referring to physical or mental impairments. *Dyspepsia* means "indigestion." The *pepsia* in this term means "digestion" in Greek. A disorder of the lower intestinal tract is *dysentery,* from *dys-* and *enteron,* the Greek word for "intestine."

Dysgraphia is the impairment of the ability to write. *Dyslexia* is a learning disability that involves difficulties in processing language. *Lexia* is from the Greek *lexis,* "word, speech." A *dysfunction* is impaired or abnormal function.

Euphemism is substituting a softer word for one that's offensive. But sometimes people turn this around and use coarse words in place of milder ones—for instance, calling a horse a "nag" or a person's nose a "beak." This is known as *dysphemism,* a word meaning "bad speech."

ECDYSIAST

In 1940, American journalist and essayist H. L. Mencken received a letter from a woman named Georgia Sothern. She wrote: "I am a practitioner of the art of strip-teasing…. there has been a great deal of…criticism leveled against my profession. Most of it…arises from the unfortunate word *strip-teasing,* which creates the wrong connotation…. if you could coin a new and more palatable word to describe this art, I and my colleagues would have easier going. I hope…[you] can find time to help the…members of my profession."

Mencken replied: "I sympathize with you in your affliction. It might be a good idea to relate strip-teasing in some way to the…zoological phenomenon of molting…which is *ecdysis.* This word produces…*ecdysiast.*"

So Georgia Sothern the stripper became Georgia Sothern the ecdysiast. Through her promotion of both the word and profession, a union arose called the Society of Ecdysiasts.

However, the Queen of Ecdysiasts, Gypsie Rose Lee, was not amused. In a 1940 interview, she leveled her guns against Mencken: "Ecdysiast, he calls me! Why, the man…has been reading books! Dictionaries! We don't wear feathers and molt them off….What does he know about stripping?"

The extent of Mencken's conversance with stripping is unknown. He did, however, know his classical languages, because the term *ecdysis* comes from a Greek term meaning "casting or stripping off." *Ecdysis* is the scientific term for the periodic molting of lobsters, crabs, snakes, and lizards.

ECHO

Echo was a wood nymph who desperately loved a handsome Greek named Narcissus. But Narcissus was vain and aloof and loved no one, though many sought to win his heart.

Echo, however, ceaselessly pursued the beautiful Narcissus. Though every day she gazed at her beloved from behind the forest foliage, she could never speak to him, because Hera, the queen of the gods, had put a strange curse upon the wood nymph.

Echo had been elected to distract the jealous Hera while her husband Zeus dallied with all the other nymphs in the forest. Chattering gaily, Echo turned Hera's head long enough for Zeus to slip away. Discovering this scheme, the enraged Hera cursed the nymph and rendered her mute, except to repeat the words of others.

Unfortunate Echo was unable to initiate a conversation with her beloved Narcissus. One day, however, the handsome youth detected her presence and addressed her. She could only repeat his words, and Narcissus believed her insane.

Echo, cruelly rejected, retreated to the shadows in shame. She thereafter refused all food and wasted away until all that was left was her lonely voice, repeating the words of others.

The word *echo* is derived from a Greek term meaning "sound." The concept of sound may be personified by the wood nymph Echo.

The word *egg* has been used as a synonym for an individual, chap, or fellow since at least the mid-19th century. Adding the modifiers *good, bad,* or *tough* creates terms of approval or disapproval. A *bad egg* is a troublesome, dishonest individual. Both rascal and rotten egg may appear wholesome at first blush, but when cracked open, their foul natures are revealed. An honest, helpful person is a *good egg,* but a *tough egg* has seen hard times and is likely to give you trouble.

An *egghead* was originally a bald person, but the word has become synonymous with "intellectual." The latter sense was made popular during the 1952 presidential campaign of Adlai Stevenson, a man with a conspicuously high forehead and high-minded political and philosophical ideals.

To *lay an egg* is to make a humiliating mistake or deliver a bad performance. The expression comes from the British game of cricket; the team failing to score was said to have *laid a duck's egg,* the shape of which suggests a zero. The phrase was taken up by American vaudeville in the late 19th century, where it signified a flop of a performance.

When you *walk on eggs,* you must proceed with wariness lest you crack the shells and ruin the contents. This metaphor conveys the desperate impossibility of a situation, since nobody can walk on eggs without breaking them.

Dame Nellie Melba (1859–1931), Australian coloratura soprano, was the inspiration for two epicurean terms. The opera diva, dieting to control her weight, ordered toast while dining at the Savoy in London. By mistake she was given some extra-crunchy, overtoasted slices of bread. She enjoyed them so much that *melba toast* was added to the menu in her honor. When Dame Nellie wasn't dieting, she enjoyed a dish consisting of ice cream, peaches, and raspberry sauce—the *peach melba* that bears her name.

Romaine lettuce, Parmesan cheese, and croutons are the basic elements of the *caesar salad*. This dish is named for the Italian-American chef Caesar Cardini, who owned a restaurant in Tijuana, Mexico. He created his namesake salad in 1924.

The *graham cracker* was named for Sylvester Graham (1794–1851), a temperance advocate who promoted abstinance from meat, fat, mustard, and sexual excess. He developed the nutritious cracker made from whole-grain, unsifted flour—and it remains an American favorite today.

A California botanist named Rudolph Boysen created a hybrid berry in 1923 by crossing blackberries and raspberries. The novel fruit was named the *boysenberry* after its developer.

EROTIC

The Greek word for lust or sexual desire is *eros*. The Greek personification of passionate love was the god of the same name, Eros, who, according to one tradition, was the son of Hermes, the messenger god, and Aphrodite, the goddess of love.

The Greeks installed statues of Eros in gymnasiums and shrines, worshipping him as a god of fertility. Presiding over sexual love, Eros was responsible for ensuring the continuity of the human species; but in villainous and chaotic moods, he smote both mortals and gods with passion for one another. *Eros,* the Greek word for lust, gives us the modern adjective *erotic.* The word is also responsible for the noun *erotica,* referring to art or literature with a sexual theme.

In the Roman tradition, the same god is called Cupid. In Roman art, he's often depicted as a blindfolded child, indiscriminately shooting arrows of desire without regard for the consequences. This image ultimately inspired the cuddly winged Cupids decorating our contemporary Valentine cards.

The name *Cupid* is associated with the noun *cupidity,* which means "excessive longing, greed, or an inordinate desire to possess something."

ETYMOLOGY, ENTOMOLOGY

The near-twin terms *entomology* and *etymology* are often mistakenly interchanged. One is associated with insects; the other with word histories. But which is which, and how can we distinguish the "bug word" from the "word word"?

Etymology is the study of word origins and histories. Etymologists pursue terms from language to language as far back in time as can be determined with reasonable certainty. Greek in origin, the word *etymology* records its family history in the terms *etymon,* which refers to the "true" sense of a word, and the suffix *-logy,* "the study of." *Etymology* is the study of a word's true meaning.

And now the etymology of *entomology.* The word arises from the observation that insects have bodies divided into head, thorax, and abdomen. *Entomon* is Greek for "segmented thing," and *entomology* is "the study of segmented things," in this case insects. *Entomology* entered the English language in the 18th century.

You'll never scramble the dangerously similar *etymology* and *entomology* if you employ this simple mnemonic formula: *ant,* the name of a common insect, sounds like the *ent* in *entomology.* Here is another helpful device: *n* is the second letter in both *entomology* and *insect.*

EUPHEMISM

There are times when all of us, in order to avoid being offensive, replace an unpalatable word with a more agreeable one. That's called *euphemism*. Over the centuries, our linguistic culture has fashioned a variety of specialized vocabularies to blunt the potency of frightening or embarrassing situations.

One thing euphemisms do is alleviate our fear of death by providing such comforting terms as *passed away, passed on,* or *gone home.*

We also use euphemisms to avoid the sacrilege of cursing by substituting words such as *gosh darn it, holy cripes,* or *shucks* for their more offensive counterparts.

Disturbing political and military realities are heavily euphemized. A political lie can be linguistically sanitized as a *plausible denial. Preemptive strike* is a military euphemism for surprise attack.

The word *euphemism* derives from the Greek prefix *eu-,* meaning "good or well," and *pheme,* "speech or saying." *Euphemism* originally denoted the avoidance of uttering ill-omened words at religious ceremonies. In recent centuries, the term has come to signify the substitution of acceptable words for unpleasant ones.

Some words referring to the anatomy are descriptive. *Molar,* for example, is from the Latin *mola,* meaning "grindstone." *Solar plexus* is derived from *sol,* Latin for "sun," and *plexus,* meaning "something woven," creating the image of an interlace of nerves radiating from a center, as rays from the sun.

Other anatomical terms are eponymous, derived from the names of the scientists and physicians who first discovered or described them. Consider *eustachian* and *fallopian,* named for two Italian anatomists.

Bartolomo Eustachius was born in San Severino, Italy, in 1524. As professor of medicine in what is now the University of Rome, he conducted research on the development and evolution of the teeth, kidneys, cranial nerves, and ear. He was the first to describe the canal connecting the back of the throat to the middle ear—the *eustachian tube,* which was named after him.

One of Eustachius' contemporaries was Gabriel Fallopius, professor of anatomy at the universities at Pisa and Padua. Fallopius was also a botanist and served as superintendent of the Padua botanical garden. But he is best remembered for his research on the ducts leading from the ovaries to the uterus—the *fallopian tubes,* which were named in his honor.

Ex-

The prefix *ex-* means out, beyond, away from, off, and former. It is an enormously useful prefix, providing meaning to hundreds of English words.

The verb *expectorate* means "to cough up and spit out." It consists of *ex-,* "out," and the Latin *pectus,* "breast." *Expectorate* is related to the adjective *pectoral,* "of the chest or breast."

The *ex-* in the word *explode* means "off," and *plode* is a form of the Latin *plaudere,* "to applaud." In the 16th century, to *explode* was to drive actors off the stage with hisses and derisive claps, literally to "applaud off." Henry Fielding in his 1749 play *Tom Jones* wrote, "In the playhouse, when he doth wrong, no critic is so apt to hiss and explode him."

To *expect* something is etymologically to "look out" for it. *Expect* is a Latin compound verb formed from *ex-,* "out," and *spectare,* "look." *Spectare* is also the source of the words *spectacle, speculate,* and *spectre.*

The words *expedite* and *expedition* are closely related. Both come from the same Latin source, *expedire,* meaning "to free the feet." The *ex-* or "out" prefix is here attached to the *ped,* or "foot" element. When you expedite an expedition, you are etymologically "freeing your feet out" to travel.

FAGGOT

Since the early 20th century, the term *faggot* has been a slur directed toward homosexual males. But this word has not always been an insult. In the 14th century, a *faggot* was simply a bundle of sticks or twigs bound together and used for fuel. The term comes ultimately from the Greek *phakelos,* "bundle."

Historical citations from the *Oxford English Dictionary* indicate that the word *faggot* was also used in reference to tied bundles of iron, steel, rushes, or even cooking herbs. Tailors are familiar with a technique called *faggot-stitching* in which loose threads are bound together by a stitch. The finished stitch resembles the bundled sticks implied in the earliest sense of the term.

The word took an opprobrious turn sometime in the 16th century, when *faggot* became an abusive nickname for a woman. A female saddled with this moniker was considered immoral, insignificant, or worthless. A *faggot woman* was dismissed as one would dismiss a bundle of sticks. In some districts, the verb form *to faggot* meant to frequent the company of immoral women. Children, too, were abused with the nickname *little faggots,* comparing them with the insignificance of small firewood.

Word watchers are uncertain why, in the early 1900s, *faggot* came to refer almost exclusively to homosexual males. One suggestion is that it parallels the development of the word *gay,* which once referred to the behavior of licentious women and was later applied to homosexual men. *Fag* is also a slang term for a cigarette. "Fag smoking" (as opposed to cigar or pipe smoking) was once considered effeminate and may have contributed to its homosexual connotations.

Farewell Terms

We often least understand those terms that are most familiar. Consider the words we employ when we part from friends: *goodbye, so long, ta ta, adios, bye-bye*. Such sentiments are tossed away as soon as they're uttered.

A look beyond the everyday sounds of these terms reveals the almost spiritual dimension of their etymologies. The most common English farewell, *goodbye*, is a contraction of the older sentiment "God be with ye," which dates to the 16th century. This valediction appears in several of Shakespeare's plays. The phrase didn't achieve its modern pronunciation until the 18th century.

The Spanish *adios* and French *adieu* mean literally "to God." The casual-sounding *so long* is an anglicization of the Islamic *salaam* and its Hebrew counterpart *shalom*, meaning "peace."

Some of our farewells are slangy. *Bye-bye* is, of course, a corruption of *goodbye*, but *ta-ta* and *toodle-oo* are in a category of a different color. Both appeared in print in the early 1900s, and both probably represent the sound of an automobile horn signaling departure. The British *pip-pip*, used in that country as a humorous affectation, is a breezy farewell imitating a bicycle horn.

FIGHTING WORDS

Countless words have been written about war: that it is hell (William T. Sherman); that it is like love, it always finds a way (Berthold Brecht); that you can no more win it than you can win an earthquake (Jeanette Rankin); that the seriousness of waging it is the one thing that stops women from laughing at men (John Fowles).

These are opinions. What is fact is that war is linguistically productive. Every war fought on or by this country has inspired words, phrases, abbreviations, and acronyms that are both familiar and useful to most Americans. Some we still consider military or battle-specific: AWOL, *doughboy, napalm, radar, the mother of all battles, kamikaze.*

But there are stockpiles of words and expressions originally manufactured by past combats which have since been decommissioned and are now living the civilian life: *flash in the pan, hit the panic button, honcho, hold down the fort.* Who can deny the usefulness of *blockbuster, to drum up, up in arms, armed to the teeth, by the seat of one's pants, basket case, pipe down*—all inspired by weaponry, warfare, and armed conflict.

FLAPPER

These days, the *flapper* girl of the 1920s lives only in caricature. She's the young woman wearing a fringed dress, with bobbed hair and a cigarette in one hand and liquor flask in the other. She kicks wildly to the Charleston or wears her boyfriend's oversized raccoon coat.

The flapper was a scandal to the establishment of her day. Swearing, drinking, wearing garish makeup but no corset, she was the antithesis of the mother and grandmother who embodied Victorian sensibilities. She boldly fashioned a new wardrobe, a new set of morals, and even a new radical lexicon. Flappers were responsible for inventing such zoologically inspired linguistic concoctions as *the bee's knees, the cat's meow, the clam's garters,* and *the eel's hips,* amongst many other novel expressions.

But where did the flapper acquire her unusual name? This word has a surprisingly tangled history. In the late 19th century, *flapper* meant both "prostitute" and "young teenage girl"—the latter from the notion that her hair was worn in a braid and tied with a large bow that "flapped" against her back.

A *flapper* was also a young duck or partridge just learning to fly. Its flight was erratic and unpredictable, just like the "flighty" young woman.

The moniker may have been reinforced by the Charleston, the dance rage of the Roaring Twenties characterized by wildly flapping limbs.

FLASH IN THE PAN

A person whose success is disappointingly short-lived is often branded a *flash in the pan*. This expression, an Americanism from the 17th century, was inspired by the firing sequence of the flintlock musket. Notoriously unreliable, the musket failed to fire, much less hit its target, with exasperating frequency.

In a Rube Goldberg–like scenario, the musketeer began by aiming his weapon and pulling the trigger. This activated a steel hammer, which struck a flint, creating a shower of sparks. The sparks, if all went well, ignited the priming powder, which rested on a piece of concave metal called the "pan." This ignition, in turn, exploded the main gunpowder charge of the musket, sending the lead ball toward its target.

If, however, the priming powder failed to ignite the main charge, the contents of the pan would flare but not detonate the gunpowder—resulting in a promising but unfulfilling flash in the pan. An elaborate scheme burning brightly with early success but quickly perishing evokes the obsolete *flash in the pan* musket technology.

FLATTERY

Sages and thinkers throughout the ages have warned against the deceits of flattery. In a translated quotation from the Roman philosopher Cicero, we read, "Let flattery, the handmaid of vice, be kept out of friendship." A German proverb says, "Flatterers, like cats, lick, then scratch."

William Shakespeare's plays are peppered with references to the subterfuge of false praise, as is the book of Proverbs in the Bible's Old Testament. In 1790, Edmund Burke warned his readers, "Flattery corrupts both the giver and receiver."

We American English speakers have our own 21st century cliché dealing with fulsome acclaim: "Flattery will get you nowhere." We've been brandishing this phrase since about the 1950s; it first appeared in print in a 1971 Ellery Queen novel. Sometimes we employ this expression ironically in response to an insult; other times we use its humorous variation, "Flattery will get you everywhere."

The origin of *flattery* is surprisingly simple. There is a flat in *flattery*. The word means to smooth down or caress with the flat of the hand, much as we would in ingratiating ourselves to a cat. When we want to "butter someone up," we pet and smooth him with glossy words and compliments. The term *flattery* came to English in the 13th century from the Old French language.

FLOTSAM AND JETSAM

We find the terms *flotsam* and *jetsam* linguistically joined at the hip. Wherever *flotsam* resides, there also is *jetsam*. Is there a difference between the two?

First, some clarification. Most contemporary English speakers use *flotsam and jetsam* in reference to general tidal deposition, such as bits of wood, glass, or shell. These twinned terms are sometimes metaphorically attached to any kind of remnants or odds and ends, or perhaps to a ragtag group of humans living on the margins of society.

Historically, however, these terms belong to the maritime industry. They refer specifically to the remains of a shipwreck. *Flotsam* is the term reserved for the floating relics of a ship's cargo or equipment after that vessel has foundered, while *jetsam* is freight purposely tossed overboard to lighten a ship in distress.

Jetsam is from the Latin verb *jactare*, "to throw," etymologically reflecting the cargo's fate of being hurled into the waves. Its cousins include *jet, jetty,* and *jettison*.

FLOWER NAMES

The pride of Holland, the *tulip,* has a name of Middle Eastern heritage. It comes from the Persian word for turban, *dulband.* With its large, upturned petals, the flower bears a fanciful resemblance to the headwear of that region. *Tulip* was adopted by English speakers in the 16th century, while the Swedes retained *tulpan,* the Danish, *tulipan,* and the Italians, *tulipano.*

Edelweiss, the blossom that blesses the Von Trapp homeland forever, is a common motif in Swiss culture. The name comes from the German *edel,* meaning "noble," and *weiss,* "white, pure."

To the Greeks, the seed of the *geranium* resembled a crane's bill. The name of this plant hails from the Greek word for crane, *geranos.* The early English name for the same flower was *cranesbill.*

The name of a flowering shrub of the Mediterranean, *laurel,* comes from the Latin *laurus.* Athletes and scholars were honored with laurel crowns in early Rome. The expression *poet laureate* echoes the Roman practice of crowning the man of words with laurel sprigs. The names *Laurence* and *Laura* are relatives of this Latin-derived term.

The *pansy,* a colorful flower of the genus *Viola,* was named for the French word for "thought," *pensee.* Most sources suggest that the "pensive" look of the blossom earned it the name. Ophelia, in Shakespeare's *Hamlet,* says, "There's pansies, that's for thoughts." By the 1920s the word had become an abusive nickname for an effeminate male or a homosexual.

FLUERE WORDS

The Latin verb *fluere,* meaning "to flow," is the wellspring of many modern English words: *fluid, fluent, affluent, influence, influenza.*

The derivative *fluid* is both adjective and noun. As an adjective, *fluid* refers to something that flows easily and is not fixed. As a noun, it denotes a flowing substance such as a liquid or a gas.

Someone who speaks a language with facility and expression is said to be *fluent.* This term implies that words figuratively "flow" out of the speaker's mouth.

Add the prefix *af-* to *fluent* and you have *affluent,* an adjective that describes a wealthy and prominent person. *Affluent* was first recorded in English circa 1413, and at that time it meant "flowing in abundance."

Influence is another sibling in the *fluere* family. This word comes directly from the verb *influere,* meaning "to flow in." It originally denoted a kind of ethereal fluid that "flowed in" from the stars and affected the lives of human beings. Today the word *influence* implies the power of persons or events to affect one's life.

The term *influence* gave rise to the term *influenza,* a malady thought by 17th and 18th century Italians to be caused by a "flowing in" of fluid from evil stars.

FLUKE

The word *fluke* has a host of definitions. It's a parasitic flatworm, a whale's tail, the flat end of each arm of an anchor, a flounder or flatfish, and an unexpected event or stroke of luck. What etymological ribbon ties these notions together?

While the flatworm and the flounder are both flukes, they're members of separate zoological families. Some flatworms, such as blood and liver flukes, are parasitic organisms with a flattened and ribbonlike conformation. Flounders, also called flukes, are likewise flattened, with eyes staring disconcertingly from only one side of their heads. The obvious biological connection between the parasite and the fish is their flatness, thus the term *fluke* to refer to both. *Fluke* comes from an Old High German word meaning "smooth." The modern German cognate, *flach,* means "flat."

The *Barnhart Dictionary of Etymology* asserts that the *fluke* that means one of the flat ends of an anchor and also the flat of a whale's tail probably arose from the resemblance of their shapes to that of the flatfish.

All these *flukes* fit comfortably in this etymological family portrait. But what about the same word meaning "unexpected event"? For reasons unclear to etymologists, it's associated with British billiard slang. When it appeared in print in 1857, this *fluke* was a lucky stroke at the billiards table. Today we use it to refer to an unusual occurrence or chance event.

FLY OFF THE HANDLE

Americans have been putting this idiom to good use since the 18th century. *To fly off the handle* is to lose one's composure and become uncontrollably angry.

The *handle* in this expression belongs to an ax whose head has detached, becoming a dangerous, hurtling missile. Early American axes were often crudely made and hafted. Sometimes Eastern manufacturers shipped only the axheads, and recipients fashioned their own handles. If the homemade handles were not crafted carefully enough to keep the head secure, the chopping blade would sooner or later part company with the handle and fly through the air with a potentially deadly mission.

The pain caused by the blade descending on a nearby human target would elicit cries of anger from the victim. *To fly off the handle* sums up the rage one might feel upon being the target of a ballistic ax head.

The expression was printed for the first time in an 1825 novel, *Brother Johnathan; or the New Englanders,* by John Neal. It turned up again in 1844, in Thomas Haliburton's Sam Slick tales.

American English cheerfully and promiscuously borrows vocabulary from almost every language on earth. We native English speakers daily employ terms that originated in Hindi, German, Italian, Chinese, Afrikaans, Turkish, Portuguese, Creole, and a host of other tongues.

From the Swedish language comes word *tungsten,* a heavy metallic element having the highest melting point of any metal. Tungsten is used in filaments of incandescent electric lamps. Meaning literally "heavy stone," the word *tungsten* was coined by K. W. Scheele in the mid-1700s and began appearing in English late in the century.

The word *behemoth,* borrowed from the Hebrews, who may have borrowed it from the Egyptians, means "monstrous beast." Some scholars believe the original Egyptian word was *p-ehe-mau,* "water-ox" or hippopotamus. The *Barnhart Dictionary of Etymology* says *behemoth* was first printed in English in 1382. Another word borrowed from the Hebrews is *cherub.* This term denotes a celestial spirit described in Genesis and Ezekiel of the Bible's Old Testament. In modern English, a cherub is a beautiful, angelic child.

From a language called Evenki, spoken in north-central Russia, comes the word *shaman,* "spiritual intercessor." Several cultures have adopted this word. Some American Indians, Buddhists, and Shinto priests call their healers and holy people *shamans.* This word appeared in English in the 1690s; *shamanism,* denoting the religious philosophy of the Evenki-speaking people of Siberia, was recorded in English in 1780.

We have the Dutch to thank for the words *booze, easel,* and *cookie. Booze* comes from the verb *buizen,* "drink to excess." *Easel* is a corruption of the Dutch *ezel*, "ass"; just as a beast of burden carryies loads, an easel bears a canvas. *Cookie* was originally the Dutch *koekje*, "little cake."

From Italian we've adopted *lava*, derived from the Latin term *lavare*, "to wash." *Parasol* is also Italian; it means "guard against the sun."

Our word *boondocks* comes from the Tagalog language of the Philippines. It means simply "mountain."

From the various dialects of India come the words *bandanna, bangle,* and *cheetah.* The latter means "speckled."

And we certainly would be linguistically impoverished without these Arabic-derived terms: *hazard, jar, magazine, coffee,* and *zenith.*

FORNICATE

In the early 1800s, Noah Webster—journalist, author, and original compiler of the famous *Webster's Dictionary*— struck the word *fornication* from a new edition of the Bible, replacing it with the more palatable term *lewdness*.

Fornication by definition is a sexual tryst between two persons not married to each other. At the heart and soul of this term, however, is not sexual misbehavior but architecture—specifically, the architecture of ancient Rome.

Below the streets of Rome were subterranean vaults that served as dwellings for vagrants, criminals, and low-class prostitutes who lacked the status to work in the official brothels. These underground Roman prostitutes often conducted business beneath an arch or a vault, which in Latin is a *fornix*. Because so much sex was bought and sold in these subterranean vaults, the word *fornix* became synonymous with what we would call a brothel.

In the 14th century, this term found its way into the English language. A *fornatrix* is a prostitute; a *fornicator,* her client; and *fornication,* their sexual activity. All these from the simple term *fornix,* Latin for "arch" or "vault."

It doesn't quite rival baseball as a national sport or pastime, but Frisbee-tossing certainly has its devotees. Since the mid-1950s, when inventor Fred Morrison marketed his first flying disc in California, Frisbees have been whizzing from hand to hand by the millions.

Though the plastic disc itself was invented and marketed in California, the story of the Frisbee's name has 19th century East Coast origins.

In the 1870s, a confectioner named William Frisbee baked and distributed pies from his Bridgeport, Connecticut, bakeshop. The pies were sold in tin pans embossed with the confectioner's family name. Both the pies and their tins were popular in New England for decades. Long after the pies had been consumed, locals used the tins as hand-tossed flying devices.

Fast forward to the West Coast of the mid-20th century. Young California inventor Fred Morrison was hoping to capitalize on the UFO craze of the 1950s when he invented a plastic disc patterned after spacecrafts depicted in alien invader movies. Morrison called his new toy Morrison's Flyin' Saucer. It quickly became a local favorite.

When the president of WHAM-O, Morrison's manufacturing company, was on an East Coast promotional tour, he discovered Yale students flinging William Frisbee's pie tins across the campus lawn. They had already been "Frisbee-ing" for years! WHAM-O then replaced the moniker Flyin' Saucer with the name of the 19th century Connecticut pie baker.

FRISKY POLYSYLLABLES

Heard these lately? *Snollygoster. Absquatulate. Cattywampus. Hornswogglement.* Though these words have nearly vanished from our 21st century vocabulary, they were fairly common in 19th century America. Writers such as Mark Twain and Herman Melville, as well as newspaper editors across the country, blithely used such lexical eccentricities as *slobgollion, galleywest,* and *obfliscated.*

Perhaps the most recognizable of these curious terms is *cattywampus,* meaning "askew or out of order." Appearing in the mid-1800s, *cattywampus* may have been influenced by *cattycorner,* meaning "diagonal from."

Snollygoster is a noun and was defined in 1895 by a Georgia newspaper editor. "A snollygoster," he wrote, "is a fellow who wants office, regardless of party, platform or principles...who...gets there by the sheer force of monumental talknophical assumnancy." Harry Truman revived the word *snollygoster* in 1952 as a term of reproach for candidates who used public prayer to win votes.

How about *absquatulate?* First recorded in print in 1830, *absquatulate* means "to flee quickly." It's most likely an elaboration of *abscond,* "to depart secretly."

If you were the victim of a 19th century swindle, you could say you got *hornswoggled.* This polysyllable curiosity was first printed in 1829 and is still featured in newly published American dictionaries. Its origin is unknown.

FUDGE

John F. Mariani, author of *The Dictionary of American Food and Drink,* has traced the origin of fudge making to American women's colleges. Mariani has uncovered late 19th century fudge recipes with names like "Wellesly Fudge" and "Vassar Fudge."

The origin of *fudge,* the noun, referring to the dark cocoa candy, and the homonymic verb meaning "to cheat," has eluded the most dedicated word hunters for decades. But the two meanings may have a single derivation.

In 17th century England lived a sea merchant named Captain Fudge, nicknamed "Lying Fudge." Returning from his voyages, Lying Fudge brought with him a shipful of pre-varications—grossly inflated fictions about himself and his exploits. The verb *to fudge,* meaning "to lie," may commemorate this fabricating captain. According to Isaac D'Israeli, father of British prime minister Benjamin Disraeli, in his *Curiosities of Literature* (1791), this seafarer lied so extravagantly that "sailors, when they hear a great lie told, cry out 'You fudge it!'"

A second theory on the origin of *fudge* asserts that a Middle English verb, *fadge,* means "to hoax or cheat." *The Dictionary of American Food and Drink* suggests that the young women of Vassar and Wellesly, purported inventors of this confection, may have used candy making as an excuse to *fadge, fudge,* or cheat their curfews.

Smith Hempstone, American ambassador to Kenya under the first President George Bush, was skeptical about U.S. involvement in Operation Restore Hope in Somalia. In early December 1992, Hempstone wrote a letter to Under Secretary of State Frank Wisner.

"I must confess," wrote Hempstone, "that I have been bemused, confused, and alarmed at the Gaderine haste with which the [U. S. government] seemingly has sought to embrace the Somali tarbaby."

The story behind this term lies in the New Testament book of Matthew. The adjective *gaderine* comes from Gadara, the name of a region situated on the south side of the Sea of Galilee. According to Matthew, chapter 8, two men possessed by devils lived in this region. The men were so violent that no chain could subdue them, so bizarre that they shrieked continually and cut themselves with stones.

One day Christ passed by the demoniacs and ordered the devils to leave the human bodies they had possessed. Not far away was grazing a herd of swine. The devils said to Christ, "If you drive us out, send us into the herd of pigs."

Jesus granted this, and the herd, possessed by many spirits, rushed into the Sea of Galilee, where every pig drowned.

Ambassador Hempstone felt an ill wind blowing out of the region of Mogadishu. Seeing the mobilization of troops and supplies to assist Somalia as confused and frenzied, he characterized it as being in *Gaderine haste,* bringing to mind the New Testament image of the herd of swine's headlong flight into the Sea of Galilee.

GAMS

The photograph displays a young blonde woman in a one-piece bathing suit. Her back is to the viewer, but the elfin face is turned around her right shoulder as she looks mischievously at the camera. She is supported by a pair of long smooth legs drawn close together, the right leg slightly crooked at the ankle.

This is the celebrated publicity photo of the 1940s starlet Betty Grable. American GIs responded enthusiastically to the photograph. They admired the famous Grable legs, affectionately calling them *gams*.

This term has been part of the American slang vocabulary since the early years of the 20th century. Though generally employed to describe women's limbs, it's not necessarily confined to female anatomy. The term has been used generically to refer to legs of any kind, be they human or animal.

Gam is the offspring of the term *gamba*, Italian for "leg." *Gamba* is not only the etymological progenitor of *gams*, it's a relative of the term *gambol*, "to leap about or kick up the legs in play."

You can detect the word *gamba* in *gambrel*, a roofing style characterized by a sharp downward bend in the roof. When viewed straight-on from the end of a building, the lines of a gambrel roof are analogous to the crooked hind leg of an animal.

German Adoptees

As a Germanic language, English contains many structural and etymological elements of that tongue. But German immigrants to North America in the 19th century added many of their terminologies to the linguistic farrago that is the American English language. These are now official members of the English vocabulary.

The word *Hinterland* was introduced to English speakers in the late 1800s. In English, *hinterland* refers to the backcountry or wilderness, but in its original language the word literally means "behind-land."

A *loafer* is perpetually idle. This word is an alteration of the German *Landläufer,* meaning literally "land-runner" but figuratively "tramp." In the late 1930s, Americans began to use the word *loafer* as a word for informal, no-lace shoes. *Loafer* is now the trademark for slip-on leather footwear.

A *glitch* is a malfunction, a mishap, a snag. English speakers inherited this word from the German verb *glitschen,* "slide, slip." Our verb *carouse* comes from the German phrase *gar aus trinken,* "drink fully." *Smut,* meaning obscene or pornographic literature, derives from *Schmutz,* German for "dirt, filth."

Our personal names, both first and last, have traceable histories like any other word. *Smith,* the most common American surname, is from a Germanic term meaning worker or craftsman. It refers, of course, to the metalworker's trade.

The name *Klein* means "small" in German. Originally this was a nickname bestowed upon those diminutive of stature. The related *Kleinbaum* means "small tree," *Kleinfeld* is "small field," and *Kleinberger* means "dweller by a small hill."

The surname *Kirsch* is German for "cherry." As a topographic title, *Kirsch* was given to one living near a cherry orchard or a wild cherry tree. *Kirsch* was also an occupational name for a gatherer or seller of cherries. It may also have been the nickname of a man with a ruddy complexion.

Klempner is another German occupational surname. Klempners may have tinkers or plumbers in their ancestries. This last name derives from the verb *klempern,* "to clamp, bolt, rivet."

Neubauer was originally a nickname given to an agriculteral worker who was new to an area. The name is a combination of *neu,* "new," and *bauer,* "farmer." An alternative suggestion is that the name may have been taken by the builder of a new house (*bauen* means "to build").

Daimler was the occupational name for a professional torturer, specifically, one who applied thumb-screws. It was also a nickname for a cruel person. *Daimler* is a derivative of the German *Daum,* "thumb."

GEYSER

The world's most famous geyser is probably Yellowstone National Park's Old Faithful. Named for its consistently predictable eruptions, Old Faithful rockets a column of steam and boiling water 100 feet in the air approximately every sixty-five minutes.

Old Faithful has at least three hundred companion geysers in the Yellowstone area. All these dramatic eruptions are the result of volcanically heated, subterranean water shooting upward through rock channels—a kind of subterranean pressure valve.

In addition to the Yellowstone group, other geyser fields are found in New Zealand, Chile, and Siberia. How did this phenomenon get its name?

The volcanic island of Iceland boasts a spectacular geothermal specimen, with eruptions cresting at 200 feet. Long ago, Icelanders named this spouter *Geysir,* "the gusher." The name comes from the verb *geysa,* "to rush forth."

English speakers borrowed the word late in the 18th century and modified its spelling to *geyser.* This Icelandic-based name has now come to refer to all spouting hot springs.

GIMLET

A gimlet is both a tool and a cocktail. As a tool, a *gimlet* is a boring implement with a metal screw tip at one end and a crosspiece handle at the other for one-handed turning. The other *gimlet* is a cocktail of gin and lime juice with perhaps a splash of soda. Is it coincidence or design that the tool and the drink have the same moniker?

First, let's take a look at the etymology of the term. English speakers adopted *gimlet* some nine hundred years ago from a Germanic word meaning "auger." It was employed in reference to the boring implement for nearly a millennium until the 1920s, when a newly invented alcoholic beverage was given the name.

Reference sources contain inconsistent stories about the relationship between these two. Some say the drink name is an eponym of its purported inventer, Sir T. O. Gimlette. He was a British naval surgeon who, concerned with the health of his peers, recommended that his fellow officers dilute their straight gin with healthful lime juice.

Other sources suggest that the cocktail was named after the tool, since its intoxicating properties penetrate the drinker with the certainty of an auger.

We find an extension of this word in the phrase *gimlet-eyed,* meaning sharp-sighted or describing someone possessing a penetrating glance. The 1889 *Century Dictionary* defines a gimlet eye as a "small, sharp, disagreeably prying eye."

The technical language of a profession, hobby, or sport is called *jargon*. This "shop talk" is necessary for the economical communication amongst peers. When jargon gets out of control, however, it can degenerate into polysyllabic gobbledygook. *Gobbledygook* is a generic term encompassing language of bureaucratese, officialese, legalese, or military parlance.

Coinage of this term is attributed to Maury Maverick, Democratic representative from Texas in 1944. As chairman of the Smaller War Parts Corporation during the Second World War, Maverick was obliged to attend bureaucratic meetings at which he endured such vague phrases as "alternative but nevertheless meaningful minimae."

On March 30, 1944, the plain-talking Maverick issued a formal order banning so-called "gobbledygook language." "Be short," he demanded, "and say what you're talking about.... Anyone using the words 'activation' or 'implementation' will be shot."

When interviewed by the *New York Times Magazine,* Maverick explained, "People ask me where I got 'gobbledygook'.... Perhaps I was thinking of the old bearded turkey gobbler back in Texas who was always gobbledy-gobbling and strutting with ludicrous pomposity."

Representative Maverick's eccentric coinage appears to have staying power; after sixty years it's still a colorful, serviceable American slang term.

God's in His Heaven

Many of our most enduring expressions come from great works of literature. The plays of Shakespeare, for example, give us the familiar phrases *into thin air, one fell swoop,* and *sound and fury.*

The 19th century poet Robert Browning is credited for the phrase *God's in his heaven, all's right with the world.* In Browning's 1841 dramatic poem *Pippa Passes,* a young Italian peasant girl strolls through the streets of her village singing traditional songs of love, nature, and heroic deeds. The lyrics are overheard by certain characters in the story whose lives are changed by Pippa's innocent songs.

In the first scene, Pippa's voice reaches the ears of a pair of lovers, one of whom has just murdered the other's rich, old husband. When Pippa sings "the lark's on the wing, the snail's on the thorn, God's in his heaven, all's right with the world," the guilty paramour is convicted of his evil crime and seeks forgiveness.

We often quote this line to express the perfection of a moment, as did Jim Murray, commenting in the February 1, 1996, edition of the *Los Angeles Times* of Magic Johnson's return to basketball: "A guy with a smile as broad as the Atlantic...had the ball in his hands and a song in his heart and, as the poet said it, God was in his heaven and all was right with the world."

GOMER

If American slang is your language of choice, or even if you're a casual user, you're likely to encounter the slightly derogatory nickname *gomer.*

In the medical profession, *gomer* has been used to indicate an old, unpleasant, or dirty patient who frequently seeks emergency treatment for minor health complaints. In this case, the epithet is explained as an acronym of "get out of my emergency room." Another theory has it that this *gomer* comes from a Hebrew root word meaning "to finish," implying that medically compromised *gomers* are in the process of finishing life on this earth.

Another breed of *gomer* is simply a slow-witted, socially maladroit male. This *gomer* is the conceptual cousin of the goof or the dope. Most word watchers agree this moniker derives from Gomer Pyle, the name of a yokel played by Jim Neighbors first in *The Andy Griffith Show,* then in the series called *Gomer Pyle, USMC.* This explains why military cadets and naïve marines are sometimes called gomers.

For a thorough explanation of the evolution of this epithet, complete with historical quotations containing *gomer,* look the word up in the excellent *Random House Historical Dictionary of American Slang,* edited by J. E. Lighter.

GOODY TWO SHOES

Parents and teachers adjure children to always be on their best behavior. The better the children behave, the more their elders approve of them.

But children quickly learn from their peers that there is such a thing as being *too* good. Obedient, cheerful automatons are inevitably scorned by their more spirited friends. A "perfect" child is sure to be saddled with the horrifying epithet *goody two shoes.*

Goody Two Shoes was the name of a character featured in an 18th century nursery tale attributed to the English novelist Oliver Goldsmith. The heroine was a poor but earnest child who had but one shoe. When she was given a matching pair, her joy was so boundless that she pointed to her little feet and exclaimed, "Two shoes!" to everyone she met.

Goldsmith wrote *The History of Little Goody Two Shoes* as a morality tale for 18th century children, illustrating how the impoverished heroine was able to achieved fame, wisdom, and riches as a result of her virtue and patience. We can compare the story of Little Goody Two Shoes to that of Pollyanna, the perky girl whose name we associate with syrupy optimism.

R umor-mongers rely on the *grapevine* to transmit and receive important social information. Local gossip, humorous anecdotes, and ruinous calumny typify grapevine news. It travels quickly and mutates as it goes, much like a game of telephone writ large.

Americans have employed the term *grapevine,* referring to informal person-to-person gossip, for at least a century and a half. This term is a clipped version of the earlier expression *grapevine telegraph,* a phrase introduced to print circa 1862. Current during the Civil War, the phrase reflected the near-telegraphic speed with which rumors of battles lost and won traveled from camp to camp.

But what of the *grapevine* in this phrase? The most plausible explanation comes from the 1942 *Dictionary of American English:* "That curious and vivid Western phrase 'grapevine telegraph' originated in 1850. A man named Colonel Bee constructed a telegraph line between Placerville and Virginia City, attaching the wire to the trees; their swaying stretched it until it lay in loops on the ground, resembling the trailing California wild grapevines."

So the phrase refers to an informal, unorganized body of chin-waggers dispatching gossip with wondrous speed through the grapevine telegraph, or grapevine.

GREEN

American English has dozens of phrases in which color terms are employed symbolically. Consider: *black sheep, golden oldies, paint the town red*. In our culture, each color has a metaphorical value; white means purity, blue for excellence, and so on.

Green packs a fairly heavy symbolic punch in American English. Some consider it the color of envy. In past centuries, envy was seen as an emotion so powerful that it literally turned a person's countenance green with sickness.

More recently, green has been putting in time symbolizing money and inexperience. The money metaphor is obvious, but what about this color representing naiveté or lack of sophistication? As the hue of young growing plants, green looks like youth and pliancy. From this image comes the notion of inexperience.

American English speakers have used the term *greenhorn* to refer to a raw recruit or a newly arrived European immigrant. The *greenhorn* refers to a young animal growing its first set of horns, a yearling buck, or bull, for example. The new horns aren't literally green but rather metaphorically so.

American westerners called newcomers *greenies* or *greeners* and took advantage of their inexperience by putting rattlesnakes in their bedrolls or saddling a bronc for them to ride. A horse with little experience under a rider was called *green-broke*.

Unfired clay is *greenware;* uncured glue holds a *green wood joint;* and eating unripe apples gives you the *green-apple quickstep.*

GROOVY

We most often associate the expression *in the groove* and its offspring *groovy* with a few brief years in the decade of the 1960s. *Groovy* showed up in the titles and lyrics of the pop tunes "Wild Thing," "59th Street Bridge Song," and "Groovy Kind of Love." Though some of this word's panache is lost in defining it, *groovy* means excellent, fine, satisfying. Being *in the groove* is to act correctly, work smoothly, or be in the proper mood.

Groove mongers of the 1960s do not have first claim on these expressions. Musicians such as Tommy Dorsey, Cab Calloway, Louis Armstrong, and Gene Krupa were slinging these terms throughout the 1930s and '40s. In a 1943 issue of the publication *Correct English,* Krupa said, "'In the groove' came out of those back-room music sessions where each musician would play the theme according to his individual notions…. One was, or was not, melodically in the groove."

According to the venerable *Dictionary of American Slang,* both expressions were common swing and jazz expressions, coming from the technology of recorded music: "When a phonograph plays, its stylus or needle is in the groove of the record."

A 1942 quotation from musician Tommy Dorsey, however, contradicts this notion: "When the boys and I hear a good record nowadays, we says it's 'groovey.' The expression has nothing to do with the grooves on the record's surface, it just means we think it's a fine piece of music."

The word *groovy* is most often used humorously or derisively in the 21st century as a linguistic conjuration of the zeitgeist of a past era.

GROTESQUE

In A.D. 64, the Roman emperor Nero initiated the construction of a colossal imperial palace he called the *Domus Aurea,* or "Golden House." It was surrounded by a park that was dotted with small grottoes where Nero's guests could dine or observe the well-tended landscape. The ceilings of these little grottoes were painted with lively and fanciful images of birds, masks, flowers, people, and animals.

About fifteen hundred years later, when Renaissance-age Romans excavated the remains of Nero's Domus Aurea, they were amazed by the fantastic artwork that remained on the walls and ceilings of the park's grottoes. The representations of grimacing masks, wildly blooming flowers, and playful animals amused the 16th century excavators.

This style of fanciful painting became known throughout Europe as the *grotesque* style, meaning literally "grotto-like," in reference to its place of origin.

Our English word *grotesque* comes from this Italian source. The term has suffered pejoration, or a decay in meaning, since the 16th and 17th centuries. To us, *grotesque* means distorted, bizarre, ugly, or misshapen. The grotesque has been further disparaged in the slang derivative *grotty,* meaning dirty, nasty, unpleasant.

GRUB

The word *grub* is a hard-working member of the English lexicon. As a verb, *to grub* means to scratch about or dig in the soil. The term is also another name for a larva. A simple meal is sometimes called *grub,* and then there are the derivatives *grubby,* meaning dirty and slovenly, and *money-grubber,* a sordid collector of wealth.

The etymological wellspring of this useful word is an ancient Germanic term meaning to dig about or scrape together. The notion of soil or dirt is embedded in every use of the term.

The *grub* meaning "larva," a word first recorded in the 15th century, was probably inspired by the notion of the creature digging and pushing its way through the soil.

The word *grub* that suggests food or a humble meal, surfacing in the English language in the 17th century, probably derives its meaning from the preference that some birds have for larvae as food.

In 19th century England, a *grub* was a dirty little child, perhaps one who had besmutted himself by scratching and digging about in the dirt. From this sense of the word we derive the adjective *grubby*, meaning grimy or dirty.

And, of course, there's *money-grubber,* suggesting someone greedy enough to scrape the soil looking for coins.

Chewing gum was introduced to Americans in February of 1871 when a New York entrepreneur named Thomas Adams manufactured and packaged small flavorless balls of a substance called *chicle.* The little chicle orbs, made from the sap of the Mexican sapodilla tree, were meant to be chewed but not swallowed. Adams called his novel product "Adams New York Gum" and sold it in boxes off the shelves of Hoboken, New Jersey, drugstores.

By the early 20th century, Americans could not get enough of this masticatory confection called *chewing gum.* William Wrigley, Jr., and Henry Fleer were responsible for later adding mint and fruit extracts to the flavorless gum.

Though American chewing gum was originally manufactured from a Mexican resource, the ultimate source of the word *gum* is the Egyptian word *kemai,* a name for tree sap. *Kemai* became the Greek *kommi,* the Latin *cummi,* and the Old French *gomme,* resulting in the English *gum.*

The gum in *gumshoe,* meaning "detective," is not the chewable type; it refers to rubber, another type of tree resin or gum. A detective, whose job requires stealth, is said to be as quiet as one wearing rubber, or gum, shoes. *Gumshoe* was first printed circa 1910.

Guppy

The guppy is one of the most popular home aquarium fish. The male, diminutive at an inch long, is handsomely bedecked in brilliant tints of blue, yellow, red, orange, green and purple, and spotted with black. During mating rituals, the male fans his fins before the female in an almost birdlike display of courtship.

After courtship, the female bears up to 180 live young. Frequently devoured by their parents, the young guppies survive by hiding in the bottom vegetation.

Guppies are native to the southern islands of the Caribbean and to northern South America. They are valued in the West Indies because they prey on the larvae of the mosquitoes that spread malaria.

The first guppy specimens to arrive in England were given to the British Museum in the late 19th century. Early on, they were known as "rainbow fish" and "millions fish." The man responsible for importing these tiny spots of swimming color was a clergyman from Trinidad who dabbled in ichthyology and was also president of the Scientific Association of Trinidad. Who was this gentleman? R. J. Lechmere Guppy, for whom the diminutive rainbow-colored fish is named.

GYPSY

There is a legend that says the Gypsy people were once birds. Year after year, they flew south during winter and then returned to their homeland when the leaves emerged on the trees. One summer, after a great famine, the Gypsies found a land fat with grain. They swooped down on the fields and feasted until they were so heavy they couldn't rise to their wings again. For many weeks they fed in the grain-fields until their wings grew useless and took the shape of arms and hands. This is how the Gypsies became human beings. Longing to fly again, they could only walk from place to place. And this is why Gypsies roam.

Historical accounts indicate that Gypsies were nomads of Hindu origin. Calling themselves Romany, they wandered throughout Asia, arriving in Europe by the 15th century. Traveling in caravans with few possessions, Gypsies were metalsmiths, tinkers, musicians, pickpockets, diviners, and animal doctors.

In 1836, British historian Samuel Roberts published a work asserting that these nomads were descendants of ancient Egyptians forced to wander the earth for their many sins. This theory is responsible for the coinage of the name *Gypsy,* it being a twist on Egyptian ("Egypsian"). Roberts's assertion also inspired the term *gyp,* "swindle," which reinforces the stereotype of the deceptive, cozening Gypsy.

HACK

Have you ever contemplated the differences between the English homonyms *hack* and *hack?*

Hack the verb means to cut or chop with repeated blows. This term comes to Modern English ultimately from a Germanic word that simply imitated the sound of chopping. The *hack* that refers to a harsh cough also hails from this source.

The *hack* meaning at once a worn-out horse, a hired writer, a taxicab driver, and a prostitute has a more complex history. The stage for this term was set in 14th century England in Hackney, a village outside London where horses were raised before being sold or hired out in the city. These horses, ubiquitous on London streets, pulled rented coaches or became saddle horses for hire. The rented Hackney, or *hack horse,* was symbolic of drudgery and listlessness.

Similarly, hired writers who handed in uninspired compositions became known as *hacks,* as did lukewarm attorneys and preachers. The opprobrium was extended to low-class, frequently abused prostitutes.

Moving into the 20th century, the word came to denote a taxicab or its driver, an echo of its earlier sense of a Hackney horse and carriage for hire.

HALCYON

The Greek goddess Alcyone and her mortal husband, Ceyx, were so in love they made the gods jealous.

Zeus and Hera spitefully conjured a strong wind to capsize the ship in which Ceyx was journeying. When Alcyone learned that the sea had claimed her husband, she threw herself into the waters to join her murdered lover. In a spirit of clemency, the gods transformed Alcyone and Ceyx into birds, called *halcyons* by the Greeks. Halcyons are known to English speakers as "kingfishers."

The halcyon couple tried to build their nest on the seashore, but the incoming waves continually destroyed it. Again moved by pity, the gods commanded the waters be still while Alcyone and Ceyx constructed their nest and incubated their eggs.

Each year as the halcyons raised their young, the sea remained tranquil. This annual brooding season was said to have occurred during the days of the winter solstice. Believing this period of serenity was divinely appointed, the Greeks called it *halcyon days.*

This expression survives in the English language. *Halcyon days* alludes to any era of peace, prosperity, and happiness.

HAM

Since the late 19th century, inexperienced, attention-starved actors have been called *hams*. To *ham it up* means to overdramatize, to command the spotlight regardless of one's theatrical gifts. Does the *ham* in these expressions have anything to do with the ham we eat?

It does, according to one theory. Around the turn of the century, minstrel actors used greasepaint for blackface roles. Inferior, poorly paid actors used lowly hamfat as a makeup base. These amateurs were called *hamfatters* and, later, *hams*. This term came to refer to the acting style of bad and consequently low-budget actors.

Or the word may come from *hamfisted,* an insult heaped upon bungling, clumsy boxers and ball players. By extension, graceless actors were called hamfisted performers, or simply *hams.*

No pork is involved in a third conjecture that asserts that the word is simply the truncation of *Hamlet,* a Shakespearean role often slaughtered by zealous but inexperienced performers.

Though etymologists are uncertain of the birthplace of *ham,* they all agree that it arrived on the mural of American English slang in about 1880.

Have a Nice Day

It's a standard parting benediction amongst American English speakers: *Have a nice day.* It has, in fact, been so mindlessly overused for so long by such great hordes of people it is now deservedly considered a cliché.

Identifying the source of a cliché is often difficult; such is the case with *Have a nice day.* It appears to have a long linguistic pedigree. Chaucer, in "The Knight's Tale" of the *Canterbury Tales,* written in the 14th century, used a form of the expression when he wrote, "Fare well, have good day."

How did this rather insipid little phrase become America's favorite formula for bidding farewell? The expression has probably been in use since the 1920s, and by the '50s it was enjoying the favor of truckers as they conversed on CB radios.

Two decades later it was on the tongues of all Americans. Who has not employed it either sincerely, sarcastically, or in its alternative form *Have a good one.*

In a word book titled *Have a Nice Day—No Problem,* lexicographer Christine Ammer notes that on January 1, 1988, the constabulary of Brunswick, Maine, was ordered by the police chief to eliminate *Have a nice day* from their on-duty vocabulary. It seems the officers had an irritating habit of punctuating the issuing of traffic tickets with an incongruous "Have a nice day!"

HAYWIRE

To *go haywire* means to become confused, go wrong, or malfunction. A *haywire outfit* is an operation poorly managed or running with shoddy equipment.

The colorful term *haywire* was invented by American English speakers in the 19th century. It had been a part of American parlance for decades before it was formally discussed in a publication called the *Forestry Bureau Bulletin,* in 1905. "'Haywire outfit,'" reads the *Bulletin,* is "a contemptuous term for loggers with poor logging equipment."

It was not uncommon for early logging outfits to repair faulty machinery with the wire used to bind hay for the camp's horses. As a temporary mend for a broken fence, horse harness, or machine, haywire was apt to break under even slight stress, in turn causing more vexation and confusion.

Farmers and other workers used recycled haywire to compensate for poor planning, antiquated equipment, or poverty. Thus, humble haywire has come linguistically to represent confusion, disorganization, and frustration.

The common American English expressions *heart of gold, hard-hearted, heart on a sleeve, heart's in the right place, heart-to-heart talk,* and *learn by heart* reflect an ancient belief that the heart was literally the seat of emotion, intellect, and memory.

Most of these phrases appear in classic literature; for example, *heart of gold,* which metaphorically describes the color of a good person's cardiac organ, was recorded in 1599 in Shakespeare's *Henry V.*

A translation of the *Odyssey* and the Old Testament book of Job include the expression *heart of stone.* The cliché *heart-to-heart talk* is by comparison a linguistic youngster, having first appeared in print about 1900. It refers to an intimate conversation wherein two hearts metaphorically face each other in honesty.

A *heavy heart* reflects feeling of sadness. This expression appears in the Old Testament book of Proverbs: "Heaviness in the heart of man maketh it stoop."

The phrase *learn by heart* means to memorize. It's a linguistic reminder of our ancestors, who believed the powers of memory lay in the heart. Though we believe we memorize with our minds, *learn by brain* frankly lacks the poetry of the older, dearer *learn by heart.*

HERMAPHRODITE

Hermaphroditus was one of the many handsome young gods in the Greek pantheon. His name was a combining of the names of his famous Olympian parents, Hermes and Aphrodite.

Hunting in the woods one day, Hermaphroditus discovered a shimmering lake, calm and perfectly translucent. As he paused to admire its waters, a local water nymph appeared before him. She stood, frankly admiring the young god.

Her name was Salmacis, she said, and would he like to come home with her? When Hermaphroditus coldly refused her, she retreated in shame. Hermaphroditus then turned back to the lovely and inviting lake, threw off his clothing, and dove in.

But as he did, a pair of arms encircled his shoulders. Salmacis again. This was her lake, said the water nymph, and now he was hers too. As Hermaphroditus struggled against her entwining limbs, Salmacis prayed the gods would make their bodies become one. Her supplication was granted, and the two merged into a being that was half male and half female.

The word *hermaphrodite,* denoting an animal or plant with both male and female reproductive organs, was inspired by this tale of Hermaphroditus. This term has been used in the English language since the 14th century.

HEROIN

In 1898, the Bayer Company of Elberfeld, Germany, introduced heroin, a synthetic substance derived from the opium poppy. In 1906, the American Medical Association approved heroin for general use and recommended it as a substitute for the dangerously addictive drug morphine. Victorian housewives, gratefully embracing Bayer's promise of a "new, nonaddicitive panacea," administered heroin to themselves, their children, and their husbands.

But this new synthetic drug proved to be as dangerous as morphine. In the early 1920s, there were an estimated 200,000 heroin addicts in the United States, many of them housewives. A growing medical awareness of narcotics addiction and a temperance movement led by the Protestant churches led to a ban of the sale of narcotics, including heroin, in 1923. Criminal syndicates, emerging to meet the illicit demands for heroin, found a new source of income in the traffic of this drug.

In 1898, Bayer believed it was gifting the world with a panacea designed to invigorate, soothe, and heal. *Heroin* is derived from the Greek *heros,* "valorous person." The inventors of the narcotic believed their new drug would comfort the patient by allowing him, for a short time, to feel like a hero.

Many creatures pass the winter in a state of near or total hibernation. In protected burrows, animals such as squirrels, snakes, turtles, and bears enter a sleeplike dormancy for months at a time. The mammals live off stored body fat until spring, when the warm weather renews their food supply.

The British scientist Erasmus Darwin (grandfather of Charles Darwin) is credited for having used the terms *hibernate* and *hibernation* in reference to the winter dormancy of animals in 1802. In other contexts, the word *hibernate* means simply "passing the winter in a suitable location." Human beings were said to "hibernate in warmer climes" when spending the coldest season on the Mediterranean.

Taken from the Latin word for winter, *hiems, hibernate* has several etymological relatives. The adjective *hibernal* means "pertaining to winter." This word appeared in English circa 1600.

The word *hibernaculum* originally denoted the winter quarters of Roman soldiers; in a more modern incarnation, the word refers to the bulbs or buds of certain plants that assist the organism in winter survival.

The old Roman name for Ireland is *Hibernia*. Most word scholars believe this moniker was influenced by the Latin word for winter. Ireland, to the Romans, was a cold, "wintry" place compared to their Mediterranean homeland.

Hick

American English speakers have available a nest of opprobrious terms to call provincial folk: *hayseed, rube, redneck, hillbilly.* But what about *hick,* the term meaning naïve, unsophisticated country dweller?

Though we all understand the insulting intention of this moniker, its origin is a bit fuzzy.

In 17th century England, Hick was a pet name for Richard (analogous to, say, Bob for Robert). American lexicographer Hugh Rawson says, "Personal names frequently are used as generic characterizations and means of addressing individuals whose real names are unknown, with the pejorative connotations coming through...when the names are shortened to their familiar forms." For example, consider Dago (a corruption of Diego) for an Italian or Heine (a form of Heinrich) for a German.

Hick, then, short for Richard, was applied to the Rural Everyman, the generic dweller of the sticks.

Hick achieved new prominence among the flappers of the 1920s, sensitive as those worldly young moderns were to the unsophisticated demeanor of rural males.

HIEROGLYPH

With his eye on the treasures of Africa, Napoleon launched a military and scientific expedition to Egypt in 1798. While working on a fortification near the port city of Rosetta at the mouth of the Nile, one of Napoleon's soldiers unearthed a slab of black granite. Engraved on the face of this stone were three distinct scripts: Egyptian hieroglyphic inscriptions, a simplified hieroglyphic style called *demotic,* and a Greek text.

Called the Rosetta stone after its place of discovery, this engraved granite slab was the key to the deciphering of ancient Egyptian hieroglyphic text. The understanding of the famous Egyptian carved characters had been obscured for centuries, but the Greek carvings included on the Rosetta stone enabled linguists to translate the Egyptian text.

Hieroglyph means "sacred carving." It is a combination of the Greek *hieros,* "sacred, holy," and *gluphe,* "carving." The Greeks applied this term to the characters carved on Egyptian buildings and monuments, which often illustrated the exploits and achievements of kings and gods. The word *hieroglyphic* was later used to classify the inscriptions of the Hittites, Mayans, and Aztecs, though those languages are unrelated to the Egyptian.

The Greek word *hieros* also appears in *hierarchy,* which means "sacred ruling"; *hierocracy,* "government of priests"; and the obscure term *hierophant,* "an expounder of sacred mysteries."

Hijack

We American English speakers cherish our home-grown words and phrases. With gusto we sling such native terms as *promo, break-dance, compassion fatigue, jazz,* and *guesstimate.* It's ironic, however, that though we can't live without our Americanisms, we're sometimes hamstrung in our efforts to identify their origins. For example, the birthplace of America's most beloved quip, *OK,* has never been positively identified.

Another Americanism of uncertain heritage is the term *hijack.* Most word watchers agree *hijack* began to proliferate in print during Prohibition (1919–1933). A hijacking in this era consisted of thieves holding up whiskey smugglers to relieve them of their contraband.

So how do we come by the term *hijack?* One story says that when the thieves aimed their guns at the driver, they commanded him to "Put 'em high, Jack," or raise his hands in surrender. Another theory says that *hijack* may be a truncation of *highway jacker* (a *jacker* being "one who holds up").

The late word pundit John Ciardi, on the other hand, wrote of evidence that *hijack* may be a corruption of a similar-sounding Chinese word meaning "ocean-robber," or as we would say, "pirate." Ciardi entertained the notion that the word originated on the high seas where piracy of cargo is common.

Hijack evolved over the decades to keep abreast of increasingly aggressive robbery techniques. The 1960s version of the word included the notion of hijackers holding human hostages; in 1961, the word *skyjacking* appeared to describe the hijacking of airplanes.

HILLBILLY

If you don't consider yourself a *hillbilly,* you'd better not call anybody else one either. This can be a very insulting moniker, loaded as it is with connotations of ignorance and crudeness.

Around the turn of the 20th century, however, the nickname simply referred to a resident of the rural southeast. For example, this passage from an April 1900 edition of the *New York Journal:* "A hill-Billie is a free and untrammeled white citizen of Alabama who lives in the hills, has no means to speak of, dresses as he can, talks as he pleases, drinks whiskey when he gets it."

But, as so often happens with terms referring to rural folk, *hillbilly* eventually acquired opprobrious connotations. By about 1930, it was an affront.

It's not clear how *billy* fits in the picture. Possibly it's an oblique rhyme of the word *hill,* or it may refer to a male goat. Most likely it follows the pattern of taking a familiar Everyman name—Billy, in this case—and employing it as a generic insult, just as the title *Reuben* spawned the pejorative *rube,* or Rustic *Reuben.* This common name attached to the word for a common landscape feature gives us *hill-Billy.*

In December 1612, the English established a trading post in the city of Surat on the west coast of India. In the ensuing three hundred years, England asserted dominion over that nation. During this long exposure to Indian culture, the English adopted many native words into their vocabulary.

Hindi is India's most widespread modern language. Many words familiar to English speakers have come from that tongue.

The word *bangle* is a variation of a Hindi term referring to a colored glass bracelet.

A *bungalow* is a small, one-story house, the kind many Europeans inhabited while living in India. The Hindi word *bungalow* means "a house built in the style of Bengal."

Ever quaffed a *toddy?* You would never have done so if not for Hindi speakers. This word refers to the fermented juice of an Indian palm tree.

The Hindi language has also given us with the word *shampoo.* It comes from *champo,* meaning "massage" (as part of the process of a Turkish bath). The verb sense "to wash the hair" evolved in the 19th century.

Dungaree is a name for sturdy pants or overalls. The Hindi word *dungri* referred to a coarse cotton twill fabric. Originally used for sails and tents, dungri cloth was eventually fashioned into durable work clothes. *Dungri* was anglicised to *dungaree* in the early 17th century.

What about *jungle?* Adopted into English from the Hindi language in the mid-1700s, the word originally meant "desert or wasteland." English speakers have pressed it into service to mean "forbidding, impenetrable forest." In 1906,

Upton Sinclair further modified the term in the title of his novel *The Jungle,* a tale involving a savage, soulless American meatpacking industry.

Pajamas were originally loose cotton or silk trousers worn by both Indian men and women. Europeans appropriated this garb for nightwear, adding a buttoned top to complete the ensemble. *Pajama* literally means "leg garment" in its original Hindi language.

Other important borrowed Hindi words are *cheetah, shawl, chintz, seersucker, pundit,* and *swastika.*

If we look at the timeline of the American slang term *hip,* meaning "aware, modern, up to date," we witness its appearance in the early 20th century and its continued popularity into the 21st century.

Though the antecedents of *hip* are unknown, several theories compete to explain the origin of the word. One was offered by Peter Tamony, in the 1939 *News Letter and Wasp:* "The sense of…hip is derived from an old phrase used in wrestling, 'to have on the hip'. When a wrestler had his opponent on the hip he had complete and effective control of him."

The über-hipster musician Cab Calloway extends another theory in the 1942 *Original Jive Dictionary:* "Nowadays you have to call a gone character a hipster. That comes from the fact that a real gone musician is said to have his boots laced right up to his hips."

The Summer 1961 issue of *Dissent* makes twins of *hip* and *hep:* "Actually, 'hep' and 'hip' are doublets; both come from a much earlier phrase, 'to be on the hip', to be a devotee of opium smoking, during which activity one lies on one's hip."

Whatever its origin, the word *hip* and its variants *hipcat, hipster, hippie,* and *hip-hop* have claimed the affection of generations of American slangsters.

Bending the scales at an astonishing four tons, the hippopotamus inhabits the rivers and marshes of Africa. The hippo spends most of its day submerged in water with only ears, eyes, and nostrils exposed. After sunset, the creature wanders ashore to feed on grasses throughout the night.

Some biblical scholars think the "behemoth" of the Old Testament and the hippopotamus are the same beast. Job, chapter 40, tells us this: "Look at the behemoth...under the lotus plants he lies, hidden among the reeds in the marsh. The lotuses conceal him in their shadow; the poplars by the stream surround him. When the river rages, he is not alarmed... though the Jordan should surge against his mouth."

While *behemoth* is of Hebrew derivation, the word *hippopotamus* comes to us from the Greek language. The creature's vague resemblance to a member of the equine species inspired the Greeks to name it *hippo-potamus*, "horse of the river."

The word has a number of etymological relatives, one of which is *hippodrome,* an arena for equestrian shows or races. *Hippocrates,* the name of the illustrious Greek physician, means "strength of horses." The mythical *hippogrif,* or "horse-griffin," has the claws and beak of a bird and the body of a horse. Even the name *Philip* contains a reduced form of the Greek *hippo,* making Philip etymologically a "horse-lover."

HOBSON'S CHOICE

Take exactly what's offered, or nothing at all. That's *Hobson's choice.*

The man immortalized in this phrase is Thomas Hobson, a 17th century livery man and innkeeper in Cambridge, England. Hobson kept approximately forty horses for renting to the students of Cambridge University and to others who traveled between Cambridge and London.

To ensure that all of his horses were given equal time under the saddle, Hobson established a rotational rental system whereby the renter was forced to ride the horse nearest the stable door and none other. This prevented his customers from habitually renting and tiring the finest horses in the stable. Though the renter may have preferred the swift black mare, for example, he could not ride her until she appeared in Hobson's scheme of rotation.

Thus, the renter's only options were either Hobson's choice of horse or a long walk on foot to his destination.

Holocaust

Though we associate it with the near-genocide that occurred in Europe less than a century ago, the word *holocaust* is ancient. Its parent elements are the Greek terms *holos,* meaning "entire or whole," and *kaustos,* which means "burnt." *Holocaust,* meaning literally "entirely burnt," was a term used in 13th century English to designate a fire that completely consumed a religious sacrifice.

In 1702 the poet John Milton employed the word to describe the flames that destroyed the Phoenix, the legendary bird that arose fully animated from the ashes of its consuming fire.

The definition of *holocaust* in the *New Century Dictionary* of 1927 is "a great and destructive fire; a great or wholesale destruction of life by fire or otherwise." This interpretation was fashioned decades before Hitler committed his genocidal crimes against the Jews of Europe. It wasn't until 1957, a decade after the Second World War, that *Holocaust,* capitalized, emerged in print to denominate the specific destruction of life under Hitler's regime. This application was introduced in the 1950s by historians who wanted a name for that particular event.

Word relatives of *holcaust* are *caustic,* that which etymologically "burns like fire," and *cauterize,* to sear an incision.

Honeymoon

A sweet-sounding word for a lover's escapade: *honeymoon*. How did this charming term come to inhabit our vocabulary?

One folkloric explanation arises from northern Europe. It is said that newlyweds would share a cup of mead, or wine mixed with honey, daily for the first month, or "moon," following the marriage.

This luscious etymology, alas, is unreliable. The word *honeymoon* most likely arises from the cynic's-eye view of married love.

The first citation of the word appeared in a 1552 glossary printed in England, called *Abcedarium Anglico Latinum*. "A term...applied to such as be new married," it reads, "The one loueth the other at the beginning exceedingly, the likelihood of their exceeding love appearing to assuage, the which time the vulgar people call the honey moon."

This early citation, and all subsequent ones, suggest that marital love can be compared to the phases of the moon. When love is new, it is full and honey sweet. But as married life progresses, love dims like lunar waning.

The custom of the honeymoon trip arose early in the 19th century, whereupon the verb form *to honeymoon* appeared in the English vocabulary.

HUSK

Does the word *husk* referring to a seedpod have anything in common with the *husky* meaning "sturdily built"? What about the thick and hoarse *husky* voice? And where does the *husky* dog breed stand amidst all these terms?

Husk has been a part of the English vocabulary since the 1400s. It appears to be an abbreviation of the Middle Dutch word *huskijn,* meaning "little house." Implied here is that the husk serves as a "little house" protecting a fruit, a seed, or an ear of corn.

The adjective *husky* means "dry and thick." What is the connection with the "little house"? When you have a "husky throat," your gullet is parched, as though it were full of husks.

Husky also means "strong and stout." The *Barnhart Dictionary of Etymology* says this shade of the term appeared in the 1869 Harriet Beecher Stowe novel *Oldtown Folks.* Stowe wrote of one who was "sturdy, like a seed husk." The *Henry Holt Encyclopedia of Word and Phrase Origins,* however, contends this adjective comes directly from the husky dog breed, famous for its stoutheartedness and endurance.

And that *husky* is the "sled dog" of the Arctic. Though this term is identical in spelling and pronunciation to the adjective, it's no relative. This *husky* seems to be a remodel of the word *Esky,* itself an abbreviation of *Eskimo.*

HYPER-

The Greek prefix *hyper-* means "above, over, excessive, extreme." This prefix heads up an array of English terms both common and obscure.

Hyperbole is a figure of speech expressing more than the truth, or an extravagant statement not intended to be understood literally. It comes from *hyper-,* "over," and *ballien,* "to throw." A *hyperbolic* statement is etymologically "thrown over" the line of credibility. *Hype,* "inflated advertising," is taken to be a slang child of *hyperbole*; it began appearing in print in the mid-1960s.

Hypertext, coined in 1965 by computer engineer T. H. Nelson, means a system of hardware and software that allows easy movement between related text, sound, and graphics. It combines *hyper-* with the Latin *texere,* "to weave."

Hyperborean pertains to the far north—arctic, frigid. In this case, it is *hyper-,* meaning "extreme," plus *Boreas,* Greek god of the North Wind.

Hypergamy—marriage above one's class or position in society—combines *hyper-,* "over," and *gamos,* "marriage" *(gamy* also appears in *bigamy* and *polygamy).*

Hypermnesia is an unusual power of recollection, an abnormally acute memory. The ability to memorize the contents of a phone book is a manifestation of hypermnesia. Here *hyper-,* "extreme," joins *mimneskesthai,* "to recall" *(amnesia,* loss of memory, is *hypermnesia's* antonym).

HYPO-

The Greek prefix meaning "under, beneath, below," *hypo-*, is the advance guard of *hypodermic, hypochondria, hypothermia, hypothesis, hypotenuse,* and the rare but interesting *hypocaust.*

Hypodermic, a syringe for injections, comes from *hypo-*, "under," and *derm,* "skin." Hypodermic injections are always administered "under the skin."

The constant, morbid concern about one's health, *hypochondria,* is from *hypo-* and *khondros,* "cartilage." "Below the cartilage" refers to the area of the abdomen beneath the ribs, formerly supposed to be the source of melancholy and morbidity. In the 17th century, hypochondria meant "depression, low spirits." By the 19th century, it came to mean "belief of being ill."

Hypothermia is below-normal body temperature and is from *hypo-* and *therme,* "heat" *(therme* also gives us *thermometer, thermostat,* and *thermos).*

From *hypo-* and *thesis,* "placing," we get *hypothesis:* an assumption or supposition that supports a line of reasoning. Hypotheses "underlie" or are etymologically "placed under" theories and ideas.

The interesting *hypocaust* was the term for a series of channels under the floors of Roman buildings designed to conduct heat from a furnace—from *hypo-* and *kaien,* "to burn" (the *caust* in hypocaust also appears in *holocaust* and *caustic).*

A *hypoteneuse* is the side of a right-angled triangle opposite the right angle and is from *hypo-* and *teinein,* "to stretch." The hypotenuse etymologically "stretches under" (or lies opposite) the right angle.

HYSTERIA

Here is the word *hysteria* as defined in the 1889 *Century Dictionary:* "A nervous disease characterized by unrestrained desire to attract attention and sympathy with more or less co-ordinated convulsions and vasomotor derangements.... Women are much more frequently affected in this way than men."

The 2003 edition of *Merriam-Webster's Collegiate Dictionary* defines hysteria this way: "Behavior exhibiting overwhelming fear or emotional excess."

A change in medical philosophy about women and their bodies is responsible for the revision of the definition of this word. *Hysteria,* coming from the Greek *hustera,* "uterus," reflects an ancient belief that the womb was responsible for female emotional disorders. Writing in the 3rd century B.C., Plato claimed that when the uterus "remains barren...it is distressed...and straying about the body and cutting off passages of the breath...it provokes all manner of diseases besides."

The notion of the womb as an unruly, wandering organ persisted for centuries, ultimately inspiring the noun *hysteria,* or "female fits of passion caused by the womb," and the adjective *hysterical,* literally "of the womb" or "prone to uncontrollable emotion" as, presumably, experienced only by females.

Hysteria and *hysterical* have lost much of their gender-specific connotations in the 21st century. *Hysterical* can mean "outrageously funny," and even men can exhibit the "emotional excesses" of hysteria.

After the first frosts of autumn, an echo of July returns to our landscape in the celebrated *Indian summer* of North America. On October 31, 1850, Henry David Thoreau wrote, "This has been the most perfect afternoon of the year. The air quite warm enough, perfectly still and dry.... Our Indian summer is the finest season of the year."

Though the phrase *Indian summer* has been on the tongues of American English speakers well over two hundred years, its origin is much disputed.

This expression was discussed at length by one Albert Matthews in the January 1902 issue of the *Monthly Weather Review*. Matthews asserted that we may never know the origin of *Indian summer* but cited a possible candidate in the writings of a Rev. James Freeman from New England. Freeman wrote in 1812:

> The southwest is the pleasantest wind which blows in
> New England. In the month of October, in particular,
> after the frosts...it frequently produces two or three weeks
> of fair weather. This charming season is called the Indian
> summer, a name which is derived from the natives, who
> believe that it is caused by the wind, which comes...
> from...their great and benevolent God Cautantowwit,
> or the southwestern God...who is superior to all other
> beings, who sends them every blessing which they enjoy.

Another possibility appeared in a correspondence in the *Philadelphia National Intelligencer* on November 26, 1857:

> The short season of pleasant weather usually occurring
> about the middle of November is called the Indian sum-
> mer, from the custom of the Indians to avail themselves of

this delightful time for harvesting their corn, and the tradition is that they were accustomed to say that 'they always had a second summer of nine days just before the winter set in.' It is a…genial time…. the sky is…filled with a haze of orange and gold intercepting the direct rays of the sun, yet passing enough light and heat to prevent sensations of gloom or chill,…and the necessary fires give cheerful forecast of the social winter evenings near at hand.

This account hints that the expression may have been inspired by an Indian proverb or meterological observation; unfortunately, the *National Intelligencer* doesn't tell us which native nation originated the belief.

A darker theory comes from writings of the late 1800s, in which the development of the expression parallels those of *Indian giver, Indian tea,* and *Indian corn.* These disparaging names, coined by colonists, designated "inferior" American items resembling the genuine articles from their European homeland. Thus, *Indian tea* and *Indian corn* were bogus, imitation items. From this vantage, *Indian summer* becomes a false summer of short duration preceding the bite of winter.

With a few exceptions, all languages currently spoken in Europe, Asia Minor, Iran, and northern India belong to an ancient linguistic family called *Indo-European*. Almost every official language in the New World is also of Indo-European origin.

Most historical linguists believe such languages as Greek, German, English, Hindi, and Russian are descendants of a single tongue spoken some 8,000 years ago in the steppe region above the Black Sea.

The people who spoke this early language cultivated and stored beans and barley. They raised sheep, goats, and swine, supplementing domesticated foodstuffs with salmon, wild apples, and honey. By about 2000 B.C., their expanding populations pushed west out of Central Europe and into Greece and Italy. In eastward-migrating waves, they eventually reached Russia, Iran, and India.

These emigrants conquered new lands not only with their technology but with the armor of language, loaning it to those they vanquished. We can see evidence of Indo-European unification across this region in the various words for *mother*. In Latin, it's *mater;* in German, *Mutter;* in Sanskrit, an ancient Indian language, it's *mata;* and in Italian, *madre*.

Sir William Jones was the first to recognize this linguistic affiliation. As a judge stationed in India in the 1870s, Jones studied native law codes in the Sanskrit language. Noting the similarities between Sanskrit, Greek, and Latin, he concluded the three were related tongues, a notion that inspired the ongoing exploration of the Indo-European phenomenon.

INFANT, INFANTRY

If you've ever suspected the words *infant* and *infantry* are related, your intuition was accurate. But the notion may have befogged you: how is a newborn like a foot soldier?

Consider the infant. Unable to walk or feed herself, she is helpless. Within a few months, however, she can walk and grasp at food on a plate. At about two years the child begins to speak in short but meaningful sentences. This is, etymologically, the moment when infancy ends. The word *infant* comes from the Latin term *infans,* which means "unable to speak," referring to a child incapable of producing meaningful linguistic sounds. English borrowed the word from the Old French *enfant* in 1384.

Traditionally, infantrymen were foot soldiers outfitted with small arms, bayonettes, or rifles. Though *infantry* is etymological kin to *infant,* foot soldiers are neither helpless nor incapable of speech. The notion that binds a foot soldier to a baby is that of youth; generally, an infantryman was too young and inexperienced to ride in the cavalry. In addition, he may not have reached the age where he could "speak for himself" in legal matters.

The Italian word for foot soldier is *infante,* "youth." A collection of young foot soldiers is *infanteria,* a term that ultimately produced our *infantry.*

IRIS

When the Olympian immortals wished to send messages to one another, they often summoned Iris, the winged courier goddess. Arrayed in colorful silken robes, Iris traversed the sky, delivering the missives of the gods.

As she flew, her brilliant garments left an arc of color hanging amongst the clouds. The Greeks considered Iris the personification of the rainbow; indeed, *iris* is the Greek word for that atmospheric phenomenon.

Throughout the millennia, English speakers have applied this goddess's name to things of remarkable hue. Consider the flowering iris, a plant cultivated to bloom in every color of the spectrum.

The colored portion of the eye also bears the name of the rainbow goddess. Throughout the animal kingdom, ocular irises display extraordinary color variation from the palest blue to brilliant yellow to black. Irises, literally, come in all colors of the rainbow.

Consider a pair of spin-offs of the word *iris*. The adjective *iridescent* means showing rainbow-like colors. The metal *iridium* was so named in 1803 by its inventor because of the striking variety of color it displayed when dissolved in acid.

IRON CURTAIN

Sir Winston Churchill did not invent the phrase *iron curtain,* but when he inserted the expression in a speech at Westminster College in Fullerton, Missouri, he certainly made it famous. His words on March 5, 1946, were, "From Stettin in the Baltic to Trieste in the Adriatic, an iron curtain has descended across the continent."

Metaphorically demarcating the ideological barrier between communist and noncommunist nations, the term was rarely employed before Churchill's Westminster College address. There is evidence of its existence as early as 1904 in the H. G. Wells novel *Food of the Gods:* "It became evident that Redwood had still imperfectly apprehended the fact that an iron curtain had dropped between him and the outer world."

The *Oxford English Dictionary* asserts that this phrase, in its nonpolitical incarnation, is at least two hundred years old. An *iron curtain* in 18th century Europe was literally that: a curtain or sheet of iron in a theater engineered to drop to prevent the spread of fire throughout the auditorium. The *Oxford English Dictionary* contains a quotation in which the expression was so used circa 1794.

The modern political implication of the term relies on the image of an impenetrable barrier separating one area from another, as in the iron theater curtain segregating stage from audience.

IRONY

In Edgar Allen Poe's short story "The Cask of Amontillado," the narrator and lead character, Montresor, complains of suffering many insults from his friend Fortunato. Montresor, seeking exquisite revenge, lures the insulting Fortunato deep into the family catacombs on the pretext of tasting a fine wine stored there. Montresor entombs Fortunato alive in the recesses of the catacombs where no one would hear his cries, and where his body could never be found.

Fortunato, the name of the victim of Montresor's base revenge, means "fortunate one" in Italian. But as the story evolves, the reader realizes the poor fellow, buried alive, was profoundly *unfortunate.* It was Poe's macabre trick of irony.

Irony is not linguistically related to *iron. Irony* came to the English language from Latin in the 16th century. The Latin speakers borrowed it from the Greek *eironeia,* meaning "simulated ignorance." In modern literature, playwrights and authors create irony in, for example, a contradiction between what a character says and what he intends that statement to mean. Or it can be Poe's trick of creating a disparity between the meaning of a character's name and his predicament. A special form of irony, *Socratic irony,* refers to the philosopher's use of feigned ignorance to point out errors in his students' reasoning.

JACK

Who is the "Jack" in *Jack Frost, jack of all trades, lumberjack, hijack, jackhammer,* and *jack-in-the-box?*

Not one specific Jack is implied here, but, perhaps, millions of them. Since at least the 12th century, Jack has been a pet form of the most common masculine name, John.

For hundreds of years, *Jack* has been a kind of omnibus title for the common man as well as a term of address for a fellow whose name is unknown. An example of this is *hijack.* One theory about this word's origin has the robber demanding that his victim thrust his hands in the air—"Stick 'em high, Jack!"

Jack Frost, the personification of winter, bears the name of the common man. So does *jack-in-the-box,* the entertaining, anonymous mannikin that springs from a little covered case. A *jack of all trades* is any man dabbling in every job.

Jack is also the name we reserve for a device or tool that can perform the labor of an unskilled man, such as a jackhammer, a boot jack, or the old reliable mechanic's jack.

An Irish legend is responsible for the distribution of the expression *jack o'lantern.* This clever Jack gambled with the Devil for his soul and won. Jack kept his soul but was sentenced to wander the earth forever. As Jack and the Devil parted company, Satan bitterly hurled a flaming coal at the one who had cheated him. Jack placed the coal inside a hollow turnip to light his endless path, thus creating the first jack o'lantern.

Many coins unearthed in Roman archaeological excavations are stamped with what appears to be a man with two faces, each seen in profile, one looking right, the other looking left. These coins depict the Roman god Janus, the patron and protector of doors, gates, and bridges.

Tradition says that Janus guarded Rome and its houses from danger. Because his countenance faced both front and back, Janus knew who was entering and leaving through doorways and over bridges. During wartime, the doors to his temple were left open so the god could observe enemy invasions and spring to the aid of the Romans in case of attack.

As his cult developed, he also became the god of beginnings, and the Romans dedicated the first hour of the day to the vigilant Janus. In about the 6th century B.C., the month *Januarius* was added to the Roman calendar; it was named for Janus, the god of beginnings, and became *January,* the first month of the calendar year. It is perhaps more than coincidence that, at this time of beginnings, we assess the year behind while looking to the months ahead, in the manner in which Janus, with his double-sided profile, is depicted on ancient Roman coins.

Janus Words

Have you ever wondered how *fast* simultaneously refers to both speed (a *fast* car) and to a static position (the nervous rider clung *fast* to the saddle horn)? Why do we think *inflammable* means both burnable and not burnable?

This duet of terms is included in a rare linguistic category called *autoantonyms,* or "Janus words." The *Janus* here refers to the Roman god of doorways and arches who's depicted with two faces, one looking forward, one looking back. *Autoantonym* means self-opposite.

The two *fasts,* meaning both quick and static, hail from one linguistic antecedent. The underlying connotation in both senses of the term is extremity or severity: a fast runner propels herself with extreme speed, while a fast friend is extremely faithful.

Technically, *inflammable* means "able to burn," from the verb *inflame,* to set afire. But this term is misleading in a language in which the prefix *in-* means "not" (as in *inhuman* and *incapable*). Serious injuries have occurred involving chemicals marked "inflammable," a word often interpreted as "*not* burnable." Consequently, many English-speaking countries have passed laws to mark burnable substances with the artificially coined but unambiguous term *flammable.*

There is at least one other autoantonym, or "Janus word," in the English language: *cleave.* Why does it mean both "to split" and "to cling to?" The secret to the schizophrenic nature of this term lies on the pages of your dictionary.

JERSEY

Fourteen miles off the northwest coast of France in the English Channel lies the island of Jersey. Though nearly within earshot of France, Jersey is a dependency of the British crown.

Across the centuries, Paleolithic and Bronze Age peoples as well as the Gauls, Normans, and Romans have left their footprints on this tiny, picturesque island. German troops occupied it during the Second World War. Today, approximately 75,000 souls of Breton and Norman descent live on Jersey's 44 square miles.

The Romans, who explored the island in the 1st century, were ultimately responsible for naming this island. In honor of the Caesars, the Romans called it *Caesarea,* "land (island) of Caesar." *Jersey* is a variant of the original Latin name.

The Jersey dairy breed, famous for its milk with high butterfat content, was developed on the island in the 18th century.

Jersey also shares its name with a type of finely woven fabric. Manufactured on the island, Jersey cloth has been used for sweaters, skirts, and stockings. Our knitted pullover tops and football clothing are ultimately named for this English Channel island.

Of course, the many Jerseys in the United States were named in imitation of the original. The third state of the union, New Jersey; Jerseyville, county seat of Jersey County, Illinois; and, as if it were a clone of the original, Jersey Island, California.

Extreme nationalism, usually accompanied by aggressive foreign policy, is known as *jingoism*. The story behind the origin of this term is interesting because the circumstances, date, and cast of characters responsible for its coinage have all been positively identified.

In 1877, in a bid to magnify its power throughout the Mediterranean, Russia attempted to capture the city of Constantinople. British prime minister Benjamin Disraeli advocated sending fleets into the area to resist the Russians. Many Britons favored Disraeli's plan, and a music hall song arose out of the ranks of these proponents:

"We don't want to fight,
but by Jingo! If we do,
We've got the ships,
We've got the men,
We've got the money, too!"

The patriots who chanted this song became known as *jingoists* because of the phrase inserted in the lyrics. The hawkish policy of these 1877 jingoists was *jingoism,* a word that currently denotes unquestioning, zealous nationalism.

The expression *by jingo* had been familiar to English speakers for at least a century before the music hall refrain was written. It is a euphemism for the religious oath "by Jesus."

JOINT

The word *joint* comes to English ultimately from the Latin *jungere*, "to join." Since about 1300, the term *joint* has meant a place at which two things or parts are connected.

But in the America of the mid-19th century, this practical term was contorted into some unusual shapes. Pushed across the slang-slinging American tongue, the term *joint* came to mean a place where swindlers and burglars congregated. By the 1890s, a joint was a generic dwelling where people gathered to eat, play cards, or take shelter for the night. It could also be a specific type of establishment, such as a juke joint, beer joint, or jazz joint.

Why was this word employed to signify these kinds of dwellings? Most lexicographers believe it is because people join together there to eat, drink, or recreate. Such pursuits are "joint" activities.

A marijuana cigarette is called a *joint* probably because it's generally shared by two or more people, or "jointly." This sense of the term was reinforced in the song "Don't Bogart That Joint, My Friend," from the film *Easy Rider*. The phrase *Don't Bogart that joint* means "Don't hang on to it; smoke it and pass it on." It refers to Humphrey Bogart's habit of holding a cigarette in his mouth for an extraordinarily long time without actually smoking it.

JURASSIC

Michael Crichton's 1990 novel *Jurassic Park* and the 1993 movie of the same name planted the word *Jurassic* firmly on our linguistic landscape.

The Jurassic geologic period endured for approximately 54 million years on our planet, during which time dinosaurs ruled the land and mammals were as small as modern rodents. Allosaurus, brontosaurus, and stegosaurus trod the earth during the Jurassic, while ichthyosaurus and plesiosaurus glided through the seas. Fossil remains of the oldest known bird, archaeopteryx, have been found in rocks of the Jurassic period.

Evidence that the climate of this time was warm and moist is provided by the remains of subtropical forests and ferns, and flowering plants first appeared during the Jurassic.

The title *Jurassic* was applied to this period in 1829 by the French geologist Alexandre Bronginart. He named it after the Jura mountains on the border of France and Switzerland. The Jura range consists principally of limestone abundant with the fossils of creatures we associate with the Jurassic period.

Keeping up with the Joneses is an exhausting, expensive affair. The phrase suggests a frantic race to remain abreast of the neighbors in material and ornamental acquisition.

The expression was invented by a New York cartoonist named Arthur R. Momand in the early 20th century. As newlyweds, Momand and his wife set up housekeeping in Cedarhurst, New York, one of Long Island's most affluent towns. Unable to both pay the bills and display the proper amount of material wealth on a cartoonist's salary, the Momands quit that urban paradise and moved to Manhattan.

Momand used his Long Island experience to launch a comic strip he called "Keeping up with The Joneses," published in the *New York Globe* from 1913 to 1931.

Momand originally wished to call the series "Keeping up with the Smiths" because of the ubiquity of that surname. One source says he changed his mind because the Momands actually had neighbors named Smith in Long Island, and the cartoonist wished to avoid offending his friends.

Another account claims Momand thought the phrase "keeping up with the Joneses" was simply more euphonious than "keeping up with the Smiths."

KETCHUP

It's hard to imagine American food without America's favorite condiment, ketchup. We consume a half-billion bottles of ketchup a year, slathering it on everything from french fries to omelets.

Despite its down-home associations, ketchup has a surprisingly exotic past, having nothing to do with tomatoes or with backyard barbecues. The progenitor of our rosy red bottled condiment was concocted somewhere in Asia, possibly Singapore, where 17th century Dutch and English sailors discovered it as a briny sauce made with pickled fish and spices.

The sailors imported it to Europe, where the fishy brine soon became a favorite. The English began experimenting with their own sauce in the late 17th century, adding such local ingredients as walnuts, cucumbers, and oysters.

While Americans, too, enjoyed these walnut and oyster sauces, it was they who added tomatoes to the mix. By 1876, American manufacturers were bottling and selling what they called "tomato ketchup."

Like the original sauce, the word *ketchup* comes from an exotic source. Etymologists have traced it to a dialectal Chinese word, *ke-tsiap,* meaning something like "fish juice." Carried around the globe by sailors and merchants, the word landed on American tongues as *ketchup.*

KINDERGARTEN

German educator Friedrich Froebel was an advocate of early childhood education, believing that children were intellectually equipped enough at age three to begin a formal education. Moreover, Froebel set forth the radical notion that children's play and their games were significant activities that prepared them for adult life.

These theories were not popular amongst Friedrich Froebel's peers in Blankenburg, Germany, in the early 19th century. When Froebel established his first school for young children in 1837, he was soundly criticized. It simply was inconceivable that children could learn anything from playing games, singing songs, and studying nature! Despite the reproach of his countrymen, Froebel nevertheless dedicated his career to establishing children's schools and training teachers for them.

The educator's methods and philosophies were adopted by the American teacher Elizabeth Palmer Peabody, who, in 1860, founded a private children's school in Boston. Thirteen years later, in 1873, the educator Susan Elizabeth Blow established the first public children's school in St. Louis (she later dedicated herself to training teachers).

Froebel and his supporters used the term *kindergarten* ("child's gardens") for their schools, reflecting the philosophy that children's minds should grow as freely as flowers in a garden.

KITE

It is exhilarating to watch a kite soar and glide against a high, sapphire sky. A kite is a beautiful plaything, a hobby, an invigorating way to spend a windy spring afternoon. But in other times and on distant shores, kites have worked hard for their makers.

The Chinese, who may have invented these high-fliers two thousand years ago, used them as military signal devices. Other kites, outfitted with flutes and bells, howled and sang in the wind to frighten enemies. "Man lifter" kites were sturdy enough to bear a soldier aloft to spy on enemy movement.

In Thailand, people sent up woven-leaf kites to attract the attention of the northeast wind which brought the annual monsoon rains. For centuries, Asians have flown "fighting kites," specially adapted fliers designed to destroy rival kites in airborne competition.

Europeans were introduced to these devices in the 17th century when English, Dutch, and Portuguese trading ships returned to their home ports with kites from the Orient.

This new species of high-flying contraption was given the moniker *kite* in the 17th century. The word, however, had been a part of the English vocabulary for three hundred years, originally denoting a type of hawk noted for its graceful, gliding flight. The colorful Asian kites reminded English speakers of the original kite—the bird of prey—so commonly seen hovering in European skies.

The phrase *knock on wood* is a verbal formula we say to avert bad luck. Time and distance have swallowed the genesis of this expression, but it most certainly is of ancient vintage.

Some etymologists believe the practice that inspired the phrase came from the Druids, who believed beneficial spirits inhabited trees, especially oaks. The Druids enlisted the help of the tree spirits by tapping on the trunk of these mighty specimens.

In a children's game called "wood tag," or "tree tag," the rules state that if you touch a tree, you're safe from the "it" person. This game could have arisen from the belief that the protective spirits inhabiting trees can be invoked by touching or knocking the wood.

Another etymological contender comes from the symbols of Christianity. Touching or holding wooden crucifixes and rosary beads brings blessing. When you knock wood, you are recalling how Christ was crucified—on the wood of a cross, the powers of which may banish evil.

LACONIC

A person of few words is often considered quiet, shy, reserved. When those few words are chosen thoughtfully and carefully, the quiet person is called *laconic*. This adjective arises out of a southern peninsula of ancient Greece, in the region called Laconia, the chief city of which was Sparta.

Dedicated to military life, the Laconians committed their sons to soldiery from age seven to age thirty. Twelve-year-old boys were grouped together and made to live outdoors, eating the coarsest of foods and fashioning rude shelters for themselves. Shunning comforts of any kind, a Laconian's worth was measured by his stoic acceptance of hardship and privation. The women, for their part, were required to bear robust sons for the state; any puny infants were put to death.

Tough, spare living produced in the Laconians a lean style of speaking: if one word was enough, two were too many. According to legend, Philip of Macedon sent a message to the Laconian leaders saying, "If I enter Laconia, I will raze Sparta to the ground." The Laconians countered with a single, terse reply: "If."

LANGUAGE ORIGIN THEORIES

One of the most intriguing and frustrating questions we humans can ask is, where did language originate? Philosophers, kings, mystics, and scientists have argued this question for thousands of years. Was language a part of our evolutionary heritage, or was it a divine gift?

We have no concrete evidence indicating where the birthplace of language was, nor who may have uttered the first meaningful syllables. We can assume language predated writing, an invention over 5,000 years old, but beyond that, all we can do is hypothesize about language origin.

There is a suite of theories devised by 18th and 19th century British and American scholars which bears repeating here. All have languished from lack of evidence, but the theories are fanciful and romantic enough to make good stories.

The *bow-wow theory* declares that speech arose through people imitating animal calls. It was short work, then, for humans to begin naming animals by the sounds the creatures made.

The *yo-he-ho theory* claims that communal work efforts induced humans to produce rhythmical grunts, chants, and eventually language.

Jean Jacques Rousseau, in the 18th century, proposed what is now called the *pooh-pooh theory*. In Rousseau's mind, humans acquired speech by uttering spontaneous cries of pain, fear, surprise, and delight.

Recent investigations into the question of language origins include the reconstruction of the vocal apparatus of Neanderthals, whom anthropologists consider our early relatives, to ascertain what sounds they may have been capable of producing. Our curiosity about the origins of language follows us into the 21st century.

They were once thought to be evil, sneaky, crippled, queer, and clumsy. Considered children of the Devil, both they and their mothers were shunned. Who were they? Left-handers, that oddball 10 percent of the world's population.

For thousands of years, and probably longer, the left side of the body has universally been associated with darkness, ineptitude, and disaster. The right side, on the other hand, represents virtue and good fortune.

The belief that evil is inherent to left-handedness has linguistic consequences. Did you know the Latin-based word *dexter,* the source of our word *dexterous,* is Latin for "right," while *sinister* refers to the left? The left hand doesn't get credit even if it's as clever as the right hand, for an *ambidextrous* person etymologically possesses "two right hands"!

The word *gauche,* which we've borrowed from the French, means contemptible or ill-mannered. In its original language—and in its standard French usage—it means "left."

In German, *linkisch* means left-handed, but it's also synonymous with "clumsy" or "awkward." Even our very word *left* comes from the ancient Germanic word *lyft,* meaning "weak or broken."

Stepping left foot first off the sleeping mattress invites disaster. If your left palm itches, you'll lose money. A family member will die if your left eyelid twitches. The archangel Michael sits at God's right hand, while the Prince of Darkness sits on the evil left. Universally, customs and traditions associating the left side with misfortune, darkness, and backwardness run deep and ancient.

Many modern expressions continue to reflect the belief that calamity and clumsiness are traits of the left-handed. The dancer with *two left feet* is awkward and rhythmless. A *left-handed compliment* is a thinly veiled insult. *Left-handed wisdom* is faulty reasoning. A *left-handed diagnosis* is incorrect. In past decades, if someone called you *bent to the left,* he was questioning your sexual preference.

In some cliches, the left is libeled by its very absence. A *right-hand man* is a valuable helper. Where does that leave the left-hand man?

When ill-tempered, we say we *got up on the wrong side of the bed.* The wrong side is of course the left side, which always attracts misfortune.

LEMON

In modern slang palaver, the word *lemon* generally refers to a car that spends more time in the repair shop than on the road. It turns out that this particular incarnation of *lemon* is just the latest in a long history of colorful uses.

The word first turns up in print in the 1860s, when a *lemon* was a sour-tempered or disagreeable person—a grouch, a pessimist.

From the 1920s on, a *lemon-sucker* was a prissy or effeminate male, or an unpleasant, pucker-faced individual.

In underworld parlance, a *lemon* was someone being hustled in a con game. The victim of a hustler was "squeezed" out of his cash, like a lemon squeezed for juice.

By the 1930s, inferior appliances and automobiles were nicknamed *lemons*. But the term gained greatest currency in the automobile industry, and by the 1990s so-called *lemon laws* were instituted to protect consumers from costs incurred from endless car repairs. It's interesting to note that a smooth-running automobile is not a disappointingly *sour lemon* but is often dubbed a *sweet ride*.

Throughout American slang history, the lemon appears as a linguistic symbol for anything disagreeable, disappointing, or inferior.

To *let the cat out of the bag* means to reveal a secret. We've repeated this cliché so often we've long forgotten the story behind the feline, the open bag, and the secret exposed. How do these apparently unrelated variables combine to create such a popular expression?

The etymology of this phrase varies from source to source, but each story has a thread of commonality. One of the stories goes as follows:

In Europe, suckling pig was often sold as food by farmers at markets and fairs. The piglets, small enough to be carried home, were often placed in cloth bags. Looking to take advantage of gullible consumers, vendors substituted a cat for the small pig, admonishing the customer to keep the bag closed to prevent escape of the animal inside.

Upon opening the bag, of course, the buyer was surprised by the worthless feline placed there by the dishonest farmer or vendor. The buyer *let the cat out of the bag,* exposing the farmer's unscrupulous secret.

Levi's

McDonald's. Firestone. Westinghouse. Stetson. These familiar brands and many more are all examples of eponyms—words taken from people's names. American English is peppered with eponyms, and each one has a tale to tell.

Levi's is a popular label of blue jeans named after Levi Strauss, a Bavarian immigrant whose arrival in the United States coincided with the 1849 California gold rush. Strauss was 24 when he landed in San Francisco with a load of canvas. Instead of becoming Levi Strauss the tent maker, as he'd planned, the young man turned to clothing manufacture.

His design for canvas trousers filled a need that local miners and farmers had for sturdy work apparel. Strauss even reinforced the pant pockets with copper rivets and dyed his white denim blue to conceal soil marks.

When he expanded into factory production, Levi Strauss sold 21,600 pair of work pants the first year. He was worth several million dollars when he died in 1902 at age 73. By then, his name had become an enduring part of the world's vocabulary—*Levi's*.

LIMELIGHT

Dozens of our common expressions have outlived the technology or circumstances that inspired their coinage. For example, *beat around the bush,* referring to indirect conversation, arose from 14th and 15th century fowling, when "beaters" flushed game birds from their hiding places and hunters captured the birds in flight. Those who beat the bushes never engaged in the actual hunt. *All balled up,* "confused, disoriented," alludes to the packed balls of sticky snow on horses' feet which caused the animals to stumble and fall, sending riders and sledges into disorder.

In the limelight, "in the center of public attention," is also a phrase surviving its original circumstance. In 1826, Scottish engineer and inventor Thomas Drummond devised the "Drummond light" to illuminate lighthouses. His invention utilized flame directed against a block of calcium oxide, or lime, and a lens to focus the light. The illumination resulting from this admixture was white, bright, and intense.

This technology was adapted for theatrical lighting in the mid-1800s and served as the most effective scheme for illuminating onstage actors before the advent of electricity. Drummond's calcium oxide, or "lime," light threw performers into the full glare of audience scrutiny. Though this technology became obsolete with the invention of arc and klieg lights, we carry the expression *in the limelight* with us into the 21st century.

"Nothing exceeds halitosis as a social offense. Nothing equals Listerine as a remedy." This Rx for bad breath appeared in a 1928 advertisement for Listerine mouthwash. In the following decades, the makers of Listerine claimed their product "killed germs by millions on contact."

The British surgeon Joseph Lister is the man for whom Listerine was named. An early champion of antiseptic medicine and a proponent of Pasteur's germ theory, Lister was the first to treat wounds with dressings soaked in carbolic acid. He also encouraged surgeons to wash their hands and sterilize their instruments before operating. After some initial resistance, British and American hospitals gradually adopted the sterile procedures promoted by Lister, resulting in a dramatic decline of postoperative mortalities.

In the wake of Dr. Lister's lauded accomplishments, one Joseph Lawrence, a Missouri physician, developed an antibacterial liquid and marketed it as a germ-killing mouthwash. Capitalizing on the recent fame of the British surgeon, Dr. Lawrence called the mouthwash *Listerine.*

Listerine is one example of an eponym, a proper name turned into a common word. Other examples of eponyms from the world of science are *pasteurize,* from the French scientist Louis Pasteur; *galvanize,* from the Italian physiologist Luigi Galvani; and *volt* from another Italian, Alessandro Volta, a physicist.

Lost Positives

If we can be reckless, ruthless, and feckless, why is it generally not linguistically possible to have reck, be full of ruth, or to be feckful? Were there ever antonyms of *reckless, ruthless,* and *feckless,* and if so, where did they go?

For reasons unknown, English speakers abandoned centuries ago the verb *reck,* which means "to care." But we did not relinquish its antonym, and so *reckless* is a lively member of our Modern English discourse.

The word *ruth* is also all but orphaned by English speakers, it being a lost positive of the common term *ruthless.* Though many dictionaries contain the word *ruth,* the noun meaning compassion or pity, it's certainly unusual for any English speaker to employ it.

Feckless is a word of a different stripe. This term originated in Scotland, where in the 15th century *feck* was simply a clipped form of the word *effect.* From *feck* was formed *feckless,* literally meaning "having no effect."

And what about the *sheveled* in *disheveled?* The *ept* in *inept?* Does *unkempt* have an antonym? What about *disgruntle?* Your dictionary contains the pedigrees of all these terms; I invite you to look them up.

LOVE WORDS

The vocabulary surrounding the aspects of affection and romance has been with English speakers for centuries. Consider the terms *charm, fascinate, passion, infatuate,* and *kiss*—evocative words of ancient origin long associated with romance and desire.

Charm originates in the Latin word *carmen,* meaning "song." The reference here is to the chanting or singing of powerful recitations designed to sway destinies.

Prior to the 17th century, the Latin-based verb *fascinate* meant to bewitch or put under a spell. Today, *fascinate* means to captivate or hold with irresistible influence.

Another Latin romance word is *infatuate.* It's the offspring of the term *fatuous,* meaning foolish or stupid. To *infatuate* is to inspire with foolish passion.

And let's talk about *passion.* This term may have the most surprising history of all. Its genesis lies in a Latin noun *passio,* originally referring to the pain of the crucified Christ. Since the 15th century it has diversified to mean "strength of emotion," be it pain, anger, philosophical conviction, or most notably, strong sexual feeling.

Kiss is an ancient term of Germanic origin, represented in Dutch *(kussen),* Swedish *(kyssa),* German *(küssen),* and Danish *(kysse).* The origin of the word is uncertain, but it's most likely the syllabic representation, or onomatopoeia, of the sound of a kiss.

LUDDITE

There are those amongst us who deeply distrust technology. A technophobe is sometimes saddled with the epithet *Luddite*. This term is an eponym, or a word taken from a proper name.

The person behind the moniker *Luddite* is one Ned Ludd, an English worker who, in about 1779, is said to have vandalized labor-saving stocking frames at his workplace.

About thirty years later, hosiery workers in the Midlands of England protested layoffs and low wages. The source of their discontent was the implementation of textile machines replacing individual craft workers. The frustrated workers organized late-night factory raids, smashing labor-saving machinery.

Whenever individual workers were accused of the vandalism, they denied the deeds, claiming "Ludd had done it," placing the blame at the doorstep of a vandal long dead— Ned Ludd. The rioters, known then as *Luddites,* were eventually repressed, some at the end of a noose.

Today, a Luddite is one who fears technology or who would eliminate automation for the work it robs from the people.

LUDUS WORDS

The Latin verb *ludere*, "to play," and the noun *ludus*, "a play, sport," lie at the heart of a sizable family of modern English terms. This linguistic family portrait, engendered by the matriarch *ludus*, includes *interlude, prelude, postlude, allude, delude, ludicrous,* and *illusion.*

Interlude means "a play between." The first interludes were light theatrical farces sandwiched between the acts of early morality and miracle plays.

Prelude is etymologically a "preliminary play or action." The term can designate the first movement of a musical suite or composition. And like the other half of a pair of etymological bookends, *postlude* indicates a concluding musical statement.

What of the more abstract *allude* and *delude?* To *allude* is etymologically "to play with or upon"; an *allusion* is an indirect reference. The expression "have an albatross around my neck" is an allusion—a "play"—to *The Rime of the Ancient Mariner,* a poem that contains the source of the metaphor. To cheat or mislead is to *delude,* a word literally meaning "to play falsely or away from."

Appearing in the 17th century, *ludicrous* originally meant "sportive, jesting, frivolous." A slight semantic shift in the 18th century gave the term a new meaning: "ridiculous, liable to excite derision."

An *illusion* is a deception or misleading image. This word derives from a form of *ludere,* a word originally meaning "mock, jest, or play with."

Without the moon there would be no tides nor months as we know them. Our vocabulary would also lack the hundreds of words and phrases inspired by our celestial satellite.

And the term *lunatic* would be among the missing. This word comes to us from *luna,* the Latin word for moon. In Roman mythology, Luna was the goddess who personified the moon.

The moon has long been implicated in cases of insanity. An English account from 1635 asserts, "The disease of lunacy is a disease whose distemper followeth the course of the moon." In Jules Verne's *From the Earth to the Moon,* the author refers to beliefs that the moon causes "nervous disorders, convulsions and malignant fevers."

The word *lunatic* was adopted by English speakers in the 13th century. Meaning "one struck by the moon," and by extension, "crazy person," this Latin-derived term has cognates in both French and Spanish.

Loony, spelled as if it's related to the name of the water bird, is actually an alteration of *lunatic.* According to the *Barnhart Dictionary of Etymology,* this slang term was first printed in 1872 by American author Bret Harte.

The venerable, twenty-volume *Oxford English Dictionary* lists seven separate definitions for the word magazine. Among the usages of the word are a storehouse, a depot, a building that houses munitions and explosives, and a chamber in which a supply of cartridges are carried.

A magazine ship is one that carries food and supplies. In his 1624 writings, Captain John Smith mentions the British "magazine ship" *Diana,* laden with provisions, arriving on the Virginia shores early in the 17th century.

A country or district as a center of commerce may also be called a *magazine.* A 17th century English writer named Digby referred to the city of London as the "magazine of money."

The most familiar definition of the term is "a periodical publication containing articles by various authors."

What concept unites these various views of the term *magazine?* How comes this word to the English language?

It springs ultimately from the Arabic word *makhzan,* "storehouse." This was adopted from the Arabic by both the Italians *(magazzino)* and the French *(magasin);* English speakers adopted it as *magazine* in about 1580. All definitions of this word include inferences to "repository" or "storehouse."

But what about the *magazine* that means "written periodical"? This too is a "storehouse," a printed repository of knowledge and information. The 1731 *Gentleman's Magazine* was the first publication to be called a *magazine.*

MAGELLAN'S WORDS

In September 1519, the Portuguese sailor Ferdinand Magellan, five ships, and 250 men set sail from the coast of Spain with a plan to find a western route to the Spice Islands of Southeast Asia. Magellan believed that the Spice Islands lay just beyond the American landmass, and he was determined to find a westward passage through modern South America. A year later, in October 1520, the mariners found their westward-trending route and followed it to the Pacific side of the continent.

Along his briny journeys, Magellan invented hundreds of geographical names, many of which are still in place. The series of islands Magellan encountered at the tip of South America he called *Tierra del Fuego,* or "Land of Fires." They were so named for the many nighttime cooking fires the Spaniards spied from their ships. In the daytime, however, the fire-makers disappeared into the forests. Magellan also named the sea to the west of the Americas *Mar Pacifico,* the Pacific Ocean, because of its tranquil disposition.

Patagonia is also a Magellenic invention. The natives, who called themselves *Tehuelches,* were purportedly large by European standards; written accounts have them standing eight feet tall. Magellan christened these monolithic people *Patagones,* or "people with the huge feet." Patagonia is etymologically "Land of the Big-Feet People."

Magpie

It's hard to ignore a magpie. Like their cousins the crows, jays, and ravens, magpies are bold and raucous. This conspicuous black and white bird is native to northern Asia, Europe, and western North America.

Intelligent and resourceful, magpies are opportunistic generalists, adapting easily to seasonal and environmental changes. A magpie menu consists of worms, insects, carrion, fruit, and grains—whatever is abundantly available. They also have a curious inclination for collecting attractive trinkets and shiny objects they find while foraging.

The bird's omnivorous appetite for edibles and collectibles has led some etymologists to suggest that the word *pie,* the pastry, comes from the last syllable in the magpie's name. Pastry pies in the Middle Ages were admixtures of miscellaneous ingredients, a reflection of the diets and collected treasures of magpies.

This bird belongs to the genus *Pica,* the same name of the common pica style of type having ten characters per inch. What's the connection between the bird and the print style? The *Barnhart Dictionary of Etymology* suggests that it was named *pica* for the stark black type on a white page, the color scheme of the magpie's plumage.

What's more, a *pica* is also an abnormal craving for non-food substances such as dirt, starch, clay, or paper. Since the 16th century, this craving has been called *pica* after the magpie, a miscellaneous, nondiscriminating feeder.

MALARIA

Malaria has bedeviled humans for millennia, scourging populations in Africa, Central and South America, parts of Asia, and the Mediterranean. The disease occurs in the swampy areas of tropical and subtropical regions. A person infected with malaria suffers attacks of headaches, intermittent fever, anemia, enlargement of the spleen, and general weakness. This disease infects an estimated 250 million people annually. Two million of these cases are fatal.

A scientific investigation of malaria in the late 19th century revealed that the malady was transmitted by a mosquito of the genus *Anopheles*. Before this revelation, nobody was certain of the source of the disease. Some thought the fevers were caught by drinking swampy water, while others believed that swamps and bogs harbored minute, fever-bearing animals that invaded the human body through the mouth and nose.

The Italians said the illness was caused by simply breathing the foul, dank air surrounding stagnant water. Their name for the malady was *mala aria*, "bad air."

This word has been used by English speakers since about 1740, when an Englishman, Horace Walpole, imported it from Italy as *malaria*. Linguistic cousins of the word *malaria* are *malignant, malice,* and *malady.*

Europeans have been trading with Malaysians and their neighboring Indonesian islanders since the 16th century. The Dutch and British, through longstanding trade and colonial contacts, adopted a number of words from the various Malay languages and dialects. Some denote plants and animals; others indicate trade goods.

The Malay *ginggang,* "striped," is the source of the English *gingham,* cotton cloth with a plaid or checked pattern. The word appeared in print in English early in the 17th century.

The great ape of the rain forests of Borneo and Sumatra so closely resembles humans that it inspired Malay speakers to give it the moniker *orang-utan,* "man of the woods." *Orangutan* was first recorded by a Dutch physician in 1691.

Early in the 17th century, English speakers adopted the onomatopoeic *gong,* a Malay word for a hanging bronze disk used as a percussion instrument.

Bamboo, also of Malay origin, comes to English through two intervening languages. First recorded by the Portuguese as *mambu,* it was claimed by Dutch speakers as *bamboes;* in 1598 it arrived on English-speaking tongues as *bamboo.*

The Malay word *amok* refers to a state of uncontrolled homicidal frenzy, a desperate engagement in battle. Loaned to English speakers in 1663, it is often paired with the verbs *go* and *run.* Captain James Cook wrote in his diaries, "To run amock is to get drunk with opium."

It was the most ridiculous tea party Alice had ever attended. The tea table was enormous but there were only three seated there: a dormouse, a March Hare, and Mad Hatter. When Alice sat at the table they shouted, "No room! No room!" though clearly it was set for a crowd. The March Hare offered her wine, though he had none. The Mad Hatter asked Alice a riddle he himself could not answer: "Why is a raven like a writing desk?" All the while the dormouse dozed and muttered. When Alice left the tea table in exasperation, the Hare and the Hatter were trying to deposit the dormouse in a teapot.

Though *mad as a march hare* and *mad as a hatter* were popularized by the lunatic characters in Lewis Carroll's *Alice's Adventures in Wonderland,* the expressions themselves predate the 1865 publication of this children's fantasy.

Chaucer (1340–1400) recorded the expression *mad as a hare;* later, the Dutch writer Erasmus (1466–1536) used *mad as a marsh hare,* stating that "hares are wilder in the marshes from the absence of hedges and cover." By Carroll's time, the expression was *march hare,* though the reason hares might be "wilder" in March than in any other month is a mystery.

Hatters of earlier centuries were often quite literally mad. The mercuric nitrate used by 18th and 19th century hatters to soften the outer stiff hairs of felt caused hallucinations, insomnia, tremors, and mental confusion. The Mad Hatter was certainly patterned after real mercury-poisoned hatters of Lewis Carroll's day.

In 1869, French food technologist Hyppolite Mège-Mouries won a national prize, offered by Napoleon III, for inventing a butter substitute. Initially called "economical butter," this substance was formulated from a complex admixture of beef fat, milk, and mammary-gland tissue extract.

When Americans embraced the notion of a substitute for butter, they combined beef fat with such stockyard by-products as udders and stomachs for a concoction known as "butterine."

A French biochemist proposed a new title for this substance: *margarine.* This is a variation of the term *margaric acid,* a fatty acid thought to be one of the constituents of the animal products used in the manufacture of margarine. *Margaric* is derived from the Greek word *margarites,* meaning "pearl." Margarine was so named because of the pearly luster of its constituent acid crystals.

In the 1890s, the word *margarine* became a metaphor for any inferior or bogus substitute. A column in Britain's *Daily News* on November 26, 1897, warns against "margarine Liberalism."

Millions of Americans used margarine for the first time in the 1940s against wartime butter shortages. It was commonly called *oleomargarine,* with *oleo* coming from the Latin *oleum,* meaning "oil."

Margarine has a trio of surprising etymological relatives: the female names *Margaret, Marguerite,* and *Margarita.* These names are daughters of the Greek *margarites,* or "pearl."

214

Maroon

A homonym is a single word with two or more meanings. The word *maroon* falls into this grammatical category. One *maroon* is a dark reddish-brown; the other, a verb, means "to abandon someone in a deserted place." The word indicating color derives from the French word *marron,* which means chestnut.

The other *maroon* has a more complicated etymology. It comes ultimately from the American Spanish term *cimarrón,* an adjective meaning "wild or untamed," from the Spanish *cima,* meaning "mountain." *Cimarrón* was originally used to indicate a domesticated animal escaped into "the mountain wilderness."

During the 17th and 18th centuries, African slaves were imported to work the plantations of Dutch Guyana and the West Indies. A slave escaping to the uncultivated mountainous areas of those regions was called a *cimarron* and, later, simply *marron,* "wild beast, savage." In 1666, John Davies, author of *History of the Carriby Isles,* said of these escaped slaves, "They will run away and get into the Mountains and Forests, where they live like so many beasts; then they are call'd Marons, that is to say Savages."

By 1709, *maroon* was a verb. Prisoners left on desolate shores to live like wild beasts and runaway slaves were said to have been *marooned.*

MASOCHISM

In 1893, the German psychiatrist Richard Krafft-Ebing invented a new word. It was *masochism,* the deriving of pleasure from being offended, dominated, or mistreated. The word was inspired by the unusual life history of Leopold von Sacher-Masoch.

Leopold, born in 1836 into an affluent Austrian family, was a respected legal scholar who earned his doctorate at age nineteen. He was also a professional actor and the author of several historical publications. Despite his success, however, Leopold was haunted by childhood demons.

The boy's earliest years were orchestrated by a formidable governess named Handscha, who captivated him with dark tales of tyrants and cruel domineering mistresses. Then, in 1848, Leopold's policeman father was involved in a series of tumultuous landowner revolutions in the city of Prague. The twelve-year-old Leopold witnessed these bloody conflicts from the windows of his home.

These cruelties and dark visions later sought expression in Leopold's relationships with women. Chasing dreams of martyrdom, he sought wives and mistresses willing to tyrannize him. He insisted his lovers be clad in furs while they thrashed him with whips. To perfect his own torture, he arranged for men to steal away his women.

Leopold von Sacher-Masoch died in an asylum in 1895, but he is immortalized in the term *masochism,* the aberration he acted out.

MAUDLIN

The Bible's New Testament contains stories of two important Marys: Mary, the mother of Christ, and Mary Magdalene, a local woman who becomes one of Christ's followers.

Interpretations of the New Testament variously portray Mary Magdalene as a reformed prostitute or simply as a sinner deeply repentant of her transgressions. The events of Mary's life are dramatic and sometimes quite touching. She is cured of disease and demon possession. It's traditionally believed that Mary Magdalene is the woman whose gratitude toward Christ compels her to wash his feet with her tears and dry them with her hair. She is also the first to discover that Jesus had been resurrected from his burial tomb.

Throughout history, this Mary has been portrayed as a woman weeping in repentance, joy, and fear. As a character in the miracle plays of the Middle Ages, she clung to and wept at the feet of Christ. In religious portraiture, she weeps at the entrance of the empty tomb.

In Britian, Mary Magdalene's name is pronounced "Maudlin." This contraction gives us the word *maudlin,* meaning sentimental or weepy, after the literary and artistic portrayals of her personality. A *maudlin drunk* is one in the stages of tearfully emotional intoxication, and the related verb *maudle* means to talk drunkenly and sentimentally.

MAUSOLEUM

Mausoleum is a modern English eponym whose namesake lived 2,300 years ago in what is now southwest Turkey.

King Mausolus was a Greek who governed a small region known as Caria on the Aegean Sea. Though he involved his empire in numerous political revolts and skirmishes, Mausolus is best remembered for an immense monument he commissioned in his own honor. Built of sparkling white marble, the edifice towered 135 feet above the ground. It was bedecked with colonades and colossal statues of the king and his wife, Artemisia.

When King Mausolus died in 353 B.C., Artemisia completed the design and construction of her husband's monument. Ultimately, both Mausolus and Artemisia were entombed there, and for 1,800 years it stood as one of the Seven Wonders of the Ancient World.

The tomb may have been destroyed in an earthquake in the 14th or 15th century. Its imposing white stones were eventually purloined for the construction of other buildings nearby.

Though the tomb of King Mausolus is gone, the ancient ruler is linguistically memorialized in our word *mausolem,* which means literally "the shrine of Mausolus." Today, a *mausolem* is a small tomb, normally built above ground, where individuals or families are laid to rest.

MEDIOCRE

To have your performance labeled *mediocre,* whether you're a student, politician, actor, or attorney, is a fairly painful slap in the face.

Mediocrity is associated with unimportant, trifling, second-rate performance. Consider the opprobrium in this quotation from Joseph Heller's 1962 novel *Catch 22:* "Some men are born mediocre, some men achieve mediocrity, and some have mediocrity thrust upon them. With Major Major it had been all three." This insult, it turns out, was borrowed from a line in Shakespeare's *Twelfth Night,* which reads, "Some men are born great, some men achieve greatness, and some have greatness thrust upon them."

A look at the pedigree of this word reveals that, etymologically, *mediocre* is not as insulting as we've made it out to be. The word is offspring of the Latin *medius,* meaning middle. It's related to such terms as *medium, mediate,* and *median.*

The *med* in *mediocre* refers to something in the middle, and *ocre* is a derivative of the Latin *ocris,* "rough stony mountain." What we have here is a word meaning "halfway up or in the middle of a long climb." Etymologically, then, those of unremarkable caliber have not achieved the summit of quality or success; instead they are mediocre, only midway up the mountain.

MELLOW

The word *mellow* has lived a more exciting existence than one might imagine. It's been around the block, etymologically speaking, having been put to good use by 17th century rogues and 20th century hep cats, be-boppers, bobby soxers, and hippies.

In its current non-slang sense, *mellow* means soft, sweet, and juicy with ripeness, as in "mellow fruit." But slang-slingers through the ages have appropriated this word to enhance their discourse.

In the street lingo of 18th century England, *mellow* meant "almost drunk." To American jazz musicians of the 1930s, a *mellow* performance was skillful, sincere, or heartfelt. Billie Holliday's 1931 recording of the song "Fine and Mellow" reinforced the word's presence in America's slang lexicon.

American high schoolers of the 1940s latched onto this term; in their teenage world, a *mellow man* was an attractive, desirable boy.

This term gave the hippies and baby boomers of the 1960s a way to articulate a feeling of agreeable relaxation, or the pleasant sensation of a slight alcohol or chemical intoxication.

The word *mellow* is of considerable antiquity, having appeared in the English language in the 15th century. Its etymological ancestor appears to be the Old English term *melu,* "ground grain," with the consequent term *mellow* suggesting the softness and richness of flour.

MENTOR

When the fabled Greek hero Odysseus left his home in Ithaca to wage war in Troy, he said goodbye to his wife, Penelope, and young son, Telemachus.

A decade passed as Penelope and Telemachus waited for the return of husband and father. Meanwhile, would-be suitors vied for the hand of the beautiful Penelope, whom they thought was surely by now a widow.

Distressed by these persistent visitors, Telemachus raged against their presence. He was only a boy, however, and the suitors mocked and taunted him.

But Telemachus was not alone. His father had provided a guardian for the boy, a trusted family friend named Mentor. Full of years and wisdom, Mentor advised the young son whenever troubles besieged him. At times, the goddess Athena assumed the guise of Mentor and appeared to Telemachus, giving him divine council.

While heeding Mentor's words, Telemachus achieved adulthood and witnessed the return of his father.

Though Mentor lived in the mythical age of ancient Greece, he's with us today in the word taken from his name. In modern English, a *mentor* is a wise teacher and trusted counselor.

Midwives have been delivering the world's babies for centuries, providing advice, comfort, and support to women in labor. They may also administer culturally sanctioned medicines or herbs to ease the birthing process.

The training of contemporary American midwives varies, from simple apprenticeship for lay midwives to a four-year professional midwife program and even more lengthy education for nurse-midwives. Traditionally, midwifery is practiced by women, but men have been active in this domain as well. In the mid-18th century, American men with medical educations began to offer the service of delivery assistance.

The *mid* in *midwife* is not the same as the one in *midday* or *midlife*. In this case, *mid* is an extinct preposition meaning "with." The modern relatives of this preposition are the German *mit,* the Dutch *met,* and the Danish and Swedish *med*. *Wife* is an Old English term that originally meant "woman." Etymologically, a midwife stays "with a woman" about to give birth.

The Latin equivalent is *obstetric*. This word arises from the Latin prefix *ob-,* meaning "before," and *stare,* "to stand." In Latin, the word for midwife is *obstetrix,* one who "stands before" the birthing bed.

MILITARY EUPHEMISM

It's human nature to linguistically sanitize unpleasant, frightening, or offensive words with euphemisms, so it isn't any wonder that military and government language is a gold mine of them. Leaders and generals of all nations inject their language with euphemisms to defend their actions and create a sheen of innocence and clear judgment upon their decisions.

In 1970, then Federal Reserve Board chairman Arthur Burns used the euphemism *liquidity crisis* for a severe shortage of expendable funds.

Warrantless investigation is an FBI substitute for illegal break-in. Lies have been linguistically diminished by various government agencies glossing them over as *erroneous reports, categorical inaccuracies,* and *terminological inexactitudes.*

The troubling realities of war demand much of military euphemists. In 1969, F-4 bombers staged raids over Laos and North Vietnam. These violent assaults were called protective reactions. In Nazi Germany, the term *Schutzhaft,* translated "protective custody," was the euphemism for imprisonment in concentration camps.

And, of course, there are these familiar military euphemisms: *ultimate sacrifice,* for death on the battlefield, and *collateral damage,* for civilian casualties.

MONEY

The origin of the word *money* is a bit hazy, but its etymology traditionally revolves around a goddess, a palace constructed in her honor, and the silver coins that were made there.

The goddess was Juno, the revered queen of the Roman immortals, the wife of Jupiter, and the protector of married women. One legend has Juno responsible for warning the Roman people of danger, alerting the city of a Gallic invasion in 390 B.C. In gratitude, the citizens built a temple on the Capitoline Hill in Rome and dedicated it to *Juno Moneta,* meaning "Juno of the Warnings."

Later, the Romans began producing silver coins in Juno's temple. They called the currency *moneta* after the protecting goddess, and the word eventually arrived in 13th century English as *money.*

Mint, a place where money is made, can also be traced, (albeit circuitously) to Juno Moneta, Juno of the Warnings.

American English speakers have fistfuls of synonyms for money: *dough, bread, scratch, bucks, fin, greenbacks, simoleons, gelt, wherewithall.*

Bread and *dough,* the fraternal twins of monitary slang, reflect the notion that money is as essential as the dietary staff of life. *Dough,* coming onto the American slang scene in about 1840, predated *bread* by a century. We see written evidence of *bread* in the 1930s, when it was used by members of the jive culture. It peaked in popularity in the 1950s, '60s, and '70s with the beat and hippie generations.

The fundamental image behind the term *scratch,* another synonym, is a chicken scraping in the dirt for bits of sustenance. *Scratch* was first recorded in writing in the 1920s.

Some use the word *fin* in slang reference to a five dollar bill. *Fin* comes from the Yiddish word *finif,* which in turn is derived from the German *fünf,* meaning five.

An older monitary synonym is *jack,* a 19th century term that referred to a small coin. It is likely the source of riches in the expression *hit the jackpot.*

Wampum is probably America's oldest currency word. It comes to English from the native Algonquin speakers of the eastern United States. This term is the abbreviation of a word that sounded something like *wampumpeak,* which refers to white shells used as trade items.

MORON

In 1906, Dr. Henry Herbert Goddard was appointed psychologist for the Training School for Feeble-Minded Boys and Girls in Vineland, New Jersey. Goddard's school provided asylum for what were then labeled "mentally defective" children.

During his appointment at the Training School, Goddard incubated several theories that would affect two generations of social and psychological thinkers. One theory sprang from his conviction that social pathology, moral deficiency, and feeble-mindedness were hereditary, engendered by the "bad blood" of an ancestor. Goddard argued that normal intelligence resulted from a dominant gene and feeble-mindedness from a recessive gene.

In 1910, the doctor invented a word and a concept to categorize a certain strain of mentally defective person. The word was *moron*. Clinically, a moron was a "high-grade" feeble-minded adult with a mental age of seven to twelve years. Morons appeared normal but lacked rationality and were considered "morally deficient." According to Dr. Goddard, morons were the source of much of society's crime, poverty, and sexual irresponsibility.

Henry Goddard coined the word *moron* from the Greek *moros,* "foolish, dull." Originally a clinical term, it migrated to our slang vocabulary in the 1920s, when it became a term of abuse. Psychology has since abandoned the use of *moron,* but the term survives in the language of insult.

Morphine

In his great opus *The Metamorphosis,* the Roman poet Ovid weaves the tale of Morpheus, the god of dreams. Morpheus was a shape-shifter who appeared to dreamers in various human guises. In naming Morpheus, Ovid borrowed the Greek word *morphe,* meaning "form or shape," to characterize this god whose nighttime appearances gave substance and shape to the dreams of mortals.

Fast-forward from antiquity to 1806, when German chemist Wilhelm Serturner isolated a new analgesic drug from the opium poppy. Those who ingested this novel substance experienced relief from both cough and chronic pain. During the Civil War, this analgesic was sent home with thousands of wounded soldiers for the relief of suffering.

Dr. Serturner was probably familiar with Ovid's tales, because he named his marvelous drug *morphine,* after the dream-god Morpheus. In doing so, the chemist linguistically proclaimed the dreamlike euphoria the drug produced.

MOXIE

Not too many decades ago, the word *moxie* was commonly employed as a slangy American synonym for courage, vigor, and spirit.

This term was born in 1884 in Lowell, Massachusetts, with the advent of a liquid tonic called Moxie Nerve Food. Its inventors asserted that the drink could cure "brain and nervous exhaustion, loss of manhood, softening of the brain and mental imbecility." Moxie Nerve Food was popular as an elixir until the 1906 Pure Food and Drug Act forced its manufacturer to abandon the medicinal claims.

It was thereafter presented as Moxie, a soda pop. Poured into car-shaped bottles called Moxiemobiles, it was the favorite drink of President Calvin Coolidge in the 1920s. Moxie's popularity peaked in 1925, after which it was gradually eclipsed by rivals Coca Cola and Pepsi Cola.

No one is certain why its inventor, Dr. Augustin Thompson, christened his elixir *Moxie,* but most word watchers contend that its synonymy with courage and vitality was a result of its early medicinal claims to restore energy and manhood. The slang sense of the word was first recorded in print in the 1930s.

MRS. BYRNE'S DICTIONARY

If you're a word lover with an appetite for the unusual, you must procure a copy of *Mrs. Byrne's Dictionary,* a collection of "6,000 of the weirdest words in the English language." According to the introductory text of this quirky work, the compiler, Mrs. Byrne (a.k.a. Josepha Heifetz Byrne), dowsed a smorgasbord of dictionaries for words "unusual, obscure, difficult, amusing and preposterous." She then corralled these terms in a compendium of her very own.

What kinds of words are we talking about here? Between the covers of *Mrs. Byrne's Dictionary* lurk such tongue-sprainers as *palilalia,* "helplessly repeating a phrase faster and faster," and *acalcula,* "the inability to work with numbers; a mental block against arithmetic."

In her word herd, Mrs. Byrne has stabled the delightful term *eyeservice,* work done only when the boss is watching.

If you're seeking a word that means fortune telling with onions, Mrs. Byrne supplies you with just the thing: *cromnyomancy.* Continuing in the clairvoyant theme, we find *belomancy,* fortune telling with arrows, and *aleuromancy,* using flour or meal to tell the future.

Mrs. Byrne has a little something for everyone. If you have large ankles, you're *scaurous* (skor-es). A *fefnicute* is a hypocrite or sneak.

Mrs. Byrne's Dictionary is not for the faint of heart. It is a treasure for those unafraid of sounding out jaw-crunchers like *omphalomancy, dromomania,* and *callipygian.*

Or try making sense of such goofy lexical offerings as *mortling* and *oubliette,* meaning, respectively, "wool taken from a dead sheep," and "a dungeon whose only opening is the ceiling."

Turning more pages: *Malacodermous* means "soft skinned." *Noctivagation* is "wandering at night." Searching for a word that refers to a euphemistic half-truth? Try *paradiastole*. If you've ever known a poor man posing as a rich man, you can call him a *stalko*.

Not all of Mrs. Byrne's offerings are addlepating esoteria; some are refreshingly useful, like *paleomnesia*, "happy memories from events far in the past," and *euneirophenia*, "peace of mind after a pleasant dream."

Most of us consult dictionaries for clarity in the spelling, definition, and histories of words. But this lexicon seems to laugh in the face of clarity in pursuit of a good time. Check your library or bookstore for *Mrs. Byrne's Dictionary*, published by University Books. Prepare for the absurd, crack the cover, and dive in.

Ms.

The female title Ms. began to receive a lot of press in the early 1970s. A compromise in spelling and pronunciation between *Miss* and *Mrs.*, *Ms.* was designed to title every woman regardless of her marital status. The popularity of the term was enhanced by the success of the feminist magazine of the same name that hit the newsstands in January of 1972.

Those who associate the title *Ms.* with the feminist movement of the '70s may be surprised to learn that the proposal for this term most likely came in the 1950s from a man with a pragmatic, rather than a social, agenda.

In 1950, a newspaperman named Roy F. Baily in Norton, Kansas, suggested that the title *Ms.* be affixed to the surname of all women, married or unmarried. This was Mr. Bailey's solution to the clerical problems engendered when women neglected to sign their names with appropriate titles. Lawyers, doctors, journalists, and others encountering these untitled names were placed in the embarrassing position of guessing the marital status of the woman in question.

Ms. was sporadically and unenthusiastically employed for the next two decades until championed by the feminist movement. Now the title is more commonplace than the *Miss* and *Mrs.* from whence it sprang and is a standard entry in every modern dictionary.

Author and verbivore Robert Hendrickson says the curious toast *Here's mud in your eye* "was originally made in the muddy trenches of World War I, or in the cafes where English and American soldiers spent their leaves trying to forget them."

This toast seems to be an expression in search of itself. Its source seems to have been lost in the shadows of etymological history. There are at least four theories of its genesis.

One has the toast coming from the Middle Ages, when bits of toasted bread were added to wine as flavoring. If a reveler inverted his goblet quickly, the bits of toast and other dregs, the "mud," could slide out and land in an eye. Thus, *Here's mud in your eye* meant "Bottoms up! Drink it all down!"

Or perhaps this expression was commonly dedicated by one horse-racing jockey to another. The jockey who proposed the toast hoped his opponent would trail behind, where the leading horses would literally kick mud in his eye.

Author James Rogers, in his *Dictionary of Clichés,* says, "One can only suppose the notion is that mud would blind one to the bad things nearby, as a series of drinks would."

Though there is no accord on the birthplace of this phrase, all agree it began appearing in print in the 1920s.

Daughters of the Greek god Zeus, the nine Muses were specialists in the studies of history, poetry, dance, song, tragedy, comedy, mime, and astronomy. These goddesses were popular entertainers at Olympian feasts because their beautiful voices, joined in song, pleased the gods and flattered their deeds and adventures. The Muses are often depicted in sculpture and paintings as young women in flowing garments, holding hands and dancing together in a circle. Each Muse carries the symbol of her study: a mask, a sphere, a lyre, or a flute.

The Muses were the personifications of the highest musical, scientific, and artistic ideals. Writers and scholars of every age have sought inspiration from these creative spirits of the ancient world.

Our word *music* was coined from the collective name of these Greek goddesses. *Music* literally means "of the Muses" and refers to the arrangement of pleasing tones with the voice or instruments—a skill at which the Muses excelled.

Museum, another term inspired by the nine daughters of Zeus, comes from the Greek *mouseion* and originally meant "shrine of the Muses." The first *mouseion* was a state-supported community of scholars founded in 290 B.C. at Alexandria, Egypt. The tradition of the museum as a repository of treasured artwork and antiquities was established in Europe in the 18th century.

In the 1940s, scientists and engineers appropriated the Greek-based prefix *nano* and applied it to a new discipline—*nanotechnology,* the manufacture and study of things exceptionally small. Technically, the prefix *nano-* refers to one billionth of a measure, or 10^{-9} power. Individual atoms are typically measured in tenths of a nanometer, and some computer memory chips are 500 nanometers.

A billionth of a second is, of course, a *nanosecond.* In 1964, General Sarnoff, former head of RCA proclaimed, "A nanosecond is to a second what a second is to 30 years."

The notion of a billionth of a measure inspired many terms with this prefix—*nanoamp, nanogram, nanoliter,* and *nanovolt* among them. Though these terms are only six decades old, making them linguistic infants, the *nano-* prefix is ancient. It comes from the Greek word *nanos,* meaning "dwarf." Related terms are *nanoid,* "dwarflike," and *nanism,* "dwarfishness or abnormally small stature."

NARCISSISM

Of all the players in the tales of ancient Greece, none was more handsome and desirable than Narcissus. A young man of remarkable beauty, Narcissus was desired by scores of nymphs, goddesses, and gods. Narcissus, for his part, was unmoved by pledges of love and rejected anyone who asked for his attention.

The handsome youth one day rebuffed the affections of a particularly amorous nymph. With tears stinging her cheeks, the nymph prayed to the gods that the cruel Narcissus would one day know the pain of rejected love.

Her prayers were answered when, after hunting in the forest, Narcissus knelt beside a clear pool to drink. Gazing back at him from the depths of the water was his own gorgeous face. Narcissus suddenly realized why he had been the object of such adoration. He fell overwhelmingly in love with his own image. Unable to leave the reflection in the pool, Narcissus died from longing for his own beauty.

This ancient story suggested the clinical term *narcissism* to a pair of 19th century psychologists, Havelock Ellis and a German named Näcke. Introduced in 1899, *narcissism* refers to a personality disorder characterized by abnormal self-admiration and a preoccupation with one's own comfort and well-being.

NEANDERTHAL

Early humans, *Homo sapiens neanderthalensis,* better known as Neanderthals, flourished in Europe and the Middle East from 100,000 to 35,000 years ago. Neanderthal's fossilized remains have been found in caves and burial sites in Germany, France, Belgium, Yugoslavia, Israel, and Iraq.

Skeletal analysis of the Neanderthals reveals that they were stouter and stronger than modern humans. The skull was low and sloping, with brow ridges protruding over the eye sockets. Evidence suggests that they were hunters and opportunistic gatherers, exploiting the resources of their varied habitats across the continents of the Old World.

Reproductions of Neanderthals produced in the 19th and 20th centuries showed them as stoop-shouldered and brutish with vacant, bovine expressions. But more recent views situate Neanderthals on equal ground with modern humans in terms of intelligence and creativity.

Academic debates have raged for decades about the Neanderthal branch on the human family tree. Some anthropologists claim Neanderthals are our direct ancestors; others posit that they were never in our immediate line of descent and that they simply became extinct approximately 35,000 years ago.

The title of these beings comes from the name of the site where the first Neanderthal skeleton was discovered, in a cave in the Neander Valley near Düsseldorf, Germany. The German word for valley is *Thal,* so *Neanderthal* simply means "Neander Valley."

The English word *nebula,* a direct borrowing from Latin, meant "cloud, mist, vapor" when it first appeared in the language in 1449. The term is ancient and widespread. Words with the same etymological ancestry as *nebula* show up in Greek *(nephos),* Old Slavic *(nebo),* Sanskrit *(nabhas),* Welsh *(niwl),* German *(Nebel),* and Dutch *(nevel).* All these related terms suggest fog, clouds, or sky.

By 1661, however, the English *nebula* referred to a film or opacity on the cornea of the eye that caused defective vision. Astronomy appropriated the term in 1729 and used it to designate a tenuous cloud of gas and dust in interstellar space. Here the word *nebula* has stabilized with no semantic alterations in three hundred years.

It has, however, engendered some interesting offspring. For example, a *nebulizer* is an instrument that converts liquid into a fine spray. A *nebule* is a cloud or fog. An artist whose work is characterized by indistinctness of outline is a *nebulist.* The *Oxford English Dictionary* tells us that a *nebulon* is a "worthless fellow." The most familiar of the *nebula* progeny is *nebulous,* "hazy, vague, formless."

NECTAR

The term *nectar* has three subtly different implications in our language. It's the botanical term for a sweet liquid secreted by flowers, it's a nickname for any delicious beverage, and, finally, it refers to the drink of the immortal gods of Mount Olympus.

The Greek poet Homer described nectar as a drink resembling red wine. At the Olympian banquet table, this magical concoction was poured and served by Hebe, the goddess of eternal youth. Mortals were forbidden to drink nectar, for in doing so they would attain immortality and become like the gods.

Nectar is a Greek-based word that means "death-overcoming." Etymologically and practically, nectar confers immortality.

This term has several notable relatives. For example, the same *nec* in *nectar* also appears in *Necropolis,* the Egyptian city of the dead, or a cemetery in general. *Necrosis* is death or decay of body tissues. *Necromancy* is fortune telling by communicating with the dead; *necrophilia* is an obsession with corpses; and *necrophobia* is a fear of the dead.

Nectarine entered the English language in about 1660. This peachlike fruit was named after its sweet "nectar-like" juice.

Negligee

Abandon everything you think you know about negligees. Forget the lace, the delicate diaphanous fabrics, the whole erotic appeal. The original negligee, designed in France in the 18th century, was a voluminous dressing gown enveloping the female body from neck to toe.

French ladies of the 17th century were obliged to corset, bunch, and pinch their figures into a fashionably correct profile. When they relaxed at home, however, these women loosed the laces and donned a sacklike garment called the *negligee,* a gown constructed of up to twenty yards of delicate silk, damask, or Indian cotton. Relatively shapeless and lacking ruffles, stays, bodice, or braids, the negligee provided comfort for a body that would otherwise be squeezed into unnatural configurations.

This laxness is implied in the etymology of *negligee.* It comes from the French verb *negliger,* "to neglect." Etymological cousins of this term are *negligence* and *negligible.*

According to the *Barnhart Dictionary of Etymology,* the modern *negligee* is simply a revival of the 18th century term. The contemporary garment, abbreviated in length and volume, and festooned with lace and ribbon, hit the nightwear market in the 1930s, infusing the word *negligee* with 20th century sex appeal.

Neo-

The Greek prefix *neo-* means "new, recent." It heads up such venerable terms as *neophyte, Neolithic, neonatal,* and *neon.*

A *neophyte* is a beginner, a novice, a new convert. Splicing *neo-* with the element *phyte,* "plant," creates a word meaning "new plant."

The word *Neolithic* was coined in 1865 by one Sir John Lubbock. This is the designation of a cultural era marked by the emergence of agriculture and sophisticated stone tools. *Neolithic* means "of the new stone age."

Neonate literally means "newly born" and is the medical classification of an infant less than four weeks old. The *nate* in this word (from the Latin *nasci,* "to be born") also appears in *nativity, nation,* and *native.*

Neoprene is a synthetic rubber. This word, coined in 1937, is a marriage of *neo-* and *chloroprene.*

Consider the term *neon,* which is *neo-* plus *n.* Scottish chemist Sir William Ramsay came up with this one in 1898 when he announced the "new" chemical element he had discovered.

English speakers use this prefix freely, adding it to nouns to create instant *neologisms* ("new words") such as *neopagan* (1869), *neoclassic* (1877), *neo-Darwinism* (1900), *neo-Nazi* (1938), and *neoliberal* (1945). Any "new" word is possible with the addition of this hospitable prefix.

NERD

Many attempts have been made to locate the birthplace of the word *nerd,* meaning "obsessively studious social maladroit." The first nerd on record is the one in Dr. Seuss's 1950 children's book *If I Ran the Zoo:*

> And then, just to show them, I'll sail to
> > Ka-Troo
> And bring back an It-Kutch, a Preep
> > and a Proo
> A Nerkle, a Nerd, and a Seersucker,
> > too!

This 1950 nerd is a fantastical creature springing from the imagination of Dr. Seuss, the pen name of Theodore Geisel. A year later, the slang *nerd* appeared in print. Attempts have been made to connect the Seuss nerd and the "socially unacceptable" nerd, but according to Linda and Roger Flavell, in their book *The Chronology of Words and Phrases,* "The trouble with this is that it is a very rapid transition from a children's rhyme to a pejorative term, for it is only one year later in 1951 that it is recorded with its slang meaning."

Another possibility has the word *nerd* an alteration of *nert,* itself a remodel of *nut,* a 20th century slang term meaning "eccentric, insane person." Some suggest the word's insulting connotation is enhanced by its rhyme with *turd,* while still others trace the term to Mortimer *Snerd,* the name of Charlie McCarthy's famous dummy.

By the 1980s, the antisocial nerd had become so legendary that he was transformed into an antihero of sorts in the 1982 movie *Revenge of the Nerds* and in the 1986 play *The Nerd.* Still, nobody knows where the bespectacled maladroit got his name.

NEWFANGLED

Something *old-fashioned* is outdated, no longer current or in vogue. Old-fashioned is generally undesirable in a society that values novelty and change.

But what about something *newfangled?* Newfangled is assuredly current and in vogue. Still, there's something cynical about this adjective. Our encounters with *newfangled technology,* for example, often leave us confused and frustrated.

What's the story behind this slightly disparaging term? All of us know what *new* means, but what about the body of this word, *fangle?*

Fangle comes ultimately from the Old English language, spoken from the 5th to 12th centuries. The ancestor of this word is an Old English verb meaning "to take or seize." When combined with the word *new,* the resulting term means "seizing or taking something novel."

Fangle is related to the modern German verb *fangen,* which means "to capture, trap, or hook." Our English word *fang* arises from this same etymological source, a *fang* being a long pointed tooth engineered to seize prey.

A sense of rapaciousness is embodied in our word *newfangled;* its etymology reflects a zealousness or even greed in grasping at that which is novel but not necessarily considered useful.

NIMROD

Nimrod was an Old Testament king whom the Bible calls a "mighty hunter before the Lord." A grandson of the ark-builder Noah, the mighty hunter Nimrod was also a founder of nations. He established the cities of Babylon, Akkad, and Nineveh, the capital of the Assyrian empire.

English speakers have used the name of this Assyrian king as a moniker for a skillful and daring hunter or sportsman. Recently, however, the word *nimrod* has suffered from disrespect. It's no longer a compliment to be considered a nimrod; it is, in fact, undesirable in most instances, because a 21st century nimrod is an obnoxious person, a jerk.

How has the mighty hunter and the founder of empires fallen so far from grace?

Evidence is meager, but this uncomplimentry sense of the word probably owes its currency to a 1940's Warner Brothers cartoon in which Bugs Bunny refers sarcastically to the hunter Elmer Fudd as a "poor little nimrod." Stripped of all dignity in this lampoonish context, the word has since become increasingly abusive.

Popular media have used the word to designate dim-witted dweebs since at least the 1960s. *Nimrod* appeared in *Newsweek* in 1963, *TV Guide* in 1995, *Harper's* in 1996, and in the script of the 1988 movie *Heathers*.

Nouns of Assemblage

Terms such as *litter of pups, flock of sheep,* and *pride of lions* are called "nouns of assemblage" or "company terms." Modern English speakers have occasional need of these expressions: *herd of cows, stand of trees.*

But our conversation has a poverty of assembly terms compared to the vocabulary of 15th century English gentlemen. Every aristocrat of that era was expected to be conversant in collective terms, especially those of the hunt. European elk of the 15th century, for example, ran in *gangs.* Roebucks, however, along with quail and larks, collected in *bevies.* Game pheasants *en masse* were called a *bouquet,* inspired by the birds' iridescent plumage.

Turning to aquatic life, we encounter the puzzling phrase *school of fish,* which generates an image of piscines sitting attentively at their neptunian desks. The image goes down the drain when we learn that *school* was simply a misprint of the word *shoal.*

Clusters of domesticated creatures were given titles as well: *a drift of hogs, drove of cattle, clowder of cats, string of ponies.*

Even humans didn't escape linguistic grouping in the England of former days: *a discretion of priests, goring of butchers, drunkenness of cobblers,* and *wandering of tinkers.* These are but a handful in the extensive litany of assemblage terms applied to humans.

NYLON

At the New York World's Fair on October 27, 1938, a spokesman for DuPont announced that a synthetic filament had been invented that was "strong as steel, as fine as a spider's web, yet more elastic than any of the common natural fibers."

It was alchemy for the 20th century—the development of nylon, the polymerized fabric that changed the textile industry forever. Throughout the 1940s, DuPont turned nylon fiber into parachutes, bomber tires, and sutures. American women fell in love with the new durable nylon stocking, superior in every way to its silk predecessor.

The name for this miracle fabric was invented by a committee of DuPont executives. After rejecting such monikers as *neosheen, norun,* and *wacara,* they deemed *nylon* the worthy candidate.

In 1940, a DuPont spokesman explained the new name this way: "The letters n-y-l-o-n have no significance, etymologically or otherwise…[but] because the names of two textile fibers in common…'cotton' and 'rayon' end with letters 'on'… it was felt that a word ending in 'on' might be desirable. A number of words were rejected…. After much deliberation, the term 'nylon' was finally adopted."

Ob-

The Latin prefix *ob-* heads up dozens of modern English words, from *obbligato* to *obverse*. This prefix has many implications, the most common of which are "against" and "completely."

The term *obese* is a combination of *ob-*, "completely," and the Latin verb *edere*, "to eat." *Obese* means "thoroughly fat from overeating."

The verb *object* means "throw against." The *ject* in this term comes from the Latin *jacere*, "to throw."

"Completely filthy" is how the word *obscene* is translated from the original Latin. *Obscene* is *ob-* plus the noun *caenum*, "filth, dirt."

Obnoxious. Here the *ob-* means "completely" and the *noxious* derives from *noxa*, Latin for "harm."

One of my favorites in this prefix sorority is the rare word *obdurate*. An adjective, it means "hardened, stubborn, not easily moved to pity." The *durate* of this word comes from the Latin *durus*. The *ob-* prefix means "completely," giving us a word meaning literally "completely hard." (*Durable* and *duress* are etymological kin.)

Obsequious, "fawning, servile," has the literal translation "follow completely." *Obstreperous* means "make a noise against." To oblige is to "bind completely"; to obey is to "hear completely."

Beware, verbivores, of *ob-* imposters. Words that do not contain this Latin prefix are *oboe, obelisk,* and *obsidian.*

ODYSSEY

The Greek hero Odysseus, king of Ithaca, is one of the most celebrated figures in all mythology. He was a warrior of both strength and cleverness, a persuasive orator and brilliant tactician.

When war broke out over the abduction of the beautiful Helen, Odysseus was called away from his wife and infant son to fight in the city of Troy. He battled there for a decade before declaring victory over his Trojan enemies.

Odysseus' return to his Ithican home was beset with obstacles. For another ten years, the hero and his men wandered the Mediterranean as errant winds blew them off course again and again. After escaping from the island of the murderous one-eyed Cyclops, Odysseus was beleaguered by cannibals, enchantresses, and a six-headed sea monster that snatched and devoured men alive from the bow of the ship.

Finally arriving in Ithaca, Odysseus discovered his home occupied by lustful, greedy men hounding his wife, Penelope. Odysseus slew them by the dozens before happily reuniting with his wife and son.

Here in the 21st century, we evoke the name of the ancient Greek hero when we speak of an *odyssey,* or "Odysseus-like" journey—a spiritual, intellectual, or physical quest characterized by discovery, shifting fortune, adventure, and danger.

OFF THE WALL

The American colloquialism *off the wall* is useful in a variety of situations. An off-the-wall comment is a non-sequiter, a remark unrelated to the topic at hand. Someone with an off-the-wall personality has traits so odd and un-coventional they defy categorization. Attempting to describe anything off the wall leaves us linguistically hamstrung, temporarily at least, until we can find the proper words to articulate its eccentricity.

Popular since the early 1960s, this expression has a cloudy history. It suggests, however, game action in the sports of racquetball, squash, and handball where walls, ceiling, and floor are fair playing surfaces. The ball, shooting about at irregular angles and speeds, may be a metaphor for unpredictability in conversation, circumstance and personality.

The *Random House Historical Dictionary of American Slang* cites a 1972 interview with a New York University student who explains his understanding of the expression: "Off the wall means crazy. Or off the ceiling, which means the same thing. Or 'he's off the wall with a spatula!' 'Off the wall for extra bases' is even worse."

A variation of this phrase, *bouncing off the wall,* is generally reserved for sugar-animated children and excited terriers. While this expression may also have a court-sport origin, it most likely arose from a crude allusion to the behavior of institutionalized patients suffering from psychosis.

OK

Lexicographer H. L. Mencken called the expression *OK* "the most shining and successful Americanism ever invented." People the world over, familiar with English or not, freely employ *OK* as an expression of approval.

Ironically, popular as this "successful Americanism" is, no phrase detective or word maven has positively identified its birthplace.

Throughout the last several decades, lexicographers have concocted a smorgasbord of theories around the origin of *OK*. Some of these sound reasonable enough, but they have been unable to withstand recent scrutiny. Amongst the questionable is that *OK* is an abbreviation for Orrins-Kendall, a brand of cracker popular with Union troops during the Civil War. Another is that it's taken from a Choctaw word, *okeh,* purportedly meaning "it is." And still another ties it to the First World War. Soldiers daily reported the number of fatalities within their troops;. *O.K.* meant "0 [zero] Killed."

Most lexicographers favor the following theory. When Martin Van Buren ran for presidential reelection in 1840, his supporters founded a political committee called the "O.K. Club." The *O.K.* in this story stands for Old Kinderhook, after Van Buren's birthplace in Kinderhook, New York. The abbreviation quickly achieved the meaning "all right," for to his followers Van Buren was the right choice for president.

OLIGO-

The geologic time chart divides earth's existence into eons, eras, periods, and epochs. You may recall studying this chart in school, committing to memory such terms as *Paleozoic, Jurassic,* and *Holocene.*

One of the chronological divisions of the geologic time chart is the Oligocene, an epoch that began about 37 million years ago and terminated about 24 million years ago. During this time, global grasslands began to expand while forested regions diminished. Early mammals such as horses, apes, and mastodons flourished where dinosaurs once roamed.

The *oligo-* in *Oligocene* is a Greek prefix meaning "few or scant." The term *Oligocene,* coined in 1854, means "few recent forms," from the belief that, while the more primitive mammals emerged during this epoch, few modern animals originated at this time.

The prefix *oligo-* heads up an obscure but engaging group of modern English terms. Consider *oligochrome,* an adjective meaning "painted or decorated in few colors." A market situation in which few producers control the supply is an *oligopoly;* compare this word with *monopoly.*

Perhaps the most easily recognizable member of the *oligo-* family is *oligarchy,* a word meaning "rule or government by the few." In a democracy the people rule, but in an oligarchy decisions and policies lie in the hands of a few powerful and well-placed individuals.

Whon we don't know the name for something, we often use a stand-in word like *doo-hickey, thingamabob,* or *jigamaree.* These handy polysyllables, called omnibus terms, fill in when the proper words are misplaced or unknown.

The same thing happens when we talk about large but unknown numerical quantities. Consider *zillion, skillion, gazillion, jillion.* These mythical numbers exaggerate quantity. Such rogue terms are of course coined in imitation of the more respectable *million, billion,* and *trillion.*

And what can we say about such omnibus terms as *oodles, scads, slew, gobs?* Of course, like *zillion* and its illegitimate relatives, these terms denote substantial but nebulous quantities.

Unfortunately, the etymologies of these words are hazy. Take *oodles,* for example. Americans have been using this term to suggest a large amount since 1870, but no one can point to its origin.

The same goes for *scads,* as in "The CEO horded scads of money." Present in American slang since 1890, *scads* has fallen through the cracks of etymological history. Ditto for *gobs,* meaning a great but uncounted quantity.

Slew, however, isn't so elusive. It comes from a Gaelic word meaning "multitude." This term has been part of the American lexicon since at least 1840.

Omnibus Terms

Humans are uniquely equipped to invent and use words to communicate. But it's also human to misplace words temporarily, especially proper and common nouns. "That's whatshisname," we say, pointing to an acquaintance across the room, or "Hand me that thingybob over there."

Whatshisname and *thingybob* are part of an eccentric lexical family called omnibus terms, soft-focus words we can employ to refer to any object or person. Consider others of this family: *doodad, thingamajig, gizmo, hootnanny, googaw, whosits.*

Some of these polysyllables have somewhat traceable histories. Let's look at the word *dingus.* One of the definitions of this term is "a thing or person whose name is forgotten." This word likely arose from the German noun *Ding,* which means simply "thing."

A small, unfamiliar contrivance is a *gadget.* One suggestion on this word's origin involves the French term *gachette,* "small hook or catch." In a travel memoir dated 1886, the author writes, "Then the names of all the…things on board a ship! I don't know half of them yet; even the sailors forget…. if the exact name of anything they want happens to slip from their memory, they call it a gadjet, a gill-guy, a timmy-noggy, or a wim-wam."

Informal and vague, omnibus terms nevertheless provide valuable linguistic service as understudy monikers for objects and people whose names have been forgotten.

Noises that make their own names—like *pop, sizzle, bang,* and *whoosh*—are examples of onomatopoeia. We've invented these words to represent vocally some of the sounds in our world.

Many bird names are onomatopoeic: *chickadee, cuckoo, shrike.* While the Modern English *hoot* is onomatopoeic for the sound an owl makes, it turns out that *owl* is itself an onomatopoeic fossil. It comes from an ancient Germanic word, *ule,* originally coined in imitation of that bird's haunting call.

The pages of your dictionary harbor some unusual sound representations. How about *ululate?* This verb, meaning "to wail," mimics the glissando howl of dogs and wolves. To *pule* is to cry or peep plaintively, as would a baby chick.

Onomatopoeia might have played a role in the development of language. Linguists in the 18th century proposed the "bow-wow" theory, which claimed that early humans began acquiring language through vocal imitations of the environment, especially animal sounds. Though the bow-wow theory has languished from lack of evidence, it is not hard to imagine our prelinguistic ancestors making up words by imitating the sounds of the creatures in their environment—prehistoric onomatopoeia.

Made from the dried juice of poppy pods, opium has been used as a narcotic as well as a medicine for thousands of years.

The Greek physician Hippocrates prescribed an infusion of opium to restore balance to the ailing body. In the 19th century, it was prescribed to relieve cough, rheumatism, fever, insomnia, and a host of common maladies.

Several literary greats of the 18th and 19th centuries used opium as both pain reliever and muse. The poet John Keats called its effects "a delightful sensation about three degrees this side of faintness." Samuel Taylor Coleridge and Elizabeth Barrett Browning were among opium's devotees.

But opium can be maleficent as well. Abusers of opiates suffer extreme lethargy, severe constipation, and frightening hallucinations. The latter affliction inspired the expression *pipe dream,* referring to delusions of the type experienced by opium-pipe smokers.

The term *yen,* meaning an intense craving such as an addict might feel for his drug, comes from a dialectal Chinese word for opium. And one theory supports the notion that the word *hippie* comes ultimately from the opium-smoker's favorite position—reclining "on the hip" to facilitate pipe-dreaming.

Orient

The word *orient* is a double agent of sorts; as a noun, it refers to Asian countries. In verb form, to *orient* means to position with respect to a point of reference, for example a prominent mountain on the horizon. The Orient. To orient. How do we reconcile the duality of this term?

A look under the hood of the two *orients* reveals a common ancestor. It turns out the source of both is a Latin verb meaning "to rise or come forth."

It's the sun rising and coming forth in this instance. An early English definition of the verb *orient* was "to cause to point eastward toward the rising sun." In other words, observing the dawn is a sure method of establishing direction.

Some early European churches were constructed with east–west axes, with the chief altar situated at the east, toward Jerusalem. Such cathedrals were literally *oriented*.

English speakers eventually appropriated the term to speak of the lands lying east of Europe, toward the rising sun, the *Oriental* direction. In a twist of etymological irony, when we orient ourselves using a modern compass, we position ourselves with respect to magnetic north, not east.

Orientation meetings are designed to familiarize novices with the parameters of a new job or task. Though such meetings are not concerned with the cardinal directions, they nevertheless point attendees in the right direction, symbolically and etymologically toward the Orient or "eastward."

ORNERY

The useful term *ordinary* entered the English language from Latin in the 14th century. The words *ordinary, order,* and *ordinance* are etymological cousins, each arising from the same Latin root, *ordinarius,* meaning "orderly, usual."

English speakers found the word *ordinary* very serviceable through the centuries, employing it as both noun and adjective. An *ordinary* is the judge of a probate court or the residential bishop of a diocese. As an adjective, the word means "commonly encountered, average or usual."

In the 19th century, English speakers began manipulating the pronunciation of the term. This wordplay began with a dialectal articulation of the term which contracted *ordinary* into *ornery*. For about a century, *ornery* was simply a substitute for the original pronunciation, but through the pens of such popular writers as Mark Twain the word gradually earned a life of its own.

In a definition of this term taken from the *New Century Dictionary,* originally published in 1927, we read that ornery is "inferior or poor; plain or homely, ugly in disposition or temper; mean or contemptible; vile, lewd."

Ornery no longer meant common or average but came to connote recalcitrance, meanness, bad temper. Embedded in this newly minted term was the attitude that the behavior of common folks was unmannered and rude—just plain ordinary, or ornery.

OSCAR

In 1928, Janet Gaynor received the first Academy Award for best actress for her roles in the films *Seventh Heaven, Street Angel,* and *Sunrise.* The best-picture award of that year went to the silent film *Wings,* which featured spectacular aerial dogfights.

The annual Academy Awards have since become a significant component of our culture, and they are symbolized by a ten-inch gold-plated statuette of a sleek, muscular man standing at perfect attention: the *Oscar.* The award was designed in 1928 by Cedric Gibbons, the art director for the Academy of Motion Picture Arts and Sciences.

In 1931, four years after the inception of the film awards, academy librarian Margaret Herrick scrutinized one of the statuettes for the first time. Something about its bearing prompted Herrick to quip, "He reminds me of my uncle Oscar," referring, in reality, to her mother's uncle, Oscar Pierce, a Texas farmer. A newspaper columnist who overheard the remark later published the statement, "Employees of the academy have affectionately dubbed their famous statuette 'Oscar.'" The name stuck.

OUIJA BOARD

In 1892, brothers Isaac and William Fuld created a business called the Southern Novelty Company in Baltimore, Maryland. Their signature product was a three-ply, twelve-by eighteen-inch pine board and an accompanying heart-shaped "planchette," or pointer. The board was printed with the letters of the alphabet, the numbers zero through nine, and the words "yes," "no," and "goodbye."

The Fuld brothers called it the *Ouija board*. It was designed for two players sitting knee to knee with the board and the pointer atop their combined laps. When the participants lightly placed their fingers on the pointer, it traveled around the board, spelling out words by pointing to the letters.

Many believed the device was activated by spiritual forces. Since its introduction in the 1890s, millions have consulted the Ouija board in making important decisions, communicating with the dead, and seeking advice in love.

Ouija board sales have waxed and waned, accelerating in times of national catastrophe. During the First World War, mothers and wives bought record numbers of Ouija boards to answer anxious questions concerning sons and husbands overseas. Sales picked up in 1944, and again following the mass occult explosion of the 1960s.

Ouija is a combination of the words *oui* and *ja,* French and German for "yes," a linguistic reflection of the positive answers the board was expected to produce.

OUT OF WHACK

Most American English speakers have had occasion to use the familiar idiom *out of whack* to describe something maladjusted or out of order. Despite the commonness of this expression, plausible theories of its origin are in short supply.

One suggestion has the *whack* in this phrase being a synonym for a hit or blow that throws something off—like a mechanism, "The car door is out of whack"; or a body part, "I threw my spine out of whack."

Possibility number two involves the word *wacky,* an older dialectal word originally meaning "foolish and left-handed." Wacky in current usage, of course, is "crazy, odd, peculiar."

Both of these options are suspect, however, because the very phrase *out of whack* implies that being *in whack* (whatever that may be) is positive.

So we look to other theories, one of which points out that an older sense of the word *whack* means a share, bargain, or agreement. Or perhaps *whack* is an onomatopoeia for an auctioneer's hammer rap signaling the establishment of a bargain or fair price. If you like these explanations, then something *out of whack* is a bad bargain or an agreement that's gone awry.

Incidentally, the fraternal twin phrase *out of kilter* has an origin equally mysterious. Though the word *kilter* has entered most contemporary dictionaries, its etymological source, like our *whack,* is unknown.

OVERWHELMED, NONPLUSED

We've all been overwhelmed when faced with daunting situations. But have you ever been whelmed? It's possible. There is, etymologically, only a subtle shade of difference between *whelming* and *overwhelming*.

Whelm comes from the Middle English verb *whelmen,* meaning "to overthrow, or to turn a vessel upside down." *Overwhelm* etymologically takes that vessel and covers it completely with water, assigning it to the briny deep. *Overwhelm* is simply an emphatic form of *whelm*.

It's a different situation with *nonplused* and *plused*. If you're so completely perplexed that you can neither think nor act, you're *nonplused*. This word comes directly from the Latin phrase *non plus,* "no more, no further." However, you can never be *plused*. It's not etymologically possible; the word simply does not exist.

This begs the question: Is there a *gruntle* in *disgruntle?* A *combobulate* in *discombobulate?* A *ruth* in *ruthless?* *Reck* in *reckless?* *Feck* in *feckless?* *Hand* in *handsome?*

The answers are in your dictionary.

OXYMORON

An oxymoron is a word or phrase that contains seemingly contradictory images: *deafening silence, sweet sorrow, living death, visible darkness.* The use of oxymorons is especially effective in poetry and rhetoric. The combining of opposites momentarily scrambles the senses, sending the reader or listener groping for logic.

Shakespeare, in the following passage from *Romeo and Juliet,* uses eleven of these expressions in one sentence.

> O brawling love, O loving hate,
> O anything of nothing first create;
> O heavy lightness, serious vanity,
> Misshapen chaos of well-seeming forms,
> Feather of lead, bright smoke, cold fire, sick health,
> Still-waking sleep, that is not what it is!

Oxymoron is a combination of the Greek terms *oxus* and *moros. Oxus* means "sharp or pointed" *(oxus* is also the linguistic progenitor of the words *acid* and *acute). Moron* is a variant of a Greek *moros,* meaning "dull, silly, foolish" (*moron* is the obsolete clinical title of an adult whose I.Q. measured between 50 and 75). Meaning "sharp-dull," *oxymoron* is in its heart of hearts contradictory.

Incidentally, the *Concise Oxford Dictionary of Literary Terms* says that the plural of this word is not *oxymorons,* like any educated fool might guess, but *oxymora.*

PAINT THE TOWN RED

The common American expression *paint the town red* means "to celebrate wildly, to party with unruly abandon." Though every American English speaker knows what the expression means, its origin is surprisingly fugitive.

One theory suggests the *paint* in this expression was actually red fire that blazed in frontier settlements after an attack by some vengeful faction. This notion provided a later metaphor for celebrants who partied with incendiary glee.

William and Mary Morris, in the *Morris Dictionary of Word and Phrase Origins,* contend that the *red* in this phrase refers to the red-light districts in western towns. A herd of rowdy workers, after visiting that shady section for whiskey and company, might decide to treat the whole town like a red-light district, thus "painting the town red."

Or perhaps the *red* in this expression is symbolic of violence and blood, giving us a phrase that figuratively means to cover the town with bloodshed and brawling.

A final contender connects this phrase with an older expression *to paint,* meaning "to drink"; the *paint* here is the red on a drunk's nose. Using this notion, to *paint the town red* is to visit every saloon on the streets.

This lively expression has a mind of its own, refusing the scrutiny of America's most earnest word watchers.

The god Pan of Greek mythology was a satyr—half-man, half-goat—who made his home in the wild mountains of the ancient world. According to one version of his history, his beastlike appearance so repulsed his mother that she abandoned her infant son in the woods, where he was found and raised by nymphs.

Pan was a noisy, riotous creature who loved laughter and music. He often entertained the other gods by playing his flute of reeds, which in his honor was named the *pan flute*. Pan's lovely and melancholy flute serenades enthralled both shepherds and mountain dwellers. The herdsmen who shared Pan's bucolic home revered him as their patron, calling upon him to protect their flocks and pastures.

But the goat god had a dark side. His legendary lustful appetites drove him in ceaseless pursuit of the charming wood nymphs, who feared his slavering chases. He also inspired terror in mountain travelers by shaking branches, hurling stones, and shrieking and snorting from the thickets. His bellows caused the local flocks of goats and sheep to bolt in blind terror.

The word *panic,* referring to the irrational fear that grips both humans and animals, was derived from the name of this raucous mountain god. *Panic* comes ultimately from the Greek *panikos,* meaning literally "of Pan."

PARA-

The Greek-based prefix *para-* can mean several things: "defense against," "supplementary," "beside," "beyond," or "contrary to."

The *para-* in *parasol* means "defense against." With the *sol* in this word coming from the Latin word for sun, *parasol* is etymologically "defense against the sun." *Parachute* means "a defense against falling." This word was coined in 1785 by French balloonist Jean-Pierre Blanchard. It gained currency when Blanchard attached a parachute to a dog and dropped the whole package from a balloon.

The *para-* that means "supplementary" is in the Greek-based word *paraphernalia.* When a woman brought her dowry into a marriage, half the goods belonged to her husband; the rest was her personal property. The wife's portion was her *paraphernalia,* from *para-,* "supplementary," and *pherne,* "dowry." Currently, the word means "miscellaneous belongings or equipment," a sense that developed in the 18th century.

Parallel lines extend in the same direction, everywhere equidistant. Here the *para-* prefix means "beside, in proximity to." With the second half of the word deriving from the Greek *allelon,* "of one another," *parallel* implies "beside each other." A *paralegal* works "beside" a law professional; a *paramedic* assists a doctor. *Paralympic* athletes participate in games "in proximity to" Olympic athletes.

The *para-* in *parasite* also means "beside," giving us a word that means "feeding beside" (*site* comes from the Greek *sitos,* "food"). A *parasite* in the Roman world was one who sat at the table of a superior, earning meals by flattery. The word that refers to an animal or plant subsisting at the expense of another organism was printed for the first time in *Chambers Cyclopedia,* in 1727.

The word *paranoia* consists of *para-,* meaning "beyond" in this case, and the Greek *nous,* "mind." This word, coined in the 19th century, designates a mental disorder characterized by delusions. The adjective *paranormal,* "beyond normal," refers to that which is not rationally explicable.

Para- can also mean "contrary to." An argument or statement contrary to expectations or common opinion is a *paradox.* The final syllable in this word comes from the Greek *doxa,* "opinion" (an element that also occurs in *orthodox* and *doxology).*

But be aware, word lovers, of the *para-* imposters. The sneaky terms p*araffin, parakeet,* and *paradise* have grown up elsewhere on the etymological landscape, as have *parade, paramour,* and *paramount.*

Peanut

The peanut plant, indigenous to South America, was cultivated in Peru as long ago as 2000 B.C. It appears that ancient people also harvested peanuts in modern Bolivia and Argentina.

By the early 1500s, the peanut had traveled from South America to Africa in the holds of Portuguese sailing vessels. The plant was established in the southeastern United States by slave traders who fed the peanuts to their captives. Later, these legumes, called *ground nuts* and *ground peas,* filled the bellies and crops of colonial-era swine and barnyard fowl.

They became widely known as *peanuts* by 1800, and showman P. T. Barnum popularized them as a snack food in the 1880s.

Peanut is a logical moniker for this legume, resembling, as it does, peas in a pod. But this word is loaded with cultural significance. The word *peanut* is associated with anything inconsequential: *peanut size* means "runty." One who labors hard for little pay is said to *work for peanuts.* The *peanut gallery* of a theater is the section with the most inferior balcony seats.

Other terms of derision: *peanut brain, peanut politics, peanut head.* These epithets arose from the era when peanuts were cheap sustenance for animals and very poor humans.

A regional Southern term for this plant is *goober,* from the African Bantu *nguba,* the slave name for the peanut.

PEDIGREE

Tall, regal, and gregarious, cranes have dwelt on the planet millions of years. Cranes are migratory birds that inhabit the wetlands of Eurasia, Africa, Australia, and North America.

The bird is conspicuous in its elaborate courtship and preening displays. The dances of cranes have been ritualistically imitated by people in Siberia, Greece, Australia, and North America. Its image adorns Egyptian hieroglyphs. Cheyenne and Crow warriors made whistles from crane wing bones and piped on them for courage in battle. In Chinese tradition, the bird is a symbol of longevity.

While the English word for this bird is Germanic in origin, the Latin and French designation is *grue,* in apparent imitation of its cry.

Medieval genealogists, in tracing royal lineage, used a three-branched diagram to show family succession. This symbol suggested a crane footprint, inspiring the medievals to call this diagram *pied du grue,* or "foot of the crane." The word has been variously recorded *pedegru, petegreu, petegree,* and *pe de gru.* It came to English as *pedigree,* "a tabular accounting of lineage," in the 15th century.

PEONY

The bountiful peony has been a favorite of gardeners and herbalists for centuries. In ancient China, Japan, the Mediterranean, and Europe, the peony has been used for both medicinal and ornamental purposes.

The Roman scholar Pliny, in A.D. 77, wrote that the peony could cure jaundice, stomach pains, and afflictions of the trachea. In 14th century England, peonies were used for seasoning and placed in the same flavor category as pepper, garlic, and fennel seed.

In North America, this plant is native to the Pacific coastal mountains, but imported peonies in hundreds of varieties are displayed in gardens across the country.

Because the origin of the word *peony* comes from Greek mythology, the story is as spectacular as the flower itself. Many versions of this tale have been woven across the millennia, but here is its essence.

Asclepius, the Greek god of medicine, had a student named Paean who eventually attained the notable skills of his mentor. When Pluto, ruler of the Underworld, was wounded in battle, Paean healed him with herbs and medicines. The teacher Asclepius became jealous and plotted to kill his talented student. But Pluto foiled this plan. He turned Paean into a flower so the physician could live eternally. This flower, which was also used in Pluto's cure, was thereafter called the *peony*, after Paean, the physician of the gods.

PERSIAN WORDS

The English language is delightfully promiscuous. Throughout its long and checkered history, it has taken in terms and phrases from dozens of the world's languages. The vocabulary of our contemporary American English tongue embraces words from the Spanish, Finnish, Japanese, Hungarian, Portuguese, Hebrew, and Turkish languages.

A nice handful of our vocabulary comes from Persian, the original language of present-day Iran. Though these terms are of Persian ancestry, many of them arrived at English via an intermediary language.

For example, the term *angel,* often considered a Greek term, is Persian in origin. In that language, *angel* meant "messenger or courier."

The word *paradise* has a similar pedigree. Although the Greeks adopted this term and passed it on to English speakers, *paradise* was originally Persian and meant "walled garden." This term appeared in English around the year 1000.

A quintet of culinary terms was bequeathed to us from Persian: *rice, yogurt, orange, julep,* and *caviar.* The sartorial words *caftan, cassock,* and *cummerbund* are Persian as well, as are *taffeta, shawl,* and *percale.*

Other terms of Persian origin are *caravan, divan, jasmine, khaki, turban,* and *lilac.*

PICTOGRAPH

In September 1940, while four young men were exploring a wooded area in southern France, their small companion dog disappeared into a hole. Searching for their pet, the explorers crawled into an immense cave, whose walls were painted with a menagerie of animals long extinct in Europe: bison, reindeer, lions, and wild horses.

The Frenchmen had discovered the famous cave at Lascaux, where, 30,000 years earlier, humans had painted fantastic images on the limestone walls. The prehistoric murals were created with paints made from ground iron oxide or charcoal. The yellow, black, and red powder was mixed with animal fat and applied to the rock with fingers and hair brushes. We call these ancient frescoes *pictographs*.

The term *pictograph* appeared in the English language in approximately 1851. It's a merging of Latin and Greek: *picto* is from the Latin *pictus*, "painted," and *graph* is a derivative of the Greek verb *graphien*, "to write." Etymologically, a *pictograph* is "painted writing."

The Latin *picto* is also found in *picture, picturesque,* and *pictorial; graphien* is the root of the words *graffiti, graphite,* and *graphic*.

PIZZAZZ

Most American English speakers agree that the word *pizzazz* means something like "flair, zest, audacity." And most etymological dictionaries agree that *pizzazz* was first spotted in print in 1937. All else is speculation about this feisty little term.

The *Barnhart Dictionary of Etymology* says it's probably American college slang, coined in the early 20th century. No, claims the *Morris Dictionary of Word and Phrase Origins,* it's a bit of jargon generated by show business and ad agencies. *Webster's New World Dictionary* asserts that it's a vocal simulation of the roar of a starting engine: Pi-ZZAZZ!

Robert Chapman, editor of the *New Dictionary of American Slang,* speculates that *pizzazz* may be influenced by a combination of *piss* and *ass,* or by the expression *piss and vinegar.*

The mighty *Oxford English Dictionary* is no help in this word hunt. It states "origin unknown" beside *pizzazz.* But it does explain that the word appeared in print in the March 1937 edition of *Harper's Bazaar:* "Pizazz...is an indefinable dynamic quality, the *je ne sais quoi* of function; as for instance, adding Scotch puts pizazz into a drink. Certain clothes have it, too.... There's pizazz in this rust evening coat."

The spelling of this word changes whimsically from writer to writer, too; its recorded variants include *bizzazz, bezaz, pezzazz, pizzazz,* and *pizazz.*

PLANT

Can you name the word that unites bears, warts, and agrarian technique?

The word is *planta,* Latin for "sole of the foot," the linguistic inspiration for several important words and concepts.

Have you ever been afflicted with *plantar warts?* If you have, you know how much they hurt. These warts grow on your soles and are called *plantar* after *planta.*

Bears, wolverines, and badgers share a trait that makes them unique in the animal kingdom. Their hind feet have soles. When their feet strike the ground, they do so in a heel-to-toe fashion, similar to the stride of humans. These animals belong to a classification of creatures called *plantigrades.* This word arises from *planta* and the Latin *gradi,* "to walk."

Planta also appears to be the linguistic parent of the word *plant.* Many of our agrarian predecessors sowed their crops not by hand but by foot, the foot folding the seed into the prepared soil. Ultimately, the sole of the foot, the *planta* that covered the seed, became linguistically linked to the seedlings that later emerged, the plants.

PLUTOCRACY

One of the lesser-known gods in the Greek pantheon is Plutus, the personification of material and monetary wealth. As the keeper of riches, Plutus bore the ponderous responsibility of distributing wealth amongst the mortals. Sculptures and paintings represent Plutus as a young man bearing the horn of plenty, but there's something about Plutus that distinguishes him from every other god. He's the only Olympian immortal lacking the sense of sight.

Blinded by Zeus, the mightiest of the gods, Plutus was unable to witness the behavior of mortals. He was thereby prevented from rewarding the righteous with wealth or withholding riches from the wicked. Plutus was obliged to distribute valuables to all mortals regardless of their conduct.

From the name of the Greek god of wealth arise our modern political terms *plutocracy* and *plutocrat*. A *plutocracy* is a state in which the wealthy rule. A *plutocrat* is of course a wealthy governer. The *crat* in this term comes from the Greek *kratia,* meaning power or authority (compare *democrat* and *aristocrat*).

POINSETTIA

The fiery poinsettia, a favorite emblem of the winter holidays, is a native of the tropics that grows wild in the highlands of Central America and southern Mexico. Long before Spanish contact, the Aztecs put the plant to practical use, extracting a dye from its leaves and incorporating the milky sap of the stem in an elixer to reduce fever.

Because the poinsettia blooms in winter, 17th century Franciscan friars incorporated the crimson plants in their nativity processions. This association with Yuletide inspired its local name *flor de nochebuena,* "flower of the blessed night."

On Christmas day in 1825, an American ambassador to Mexico, Joel R. Poinsette, visited one of the Franciscan churches that had been lavishly bedecked with the flower of the blessed night. The ambassador, an amateur botanist, was captivated by the unusual shape and color of the plant and sent samples of it to his home in South Carolina. He later propagated the flower and shared it with friends and botanical gardens around the country.

By the 1850s, Americans had embraced the ambassador's scarlet flower as a lasting Christmas symbol. It was named the poinsettia, after its most ardent promoter, Joel R. Poinsette.

The Pomeranian is a little dog with a big history. Coursing through the veins of this lilliputian canine is the blood of its robust ancestor—a large white spitz dog descended from the sledge dogs of Lapland. It also shares certain characteristics (a pointed muzzle, erect ears, and a curly plumed tail) with its cousins the Norwegian elkhound and the Samoyed. Like many toy dogs, the Pomeranian breed has been gradually miniaturized to a microscopic version of its former self.

The breed was refined in the land of its namesake, Pomerania, a former maritime province of Prussia lying along the Baltic coastal plain. In the early 19th century, the nobility of Pomerania began miniaturizing a local breed for lap dogs. This original stock consisted of working animals weighing about thirty pounds. The average toy Pomeranian today is a mere pocket-barker weighing in at five to seven pounds.

In 1870, this foxlike creature was allowed for the first time to compete in England's show-rings. By 1900, an American Pomeranian Society was instituted.

The name *Pomerania* comes from the name of a Slavic tribe, the Pomerani, that inhabited the Baltic coast territory circa A.D. 600.

Pomona

Pomona was the goddess responsible for the protection and procreation of fruit in the ancient Roman world. The name *Pomona*, and the Latin word for fruit in general, *pomum*, are responsible for germinating such modern English terms as *pomade, pommel, pomology, pomegranate*, and *Pomona,* California.

Pomology, a word invented in 1818, refers to the branch of horticulture concentrating on the science and practice of growing fruit. *Pomade* was originally a fragrant ointment for the skin and hair prepared with lard and the pulp of apples. A *pomander* is a clove-studded apple or orange used as an aromatic.

The knob on the hilt of a sword is a *pommel;* so is the "horn" of a western saddle. Both are named for their resemblance to an apple or a piece of round fruit. To *pummel* someone is etymologically to beat him repeatedly with something shaped "like an apple"—the fist, for example, or the pommel of a sword.

The fruit with the delicious, ruby-colored seeds is the *pomegranate,* a word meaning "many-grained apple." (The *granate* of this term is related to *grain* and *granular.*)

The city of *Pomona,* California, founded on citrus and olive enterprises, was named in 1875 by citrus cultivator Solomon Gates for the Roman goddess of orchards and fruit.

PONDEROSA

With a name made famous by the 1960s television western *Bonanza,* the Ponderosa pine is a stately guardian of the forests of western North America. Its range extends from British Columbia in the north, east to Montana, and south into Baja California.

The Ponderosa has always been a significant player in the development of the West. The lumber milled from this tree has been transformed into telegraph poles, railroad ties, mine shoring timbers, and a variety of building materials.

It was given the Latin designation *Pinus ponderosa* in 1834 by Scottish botanist David Douglas, for whom the Douglas fir is named. The botanist borrowed the designation *ponderosa* from the Latin *ponderosus,* meaning "heavy, weighty, significant." In naming the tree, Douglas wanted to suggest its immense character and presence. Some of these massive sentinels can grow to two hundred feet and live more than five hundred years.

Ponderosa is related etymologically to *ponderous, preponderate,* and *ponder,* a verb meaning to consider or to "weigh" a matter. *Pound,* a unit of weight, is also a cousin of the word *ponderosa.*

PORTMANTEAU WORDS

In 1895, the word *brunch* was printed for the first time in the British publication *Hunter's Weekly*. A fusion of *breakfast* and *lunch*, this word quickly became an indispensable member of our vocabulary.

We've embraced dozens of such cleverly fused words. *Motel,* invented in 1925, is a blend of *motor* and *hotel, blurt* combines *blow* and *spurt,* and *splutter* is a melding of *splash* and *sputter.*

The writer Lewis Carroll called these alloys "portmanteau words." In Carroll's *Through the Looking Glass,* Humpty Dumpty explains to Alice his use of the word *slithy,* a combination of *lithe* and *slimy:* "You see," he says, "it's like a portmanteau.... there are two meanings packed up into one word." The portmanteau, a large traveling bag with two separate compartments, provides a metaphor for the "packing" together of two words into a novel linguistic construction.

Other blended terms are *squinch,* from *squint* and *pinch,* first recorded in 1835. The portmanteau of *chuckle* and *snort* produces *chortle; squall* and *squeak* combined give us *squawk.* The portmanteau word *stagflation* was invented in 1965 from *stagnation* and *inflation. Stagflation* is persistent *inflation* combined with *stagnant* consumer demand and high unemployment.

Potemkin Village

The story behind the expression *Potemkin village* involves famous personalities in a tale of love, power, royalty, and chicanery.

Grigory Aleksandrovich Potemkin was not only commander-in-chief of the Russian Army in the late 18th century, he was also promoter and paramour of Catherine the Great. In about 1787, eager to impress and delight his empress, Potemkin invited Catherine to tour provinces newly acquired under his administration.

One account has it that Potemkin constructed sham villages along Catherine's route, each settlement designed to give the impression of prosperity. Some sources report that Potemkin even stocked these outposts with "contented peasants," which he shuffled from one village to the next just ahead of Catherine's entourage.

Today, a *Potemkin village* is a thing or situation that at first appears elaborate or impressive but in fact has little substance.

Though this tale of the Potemkin villages is anecdotal, it nevertheless lends verve to our language. And the expression is colorful shorthand for describing an imposing façade constructed to disguise tawdriness.

PRAIRIE EXPRESSIONS

When the Spanish and French arrived in the New World in the 16th and 17th centuries, they were overwhelmed by the oceans of grass rippling over the heart of the continent. The French named the grasslands *pre,* their word for meadow or farm field, which comes ultimately from the Latin *praetum,* "meadow."

The prairie ecosystem, blanketing 1.4 million American acres, had a tremendous psychological impact on all who beheld it. The word *prairie* consequently buried itself deep into our language, sprouting new phrases across the English wordscape.

By the early 19th century, *prairie dog,* a term recorded in the journals of Meriwether Lewis and William Clark, emerged to designate the burrowing rodent so common on the plains. The covered wagons plying the sea of grass in the mid 1800s were *prairie schooners.*

Illinois adopted the nickname Prairie State in 1842, and Manitoba, Saskatchewan, and Alberta are the Canadian *Prairie Provinces.*

Prairie chicken and *prairie falcon* designate a pair of avian denizens of the North American grasslands.

Perhaps the most colorful expression in this genus is *prairie squint,* lines on the face caused by optical battles with the bright, harsh, grassland sun.

PRECOCIOUS

A *precocious* child grasps certain concepts long before her average peers. Precocious children can be unusually perceptive, comprehending abstractions that may confound the average adult.

Certain birds, like some humans, mature more quickly than others. Consider the newly hatched chick, quickly arising to peck and scratch at the ground. Ducklings and goslings begin to swim hours out of the egg. These birds are *precocial,* or early maturing creatures. Like precocious children, they develop more quickly than, say, robins or hawks, which spend many blind and featherless weeks in the nest before emerging as fledglings.

Trees and fruits that flower and ripen early were called *precocious* by English speakers in the 17th century. The apricot is early maturing, with blossoms appearing on its branches even before the leaves emerge. The fruit is ready to pick in late spring.

The word *precocious* is an etymological mirror of all this early ripening. It consists of the prefix *pre-,* or "before," and the Latin verb *coquere,* "to cook." Etymologically, a precocious child or bird or fruit is "precooked," or "cooked before its time."

Apricot is a direct relative of *precocious.* Originally called *malum praecocum,* "early ripening apple," by the Romans, the fruit came to be known to early English speakers as the *apricock.* Both monikers come from *praecox,* "early ripe."

PROCRUSTEAN

O n the road to Athens in ancient Greece lived a character named Procrustes. In some legends, he's an innkeeper; in others, a robber, a thug or a highwayman. In every account, though, Procrustes is a sadist.

Procrustes abducted travelers on their ways to and from Athens and subjected them to torture of the most bizarre kind. He had two iron beds—one tall, one short. In the short bed, he tied the taller prisoners. Shorter victims were made to lie in the long bed. If the tall travelers were too long for the short bed, Procrustes literally amputated their parts until they were cut to size. The short victims he stretched on a rack until they fit.

Procrustes, whose name means "The Stretcher," was justly punished when the Greek hero Theseus tied this strange character to one of his own beds and cut him to fit.

Though he died by his own device, Procrustes lives on in metaphor. The adjective *procrustean* describes something designed to promote uniformity without allowing for individuality. In the word book *Marvelous Monikers,* author Tad Tuleja cites some *procrustean* examples: "The researcher who falsifies test results to fit a predetermined conclusion, the accountant who uses 'creative financing' to balance an unbalanceable ledger, the demagogue who demands unanimity of popular opinion—all may be said to be engaging in procrustean behavior."

PULLING WOOL AND LEGS

To *pull someone's leg* is to engage someone in verbal trickery, or to harmlessly deceive or fool your victim. What circumstances have conspired to yoke together the notions of leg-pulling and prevarication?

One theory has this phrase coming from 19th century England, where muggers worked in pairs. One tripped their victim with a hooked stick, while the other snatched his purse. From this scenario may come the extended meaning of mentally tripping someone, figuratively "pulling a leg," with deception in mind. In earlier writings, the expression was *draw a leg,* which provides the figurative image of gently distracting someone from reaching his destination.

A second cliché involving deception and "pulling" is *pull the wool over (someone's) eyes.* This saying is probably English born and from the 18th and 19th centuries, when monumental curly woolen wigs were fashionable. Purse snatchers who literally pulled the wool over the eyes of their victims would take money from the "sightless" prey as he struggled for composure. Another possibility comes from the notion of a clever lawyer pulling the wool wig of a courtroom judge, temporarily "blinding" him to the truth. This expression was first recorded in America in 1839.

The tradition of puppetry is thousands of years old. Audiences in ancient Egypt, Greece, and China gathered to watch stories writ small on puppet stages.

Traditional Western puppet theaters are miniature versions of fair booths or proscenium stages. Javanese puppet shows are performed in silhouette, with the mannequins appearing as shadows on a translucent background.

Historically, puppet performances enact mythical stories, epics, heroic dramas, and satires, sometimes accompanied by narrators and music.

What are the differences, mechanically and etymologically, between *puppets* and *marionettes?* Puppets are literally pulled over the hand like a glove or mitten and manipulated with the fingers. Sometimes they are mounted on sticks, with the limbs manipulated from below the stage by rods.

The word *puppet* is a direct descendant of the Latin term *pupa*. *Pupa* originally meant "little girl" or "little doll" and also gives us the word meaning the immature larva of a butterfly or moth. Both *puppet* and *pupa* connote something small and immature.

A *marionette* is an articulated puppet operated by strings from above the stage. Marionettes were originally featured in medieval European religious presentations. One common Middle Ages story was the Feast of the Assumption of the Virgin Mary into heaven. The leading lady was "Marionette," an affectionate French name for the Virgin. In time, every string-operated figure became a *marionette,* or "Little Mary."

PUT ON THE DOG

The dog has not always been admired as the quintessence of devotion and fidelity. Wherever the dog is not considered man's best friend or working partner, this animal is food robber, livestock chaser, and flea bearer.

Consider all the English expressions reflecting a negative sentiment toward *Canis familiaris: dog face* (an ugly person) *dog breath* (an offensive person), *dog meat* (one who is doomed or in disfavor), *dog's breakfast* (a mess or confused mixture), *dog tired, sick as a dog, dog cheap, dog in the manger.*

One expression involving our four-legged friends stands in opposition to those above: to *put on the dog* means to dress in fine and fashionable toggery. This popular American English idiom resists scrutiny. No one knows its origin, nor why a dog in this case is associated with fashion, but the expression has been popular with Americans since at least the 1860s.

The most reasonable explanation for the emergence of this phrase is the rage for fancy lap and leash dogs in the 1800s. Those with enough money and leisure to pamper a nonworking dog were certainly able to afford quality personal wardrobes as well. One who strolled about in fine threads with a groomed canine in tow was said to be *putting on the dog.*

QUEER

The *Oxford English Dictionary*'s first citation of the word *queer* is from 1508, when it meant simply "odd" or "peculiar." Its antecedent is most likely the German word *quer,* "oblique, aslant, off-center."

As centuries passed, the word took on more meanings. In the 18th century, for example, a *queer bird* was a rogue released from prison. Men who used to fake drowning in order to be compensated by the Humane Society for their trauma and hardship were called *queer plungers.*

This word has often been associated with the production of counterfeit currency. A British publication from 1848 explained that *queer screen* were fake bills and *queer wedge* was bogus silver coin. Even as recently as 1942, Americans *living on the queer* were those involved in forging currency.

As a verb, the word has come to mean "spoil or ruin." Historical citations from the *Oxford English Dictionary* speak of *queering a deal*—spoiling carefully made plans.

But all of these meanings of *queer* have been eclipsed by its most common contemporary usage as a reference to homosexuality. This sense of the word emerged in America in the 1920s, with the first citation appearing in a U.S. Department of Labor publication referring to young men with "queer" tendencies. In current usage, a pejorative sense of the word has gained prominence over all its other meanings.

QUICK

There are numerous references in the Bible's New Testament to the end times, when Christ will return to the earth to "judge the quick and the dead." The disposition of the latter souls is obvious, but who or what are the *quick?*

And what about the *quick* in *quicksand, quicksilver,* and the expression *cut to the quick?* Do these belong to the same etymological clan as the word that means "fast, hasty, rapid"?

Though the relationship isn't immediately apparent, all these *quicks* come from the same source: the Old English *cwic,* meaning "living, alive." The Biblical *quick and the dead,* then, refers to the living and the dead.

To *cut to the quick* is to deeply hurt someone's feelings; it's a metaphor for piercing "living flesh" with cruel words. To pare a fingernail vigorously enough to cause pain and bleeding is literally to cut it to the quick, the sensitive skin beneath.

Quicksilver, another name for the element mercury, means "living silver"—an etymological reference to its fluidity. *Quicksand* moves as if it were alive and animated.

The adjective *quick* meaning "rapid in movement" emerged in the English language between the 12th and 14th centuries. It comes from the notion that "living" creatures are capable of moving with rapidity and spontaneity.

QUIZ

The scores of etymologists who have attempted to locate the origin of the word *quiz* have come up empty-handed. This term, meaning simply "a short test," has puzzled word watchers since it appeared in print in the late 18th century.

A story often associated with the coinage of the word *quiz* involves a Dublin, Ireland, theater manager named James Daly, who boasted that he could invent a meaningless word and make it instantly popular. Daly hired Dublin schoolboys to chalk his nonsense word on every chalkable surface in the city. The word was *quiz,* and within days Dublin was abuzz with speculations of its meaning. This makes a good story, but no written authentication for the tale exists.

More scholarly speculations come from lexicographer John Ayto, editor of *Dictionary of Word Origins.* Ayto writes that in Britain in the late 1900s, *quiz,* the noun, meant "odd person"; the verb meant "make fun of." Later, *quiz* meant "look at mockingly or questioningly through a monocle"; this action may have inspired the later meaning "to interrogate, test."

The *Dictionary of Word Origins* also observes that *quiz* has been associated with the word *inquisitive* and the Latin interrogative *quis,* "who, what?"

In the 1940s, the word gained new life with the introduction of popular radio and television quiz shows. These programs inspired the short-lived noun *quizee,* "contestant on a television quiz program."

RADICAL

The adjective *radical* wears a number of hats here in 21st century America. Political radicals seek the source of social and economic wrongs and advocate extreme action to rectify them. American history has seen radical abolitionists of slavery and alcohol, radical religions, and radical socialists.

In surfer- and skateboard-speak, *radical* is a term of high approval, meaning "excellent" and "fine." It also refers to athletic moves pushed the limits of safety and sanity. The truncated form *rad* always means "very good, fabulous."

Despite its motley 21st century appearance, this term has a respectable linguistic pedigree. *Radical* comes from the Latin word for root, *radix*. Radicals, therefore, etymologically strive to eliminate the fundamentals, or "roots," of political and social evil. The expression *grassroots* is an oblique relative of this term.

Rad, meaning "excellent," probably owes its existence to the notion that anything radical is extreme or noteworthy.

The mathematical *radical* is the "root" of a quantity. When multiplied by itself, the radical yields a given quantity.

Relatives of radical include *radish,* also derived from the Latin *radix;* it is etymologically the "root" vegetable. To *eradicate* is to "destroy at the root."

RAGLAN

A *raglan* is a loose-fitting coat or jacket with sleeves extending in one line from the collar to the wrist. A shirt or blouse outfitted with a *raglan sleeve* has slanted shoulder seams that extend to the neckline. Though the raglan is little more than a footnote in the fashion world, it is the eponym of an uncommonly courageous man.

Fitzroy Somerset, better known as first Lord Raglan, was the Duke of Wellington's aide-de-camp during the Battle of Waterloo. On June 18, 1815, the 23-year-old Lord Raglan had his right arm amputated after it had been shattered by a musketball. As the field surgeon was about to dispose of the limb, Lord Raglan cried out, "I say, bring back my arm! The ring my wife gave me is on the finger!"

Forty years later Raglan was appointed commander in chief of the British forces in the Crimea. He and his men suffered terribly during the brutal Crimean winter of 1854–55. Fifteen hundred British were lost that year in the campaign against the Russians. Never abandoning his position, he fraternized with the soldiers in his trademark big-sleeved frock to which he lent his name.

Though Raglan did all he could for his troops, he was blamed for the hardship and slowness of the war. Facing criticism from his men and his government, Raglan became ill and despondent; and on July 3, 1855, he died in the Crimea. Though the medical report cited cholera as the cause of death, Raglan's doctors said he perished of a broken heart.

Raining Cats and Dogs

Any torrential downpour causes most English speakers reflexively to claim that it's *raining cats and dogs* out there. But who amongst us has seen felines and canines literally cascading from the heavens?

Time has erased the origin of this expression, but phrase dictionaries offer several theories. One has it inspired by Norse mythology, wherein dogs were often depicted as attendants of the storm god Odin, while cats were believed to have the power to cause tempests. Another fashions an analogy between a violent storm and the sound of fighting cats and dogs.

The theory most widely accepted by phrase watchers comes out of 16th or 17th century Europe, where feral cats and dogs proliferated in the cities and villages. Vulnerable to disease and hunger, many sickened and died on the streets and byways. The animals lay where they fell until a downpour turned the streets into raging rivers of garbage, filth, and carcasses. It appeared as though the creatures fell out of the sky with the rain. In 1738, Jonathan Swift wrote in *Polite Conversation,* "I know Sir John will go, though he was sure it would rain cats and dogs; but pray, stay, Sir John."

The *Henry Holt Encyclopedia of Word and Phrase Origins* observes that early American English speakers coined their own variations of this British expression: *raining pitchforks, darning needles, hammer handles,* and *chicken coops.*

REDUPLICATION

Is it poetry? *Okiedokie, mumbo jumbo, hanky-panky, walkie-talkie.* These rhyming word combinations are examples of what linguists call reduplications. Some reduplications consist of a conjoined pair of rhyming words, like *hanky-panky* and *boo-hoo.* Others, like *bang-bang* and *hush-hush,* are simply word repetitions.

This type of word formation is particularly interesting in its variety of expression. For example, reduplication can convey mockery. Useless talk or empty ritual is called *mumbo jumbo* or *claptrap.* Someone who pretends at sophistication is *hoity-toity.* We *boo-hoo* someone who whines needlessly.

On the other hand, reduplications can indicate affection in so-called baby talk: *bye-bye, honey-bunny, night-night.* Any word can be reduplicated in baby talk, usually by substituting the initial consonant with a *w* to get such constructions as *juicy-wuicy* and *footsie-wootsie.*

Reduplications are used to imitate repetitious sounds: *yack-yack, knock-knock, beep-beep.* A dog endlessly barking *bow-wow-wows.* This linguistic construction can also suggest alternative movement, as in *dingdong, clip-clop, pitter-patter,* and *ping-pong.* Meaning is intensified in some reduplicative expressions, like *teeny-weenie* and *tip-top.*

English speakers are not the only ones to use this type of word construction. The Indonesian language uses the device to form the plurals of nouns. *Rumah* means "house"; *rumah-rumah* means "houses." *Ibu* is "mother"; *ibuibu* is the plural.

Competitors for the same thing are called *rivals.* These contestants can be rivals in love, or rivals for the same coveted job or position. A close look at the etymology of this term, however, reveals that the original rivals clashed over water.

The ancestor of the modern *rival* is the Latin term *rivus,* meaning "stream." Ancient rivals lived on opposite streambanks and vied for rights to their common source of water. Too, they may have been culturally and linguistically divided, for streams and rivers have always been natural barriers. Little has changed in the philosophy behind this term. Contemporary humans around the globe are, now more than ever, *rivaling* for water rights.

The word *river* comes from the Latin *ripa,* "[river] bank." Etymologically, *river* refers to the banks of a river, rather than the water that courses between them. The adjective *riparian,* "of a river bank," is a descendant of *ripa.* The Italian word for "bank," *riviera,* also belongs to this etymological grouping.

A river hides in the term *arrive.* This word literally means "to the river bank" and implies the end of a (river) journey. A contemporary *arrival* is the termination of any journey, whether by water or land.

ROBOT

Early in the 20th century, Czechoslovakian playwright and author Karel Capek envisioned a world ruled by automated machines. Capek crystallized this dark vision in the 1920 play *R.U.R.* The initials stood for "Rossum's Universal Robots."

Rossum's Universal Robots was Capek's fictional British firm that mass-produced robots designed to work as mechanical slaves. The grand scheme behind this design was to create a better world for humankind by eliminating menial labor. Ultimately, however, the machines arose in rebellion, destroyed humanity and created a new world of their own.

Capek extracted the term *robot* from his native language. Derived from the Czeck word *robota,* meaning "involuntary service," *robot* is etymologically a "machine that performs forced labor." By 1930, only a decade after the production of *R.U.R., robot* was a well-used English word. It has since found a place in our slang vocabulary as a "mindless, insensitive person."

In 1941, the related word *robotics* was coined by science fiction guru Isaac Asimov in the short story "Runaround."

Rude

The word *rude* has responded to the call of many shades of meaning over the centuries. In its gentlest guise, it means "unfashioned or shapeless," as in a *rude* mass of clay yet untouched by a potter.

Early anthropologists of the 19th century felt compelled to use this adjective to describe non-European tribespeople. *Rude* in this context meant "savage, untaught, or ignorant."

In *A Midsummer Night's Dream,* Shakespeare used the word to describe an ocean gale: "The rude sea grew civil at [the mermaid's] song."

Contemporary English speakers most often use the word to refer to an impolite or coarse person. Rude is the individual who cuts you off in a line of traffic.

The patriarch of this term is the Latin *rudis,* meaning "rough, unpolished stone" or "broken rubble."

Rudiment and *erudite* belong to this linguistic grouping. *Rudiment* indicates that which must be learned first, when the student is still unpolished or unrefined. *Erudite* is the etymological opposite of *rude.* Meaning "scholarly, refined," this term consists of the prefix *e-,* "away," and *rudis,* "rough stone." It literally means "away or free from roughness."

RUMINATE

Sheep, cattle, deer, elk, camels, and giraffes are members of a division of creatures called *ruminants*. Chewing and swallowing quickly, ruminants send their graze to the rumen, the first of the animal's four stomach cavities.

From there, the food passes through a multiplicity of digestive processes, one of which involves cud, partially digested graze the ruminant animal rechews and then swallows. Anyone familiar with cattle or sheep knows well the slow, rhythmic cud-chewing of the resting creatures.

The word *ruminant* comes from the Latin term *rumen*, meaning "throat or gullet," pointing to the many swallowings and regurgitations of these animals.

Though humans are not ruminants, we nevertheless *ruminate,* in a sense. When we brood on a problem, for example, we figuratively ruminate, chewing on the situation again and again, like a cow molaring her cud. Shakespeare used the term in this sense in his play *Henry VI,* wherein he has a character utter, "Conduct me where, from company, I may revolve and ruminate my grief."

The Latin verb *rumpere* means "break or burst." This verb shows up as *rupt* in the modern English terms *interrupt, disrupt, erupt, bankrupt,* and *rupture.*

To *interrupt* is etymologically to "break between."

The word *disrupt* is led by the prefix *dis-,* meaning "apart." To disrupt is etymologically to "burst apart" or "throw into disorder."

Volcanoes, geysers, and angry people *erupt.* This word means "burst forth," with *e-* meaning "out."

Someone legally declared unable to pay debts is *bankrupt.* Money changers in ancient times sat on benches (the Italian word for bench is *banca*) near the temple door. Insolvent money changers were symbolized by a "broken bench," *banca rotta,* which translated as the English *bankrupt.*

To *corrupt* is to degrade, pervert, debauch. The Latin ancestor of this word is *corrumpere,* "destroy completely." This word was put to noble use in the famous quotation from the English historian Lord Acton: "Power tends to corrupt, and absolute power corrupts absolutely."

A *rupture* is a split, break, or fracture. In fidelity to its etymological family, this word means "a burst or break."

English slang provides many derogatory terms for the country dweller: *clodhopper, Rube, hayseed, bumpkin.*

Some of these disparaging terms come from the crops raised by farmers. The term *cotton-pickin'* fits in this family of terms. Long regarded as a lowly task, picking cotton is associated with ignorance and crudeness. *Corny* is another example. This adjective goes back to the 1890s when midwestern seed corn catalogues printed jokes, riddles, and cartoons in their publications. Tired and overworked, the humorous stories became known as "corn catalog jokes" or simply "corn jokes." Eventually, any time-worn humor became *corny.* Other crop-related insults are *hayseed, pea-picker,* and *buckwheat.*

Personal names are also included in the arsenal of disparaging rural terms. *Rube,* referring to a naïve country lout, is the abbreviation of *Reuben,* from the 19th century term *Rustic Reuben.*

Another opprobrious country term is *clodhopper,* a 17th century name for one who labored in the dirt. *Bumpkin* comes from the Dutch word *boomkin,* meaning "little tree." The more recent *redneck* was originally an American southernism, alluding to the perpetually sunburnt neck of a field hand.

Rushmore

On July 4, 1930, a crowd of 2,500 souls gathered in the Black Hills region of South Dakota to watch the unveiling of a colossal likeness of George Washington's face carved into a granite cliff. Subsequent ceremonies would celebrate the installation of the images of presidents Jefferson, Roosevelt, and Lincoln, carved in a row across the face of the mountain.

This massive granite landmark is South Dakota's Mount Rushmore National Memorial, designed and executed by the American sculptor Gutzon Borglum, who, before his death in 1941, nicknamed his opus a "shrine to democracy."

Its more popular name, *Rushmore,* was given to the mountain decades before Borglum's arrival. In the 1800s, tin was being extracted from the Black Hills. The Harney Peak Tin Mining Company of New York sent west a young attorney, Charles Rushmore, to handle the acquisition of tin mining claims. While touring the Black Hills area with a local prospector, Rushmore pointed to a spectacular granite cliff and asked its name. The prospector joshed, "Never had any, but we'll call the damn thing Rushmore." Fifty years later, the damn thing, named *Mount Rushmore,* was carved with a stoic quartet of presidential visages.

SALMON, SAUTE, SALLY, SALACIOUS

Somewhere in their historical development, the phenomena represented by the words *salmon, saute, sally,* and *salacious* have "jumped." In tracing the etymological breadcrumbs back to the source of these words, we arrive at a common ancestor: the Latin *salire,* "to jump, leap."

After growing to maturity in ocean waters, *salmon* begin an arduous journey up the river in which they were born. In a mighty struggle against rapids and tumbling waterfalls, the fish leap upstream to spawn and die in their natal waters. Etymologically, *salmon* are the "jumping fish."

Salmon are not the only creatures to "jump." Certain male animals, when copulating with females, jump upon their mates. This gives us the word *salacious,* which originally denominated these leaping males. In contemporary English, *salacious* means "lewd or lustful," driven with the energy of an animal lunging in the rut.

Sally is also a member of this linguistic congregation— not the name Sally, but the term for a sudden military attack, a sortie. A *sally* is etymologically a "leaping out" at the enemy from a fortified position.

When you *sauté* vegetables, you quickly stir them in the pan so they will not overcook. To *sauté* is etymologically to make the food "jump." This term, too, is the offspring of the Latin *salire*.

For millennia, humans have harvested, processed, and traded salt. Prized as a preservative and a seasoning, salt has been used as currency and even taxed. Its acquisition has altered landscapes and shaped cultures. The ancient city of Jericho, for example, was founded as a salt trading center. Salzburg ("Salt Village") in Austria was established in the 8th century, built entirely on the revenue from nearby salt mines.

The progenitor *salt* comes from the ancient Indo-European language—source of many of the world's modern languages. The word for salt sounds similar amongst the German, Dutch, Latin, Greek, French, and Italian tongues.

Roman soldiers were sometimes paid with salt, so valuable was this commodity in the ancient world. This allowance was called *salarium,* from the Latin word for salt, *sal. Salarium* eventually became the modern English *salary,* which means today a fixed payment for work. And if you are *worth your salt,* you are a valuable employee who works hard for your pay.

The word *salad* also comes from Latin *sal.* The Roman style of salad was vegetables or greens dressed with a salty brine sauce. Other gastronomic items named after this most important constituent include *salsa, sauce,* and *sausage.*

The history of the expression *to take with a grain of salt* is somewhat hazy. One suggestion is that a pinch of salt renders a mysterious-tasting meal just a bit more palatable. Metaphorically, then, a story of questionable veracity should be swallowed only after salting it with a tad of skepticism.

The expression *salt of the earth* is a compliment for the true and noble. This saying originates in Matthew 5:13, where Jesus compares his devoted followers to salt—that most valuable and precious, yet most basic, of all commodities.

SANDWICH

A traditional tale claims that the world's first *sandwich* was invented and eaten at 5:00 A.M. on August 6, 1762. It was consumed by an Englishman, John Montague—career politician, postmaster general, Lord of the British Admiralty, and a member of the House of Lords. Historical accounts characterize Montague as an eloquent speaker, a proponent of needed dockyard reforms and a successful politician.

He is probably best remembered, however, as a rake, womanizer, and gambler. He belonged to an association called the Hellfire Club whose members mocked Catholicism by holding drunken orgies in monk's habits. Montague left his wife and four children for his sixteen-year-old mistress, a "commoner" whom he educated at the finest Parisian schools.

Montague's insatiable gambling habits held him at the gaming tables for days at a time. Early one morning, after hours of cards, Montague perceived that he was hungry. Too engrossed in his game to leave the table, he had a servant bring him a slab of meat between two pieces of toasted bread. Because Montague's inherited title was the Fourth Earl of Sandwich, legend has it that this novel fusion of gastronomic items was named in his honor.

So too were the *Sandwich Islands.* In 1778, the explorer Captain James Cook bestowed this name on what would become the Hawaiian Islands in honor of his contemporary John Montague.

Scapegoat

A *scapegoat* is a person who takes the blame for the sins and mistakes of others. The original scapegoat was a player in one of the dramas of the Bible's Old Testament.

The book of Leviticus describes in detail the rituals and sacrifices of the Israelite people. One of the Levitican ceremonies, enacted on the Day of Atonement, sets the precedent for the modern observance of Yom Kippur.

Leviticus, chapter 16, says that on the Day of Atonement, God ordered the patriarch Moses to lead a live goat before a holy altar. There, a priest was to lay his hands upon the head of the goat and "confess over it all the wickedness and rebellion of the Israelites, all their sins, and put them on the goat's head." The sin-burdened goat was then to be led away and released into the desert wilderness.

A 21st century *scapegoat*—who is not a goat at all but a human—is likewise a target of blame for the errors of others.

The term *scapegoat* was originally *escape goat*. The *e* at the front of *escape* was eventually dropped through aphesis, the loss of an unaccented initial vowel. Other examples of aphesis are *cross* for *across* and *squire* for *esquire*.

The words *manuscript, prescribe, scripture,* and *postscript* are all cousins. The matriarch of this family is the Latin verb *scribere,* "to write."

A *scribe* is etymologically "one who writes manuscripts." *Describe* originally meant "to write something down" or "to give a written account of." Today, a *description* can be either written or spoken.

Prescribe means "to write before." A *prescription* is a recipe for medication; originally such instructions consisted of words written down to be followed, as by a physician.

The word *script* also claims membership in the *scribere* family. A *script* is a piece of writing, such as the printed form of a play. *Scripture* implies holy or inspired documents. The P.S. written at the conclusion of a note abbreviates *postscript.* Coming from the Latin *postscriptum,* this phrase means "after writing."

The word *manuscript* means "document written by hand" (*manu* also occurs in *manual, manufacture,* and *manicure,* from the Latin *manus,* "hand"). Monks dedicated to the preservation of sacred documents copied manuscripts in special rooms called *scriptoriums.*

Scribble, the less reputable member of the *scribere* family, means "write hastily or illegibly." Inferior writers and hacks are sometimes labeled *scribblers.*

SCRUPULOUS

A *scrupulous* person is one who attends to detail, someone cautious and thoughtful. One can be scrupulously clean, or honest, or considerate. A *scruple* is a thought or doubt troubling the conscience.

The story behind this term opens in the Latin-speaking world, where the word *scrupus* meant "small, sharp stone." One such stone lodged in a sandal could be a painful impediment.

The metaphorical connection between a pebble in the shoe and a troubled pricking of the conscience eventually gave English speakers the modern words *scruple* and *scrupulous*.

An apothecaries' weight of ⅓ drachm or ½₄ ounce is also called a *scruple,* from the sense of "small stone." The word can denote a small unit of time: a *scruple of an hour* is the sixtieth part of an hour, or one minute. A Roman land measure of 10 square feet is also called a *scruple;* so is ½₂ of an inch.

An *Oxford English Dictionary* citation from 1830 says, "In the choice of a second wife, one scruple of prudence is worth a pound of passion."

There is a story about the woman who declared that Shakespeare might indeed have been a fine playwright had he not been so bloody addicted to clichés.

This anecdote illustrates, by twisted logic, the endurance of Shakespeare's language in the English speaking world. Consciously or not, we 21st century moderns quote this 16th century bard on a daily basis. Shakespeare's words and phrases arguably shape our thoughts and often provide linguistic shortcuts to our expression. Consider these familiar Shakespearean phrases: *cold comfort, flesh and blood, vanish into thin air, in my mind's eye, it's Greek to me,* and *we've seen better days.*

The English of Shakespeare's day was exploding with new terms borrowed from Latin, Greek, French, Italian, and Spanish. The Bard appeared to relish these novel words, for dozens of them appear in print for the first time on the pages of his scripts, these among them: *excellent, gust, summit, obscene, leapfrog, submerge, lonely.*

How would we manage without these words and phrases? We English speakers owe a tremendous debt of gratitude to the Bard of Avon, and to those who preserved his manuscripts.

SILHOUETTE

The word for the simple black profile portrait typically mounted in a graceful oval frame is the eponym of 18th century Parisian Etienne de Silhouette.

In 1759, the fifty-year-old Silhouette, son of a tax collector, became France's minister of finance under Louis XV. Silhouette inherited an insurmountable task. Though the coffers of France were empty, and the nation's economy lay in ruins, titanic sums of money were needed just then to finance the emerging Seven Years' War.

Silhouette rose to the occasion by requiring all government officials to pay taxes. Next, he restricted the amount of government pensions received by France's courtiers. The minister of finance assessed a property tax on each member of the nobility. Duke and mistress found their purses lighter under the new financial regime.

Finally, Silhouette whittled at the king's amusement funds. He suggested the royalty curtail its mania for expensive oil portraits. Would not simple profile representations in black paper be more prudent?

For these and other parsimonious notions, such as eliminating trouser cuffs and pockets to save money, Silhouette fell out of favor with the royalty and the people. After only eight months in the ministry, he was replaced. His name was thereafter associated with the simple, inexpensive portraiture known as the *silhouette*.

SIREN

The three Sirens of Greek mythology were half-bird and half-woman creatures who inhabited the island of Cyrene in the Mediterranean. Their sweet and beguiling voices lured passing mariners to their island's rocky shores. When the sailing ships were dashed to bits, the bird-women rushed in to devour the marooned men. The Greek hero Odysseus escaped the Siren's songs by ordering his sailors to stop their ears with wax and then lashing himself to the mast of the ship to prevent himself from jumping overboard to join the bewitching trio.

In 1590, Shakespeare used the word *siren* to refer figuratively to an enticing woman, in allusion to the beguiling singers who lured sailors to their deaths. In the 20th century, the word was applied to the warning devices on police cars, ambulances, and fire engines. The link between sirens and danger is most vividly illustrated by the wailing devices used in the United Kingdom during the Second World War to warn citizens of impending air raids.

Dugongs and manatees, sunning themselves on the shore, are said to resemble human females. Because of this, and their association with islands, these creatures have been given the order name Sirenia after the ancient Sirens of the Mediterranean Sea.

Sisyphean Task

In the murky light of the Greek Underworld, we witness a strange spectacle. A man stands beside a massive boulder at the bottom of a hill. Spreading his arms around the rock, the man begins to move it up the incline.

The man coaxes his burden upward until he miraculously nears the crest. At the plateau, the man loses his footing, and he and the boulder crash to the bottom. As we watch, though, he stands up and begins to renew his bizarre task.

The man is a Greek mortal named Sisyphus. His wretched labor is punishment for having twice outwitted the gods.

When it came time for Sisyphus to die, he captured and bound Hades, the god of the dead. Hades was not able to claim him. When his second call to the Underworld came, Sisyphus again escaped to the land of the living. Captured by Hades a third and final time, Sisyphus was sentenced forever to push an enormous boulder uphill, only to have it roll down before reaching the top.

Today, the phrase *Sisyphean task* refers to an endless burden or labor. On April 12, 1989, *New York Times* writer Lisa Foderero commented on official efforts to urge New Yorkers to improve their diets: "While undoing well-worn habits is something of a Sisyphean task, the state is determined to try."

SKINFLINT

A *skinflint* is a miser, a scrooge, a pinchpenny. The coinage of this word was inspired by the technology of the flintlock musket. Craig M. Carver, lexicographer and managing editor of the *Dictionary of American Regional English,* says this about the evolution of *skinflint:*

> [The musket] used a piece of flint held in a hammerlike device, or 'cock.' When the trigger was pulled, the spring-loaded cock struck the flint against a steel plate, or 'frizzen,' creating a shower of sparks. If all went well, the flash of the priming powder in the pan just beneath the frizzen ignited the charge in the bore and fired the weapon.... After repeated firings, the flint wore down, causing inadequate sparking. Most riflemen merely replaced the flint, but some penny-pinchers 'skinned' or sharpened their flints with a knife.

Washington Irving alluded to this practice with derision: "The fool...who, in skinning a flint worth a farthing, spoiled a knife worth fifty times the sum." The *Oxford English Dictionary* defines a *skinflint* as "one who would skin a flint to save or gain something; an avaricious, penurious, mean or niggardly person; a miser." *Skinflint* first appeared in print in 1700.

SLEAZY

The word *sleazy* is an especially expressive member of America's arsenal of insults. This adjective describes things inferior, cheap, squalorous, dirty. It's opprobrious quality is made complete by its rhyming with *greasy,* and the initial *sl* sound found in so many pejoratives: *slimy, slob, slut, slothful, slipshod, slug, slum, sloppy.*

The chronicle of *sleazy* remains uncharted. The authoritative *Oxford English Dictionary* cites scant evidence for a conclusive word history; ditto the *Barnhart Dictionary of Etymology.* Several other sources, however, step forward with speculations of the history of this word, all containing variations on the following theme, as follows:

A region in eastern Europe called *Silesia* was once famous for its manufacture of a superior linen fabric. The linen, originally called *cloth of Silesia,* gradually became *Silesia cloth,* and finally *sleazy cloth.*

The slow spiral of etymological degradation began when foreign clothmakers tried to imitate Silesia's fine product. The name *sleazy cloth* became associated with the second-rate foreign fabrics, giving us the *sleazy* that means "cheap, flimsy, worthless."

The term has become a stinging dart of abuse in the mouths of American English speakers. It's even spawned a nasty little brood of related insults: *sleazeball, sleazebag,* and *sleazoid.*

SLOGAN

Slogans are an essential component to successful American advertising: "The pause that refreshes." "A diamond is forever." "The beauty of all-wheel drive."

Slogans are designed to involve the listener or reader in a product or philosophy. Relying on both rhyme ("I like Ike") and alliteration ("There's a Ford in your Future"), slogans burrow into our minds and attempt to induce us to buy or vote. Distributors of every significant American product count on slogans to render their goods familiar to the public.

Our English word *slogan* is Gaelic in origin. Coming to us after many mutations, this term was originally a pair of Gaelic words, *slaugh-ghairm,* meaning "battle-cry." Soldiers, advancing into the fray, shouted in unison the name of their clan or clan leader. This was their war cry, their *slogan.*

A modern slogan attempts to rally people behind a cause or product, unifying them in a common mantra, just as ancient soldiers chanted the names that inspired their loyalty.

The *Dictionary of Word Origins,* by John Ayto, tells us that English speakers adopted *slogan* in the 16th century in its original Gaelic sense. By the 18th century, the metaphorical sense of a "catchphrase" began to emerge in our language.

Snipe

The snipe is a long-billed member of the sandpiper family. At home on almost every continent, snipe favor swamp and marshland habitats. They are most active in early morning or evening, when they probe the shallows for insects with their flexible bills. Nervous and shy, these birds prefer the security of brushy cover.

The snipe has long been a favorite gamebird both here and abroad. It's difficult quarry because of its erratic, zigzag startle flight.

In earlier centuries, snipe were captured with nets because of the near impossibility of a bow and arrow kill. Even armed with accurate shotguns, modern bird hunters find snipe challenging targets.

In the past, hunters often concealed themselves in the underbrush to avoid startling the bird. A hunter who was both stealthy and precise gained the distinction of being a *sniper*, a moniker that has come down through the decades to denominate any marksman shooting from a concealed space.

Likewise, someone who utters malicious, underhanded remarks at another is also a *sniper*, making indirect verbal snipes as if concealed by metaphorical underbrush.

SODA JERK JARGON

The ice cream clerks who invented and dispensed America's favorite dairy confections from the 1920s through the 1950s were affectionately called *soda jerks*. The *jerk* in their title was not the same as the one meaning "worthless fool"; rather, it described what they did for a living, "jerking" the soda dispenser handle all day long. The jargon invented by these ice cream parlor heroes was a kind of slangy short-hand necessitated by the short-order atmosphere of the soda fountain.

One soda jerker expression still used by restaurant work-ers is *eighty-six,* meaning "we're out of whatever it is you ordered." *Eighty-six* is said to rhyme with *nix,* meaning "no" or "nothing."

The numeric shorthand didn't stop there. *Eighty-seven and a half* meant "a pretty woman just walked in." *Ninety-five* signaled "a customer who didn't pay is walking out the door"; and *thirteen* was "the boss just walked in."

Food orders were condensed with jargon like *a-pie, c-pie,* or *coke-pie,* meaning "apple, cherry, or coconut pie." *Dog and maggot* indicated crackers and cheese. *Burn it and let it swim* was an ice cream float; a large Coca-Cola was *stretch one.* A cup of coffee was *draw one.* Two cups of coffee? *A pair of drawers!*

Though the disappearance of the neighborhood ice cream parlor has rendered soda jerk jargon obsolete, much of that slangy vocabulary has nevertheless been lovingly pre-served in many specialized dictionaries.

SOLSTICE, EQUINOX

Twice a year, on June 21 and December 22, we observe the summer and winter *solstices*. In June, when the sun is farthest north of the equator in our hemisphere, it rises at its northernmost point on the horizon and appears to halt in its progression. It then reverses its movement, rising farther and farther to the south until the day of winter solstice, when it again appears stationary on the horizon. Each solstice occurs on the day the sun "stops" in its progression.

The sun etymologically "stands still" on the two days of solstice. The antecedents of this word are the Latin *sol*, "sun," and *sistere*, "stand still." The German version of *solstice* is *Sonnenwende*, "the sun's turning point."

The *equinoxes* occur twice a year when the sun crosses directly above the equator. The *vernal equinox* arrives on March 21, the *autumnal equinox* on about September 22. On these two occasions, the hours of daylight and darkness are equal on all points of the earth. The word *equinox* reflects this phenomenon: it comes from a combination of the Latin *aequi*, "equal," and *noctis*, "night." In German, *equinox* is *Tagundnachtgleiche*, "day and night equality."

The expression *son of a gun,* coined around 1700, has a variety of uses and a hazy history. Sometimes a term of affection between friends ("you old son of a gun"), it is also a mild expression of surprise (I'll be a son of a gun!").

Theories of its origin vary. One has a *son of a gun* an illegitimate child born of a woman who had dallied with a sailor or a soldier (the "gun"). Another claims the phrase is a euphemism for the more objectionable *son of a bitch,* with *son of a gun* owing its staying power to its rhyme.

Another variation on its genesis has it that wives of British sailors were often allowed to accompany their husbands on long voyages. Children of the seafaring couples were delivered on the gun deck, which could be screened off for privacy. The birth occurred "under the gun," and any boy child was a *son of a gun.*

In the *Sailors Word Book* of 1867, author Admiral William Smith wrote that *son of a gun* was "an epithet conveying contempt in a slight degree, and originally applied to boys born afloat, when women were permitted to accompany their husbands to sea; one admiral declared he literally was thus cradled, under the breast of a gun-carriage."

Sophos Words

The names *Sophia* and *Sophie* come from the Greek word *sophos,* meaning "wisdom." Many English girls were christened Sophia after Sophia Weston, the heroine in Henry Fielding's 1749 novel *Tom Jones.* The Russian name *Sonya* is a pet form of Sophia.

The Greek *sophos* is the origin of the name, and of the words *sophist, sophism, sophisticate,* and *sophomore* as well.

The original Greek *sophists* were, as the term suggests, "wise men," teachers of rhetoric and reasoning. By the 5th century B.C., sophists were instructing young men in the art of political persuasion. Students of sophistry learned to confuse and mislead with clever arguments, making a sophist "wise" in the art of fallacious or specious reasoning.

A *sophisticate* of the 21st century is worldly wise, urbane, well traveled. We view this positively, but *sophistication* of the 15th and 16th centuries was considered unhealthy. It meant that one had become artificial, corrupt, and impure in seeking worldly wisdom.

Originally, a *sophomore* was a second-year university student taking part in dialectic exercises. Some sources say the word *sophomore* is a blend of *sophos,* "wise," and *moros,* "foolish or dull." The adjective *sophomoric* appeared in print in 1813 and implies the behavior of a boor playing at academic refinement.

The left side has been associated with calamity, evil, and clumsiness in almost every culture. The Latin word for left is *sinister;* in French it's *gauche;* and the German *linkisch* means both "left" and "clumsy." The modern English word *left* comes from the ancient Germanic term *lyft,* meaning "broken." A *left-handed compliment* is a thinly veiled insult, and if you *got up on the wrong side of the bed,* you have arisen from your mattress on the left, the side that surely brings misadventure.

In the roster of all the biased etymologies aimed at left-handers, the moniker *southpaw* may be the kindest of all. For over a century, American lefties have been bethumped with this good-natured nickname.

It's source is the game of baseball. Robert A. Palmatier and Harold L. Ray, editors of *Sports Talk: A Dictionary of Sports Metaphors,* have tracked its birthplace to Chicago's Comiskey Park. Pitchers playing that field faced west. A left-hander, therefore, threw the ball with the hand, or "paw," that pointed south. Finley Peter Dunne, humorist and sports-writer for the *Chicago News,* is credited with inventing the whimsical title *southpaw* in the 1880s.

SPITTIN' IMAGE

The origin of the expression *spittin' image* has eluded lexicographers for decades. Its spelling and pronunciation have been contested as well: is it *spittin' image, spit and image,* or a contraction of the phrase *spirit and image?*

Everyone agrees that this cliché means "exact duplicate of" or "the very likeness of." Variants of *spittin' image* have been uttered by English speakers for centuries. According to the *Morris Dictionary of Word and Phrase Origins,* by William and Mary Morris, elements of this expression can be found in writings dating to 1602.

The *spit* in this colloquialism may literally refer to saliva. Some etymologists believe *spittin' image,* or *spit and image,* reflects the belief that a child may so resemble her parent, it's as if the elder spat the younger right out of her mouth. A book published in 1895 called *The Light of Scarthy,* by one Edgerton Castle, has the line, "She's like the poor lady that's dead and gone, the spit an' image she is."

Another suggestion is that *spittin' image* is a corruption of *spirit and image.* If so, the expression would allude to the child who resembles his father as having both the spirit (or personality) and the appearance of his parent.

Mary Ann Evans, a.k.a. George Eliot, said, "The stars are golden fruit upon a tree—all out of reach."

For millennia, humans have studied the stars with profound longing and curiosity. They provide navigation for the traveler, metaphor for the poet and theory for the scientist.

Stars also bespangle our vocabulary. The English word *star* comes ultimately from the Greek word for the same, *aster.* Consider some other terms from this Greek source:

The flowering plants of the *aster* family are named after their starlike blossoms.

Very tiny planets in our solar system are called *asteroids,* a word coined in 1802 when the first one was identified. When viewed from a telescope, these minor planets look like stars. They differ in that they move across the sky against the more static heavenly objects. *Asteroid* is Greek for "starlike."

Astronomy is the study of the universe. The word literally means "the naming, arrangement, or classifying of the stars."

A "sailor of the stars" is an *astronaut.* (The *naut* in this word is the same as the one in *nautical* and *nausea,* a sensation felt by "those who sailed.") *Astronaut* was coined in 1929 and widely popularized in 1961.

The term *astrology* appeared in the English language in the 14th century. Astrology is etymologically the "study of the stars."

And the little punctuation mark called the *asterisk* (★) was so named for its obvious shape.

John Dennis was born in 1657, the son of a London saddle maker. He was educated at Trinity Hall until his studies came to an awkward halt when he was expelled for assaulting and wounding a fellow student with a sword.

John Dennis thereafter took up playwriting in London. His scripts, however, were less than inspiring. Both *Gibraltar, or the Spanish Adventure* and *The Comical Gallant, or the Amours of Sir John Falstaff* quickly withered and died under scorching reviews.

In 1709, in a final grasp at theatrical success, Dennis wrote and produced a tragedy called *Appius and Virginia*.

For this production, Dennis developed a new and convincing method for simulating stage thunder, which consisted of rattling a sheet of tin. Critics applauded the verisimilitude of this technique, but their reviews of the play were harsh and scornful.

The embittered John Dennis later returned to the same theater to watch a performance of *Macbeth*. When he heard his own thunder rumbling from the stage, he leapt to his feet and raged, "That is my thunder, by God! The villains will play my thunder but not my plays!"

Nobody celebrates this obscure British playwright, but we evoke his memory whenever we use the phrase *to steal someone's thunder,* meaning to take credit for someone else's work or to upstage the effect of someone's remarks or actions.

Sundae

The first written evidence of ice cream in the New World is from Maryland in 1702. At that time, few people had heard of ice cream. But by the late 19th century, soda fountains and ice cream parlors were springing up across America like dandelions on a spring lawn.

This burgeoning industry was a nursery of new terminology. The words *parfait, banana split, sherbet,* and *syrup* were all made popular by the American ice cream phenomenon, with *sundae* perhaps the most familiar of all.

Circa 1890, at a soda fountain in Wisconsin, a young boy asked for a dish of ice cream topped with the flavored syrup normally reserved for ice cream sodas. Within months, this novel concoction became a local favorite. Soda fountain owner George Giffy began selling this treat for a nickel on Sundays to attract a larger Sabbath crowd. It worked. Soon Mr. Giffy was making money on this recipe.

Many etymologists think it was he who originally titled it the *ice cream sundae,* after the day on which it was served. Why the word *sundae* is spelled with an -*ae* on the end rather than an -*ay* is a mystery. The word may originally have been spelled *sunday* and later been altered out of respect for the Sabbath day.

SUPERLATIVES

American English speakers are fond of positive superlatives: *sensational, fantastic, phenomenal, super, terrific, excellent, amazing, awesome, incredible.* These terms are so common that they've become blurred and nonspecific; their linguistic muscles have atrophied. A look behind the glitzy curtain of these superlatives reveals the depth and color these words have forfeited.

Consider *fantastic,* a word that for centuries meant "existing only in the imagination" (compare its relative *fantasy,* "fanciful daydream"). Only since the late 1940s has *fantastic* been synonymous with good and wonderful.

Fabulous, from the Latin *fabula,* originally meant "of or like a fable." By the early 1600s it had acquired the sense of "astonishing, wonderful." By the 1960s slang-slinging teenagers had transformed it to *fab,* a term of highest approval.

From the Latin *excellere, excellent* is etymologically "lofty." Another Latin-based term, *super,* comes from a word meaning "above, on top of, beyond." This word surrendered to the reduplication "super-dooper" in the 1940s.

Some slangy superlatives are bad words gone good. *Terrific* is the heir of a Latin verb meaning "to terrify." *Amazing* comes from the Old English word *amasian,* "to confuse, bewilder" (the word *maze,* "confusing structure," is related). More modern examples of somersaulted negatives are the *bad* that means "excellent", the *mean* that is "good" ("she makes a *mean* jello salad"), and the wicked that is "admirable."

Throughout history, all peoples have avoided swearing by or invoking the names of their sacred dieties. American English speakers often use terms that euphemize, but mimic, religious oath-taking.

For example, *God* is remodeled into *gosh, gol, golly, gad,* and *egad.* Mark Twain, in his 1876 *Adventures of Tom Sawyer,* has his characters use the euphemism *dad fetch it.* Another common substitution for God, *dad* is serviceable in constituting such oaths as *dadblame, dadgum, dadblast,* and *dadburn.*

The name *Jesus Christ* has many creative euphemisms: *gee whiz, jeepers creepers, jiminy christmas, gee willikers.* And consider the *holy* family of euphemisms: *holy cats, holy cripes, holy Moses, holy smokes.*

In the early 20th century, newspaper editors refused to print the word *hell.* It was represented "h—l" in print and verbally sanitized as *heck, Sam Hill, blazes,* and *Hades.* Even the seemingly innocuous *damn* has been disinfected in *darn* and *dang.*

SYRINX

The goat-god Pan of Greek legend was famous for his lecherous pursuit of wood nymphs. One afternoon, while Pan was dozing in a sun-warmed thicket, he heard the sound of footsteps nearby. Peeking through the underbrush, he saw a nymph named Syrinx returning to her home after a day of hunting in the mountains.

Pan, always ready to dally with a nymph, stepped onto the path in front of Syrinx and leered at her. This particular nymph was horrified at the sight of the goat-god, for she had pledged herself to chastity and knew well Pan's reputation. She sprang away through the trees, with the amorous Pan in pursuit. She was able to outrun him until she came to a riverbank, where Pan managed to throw his arms around her.

Syrinx cried out to the river gods for help and was instantly turned into a tuft of reeds. Pan sighed at the loss, and when he did, his breath through the reeds produced a sweet melody. Charmed by the sound, Pan made a flute of reeds and named it *Syrinx* in honor of the nymph.

This type of flute is today called the *pan-pipe* or *syrinx*. The name of the wood nymph is also preserved in a biological use of the same word. The *syrinx* is the pipelike or tube-like vocal apparatus of birds.

TACKY

If it's cheap, shoddy, gaudy, in bad taste, it's *tacky*. In a 1960s song called "Little Boxes," suburban homes were described as "little boxes made of ticky-tacky," or shabby, flimsy materials. This *tacky* is not connected to the one that means "sticky." How did the "cheap, inferior" *tacky* come to our slang vocabulary?

This mid-19th century Americanism began life as a term for a small, ill-kept pony or horse of little value. The scrubby little tackys were eventually associated with anything inferior and useless. In the South, this word became an insult launched against the poor, especially impoverished whites whose limited means prevented them from owning anything but second-rate tackys.

It became a Southern fashion in the early 1900s to throw "tacky parties" where guests dressed as hillbillies and hayseeds. The society section of the *Charlotte Observer* reported that a "tacky party" was given at the home of Mrs. G. W. Smithson on the evening of September 2, 1902.

The 1960s elaboration *ticky-tacky* is a reduplication, the repetition or rhyming of a word or syllable. This type of word formation almost always implies sarcasm and insult. It's not hard to hear the derision in the expression *ticky-tacky*.

Tantalus was a king of ancient Phrygia, a region situated in modern-day central Turkey. Some legends give Tantalus immortal status; other accounts tell us he was simply a mortal beloved of the Greek gods.

A frequent guest at the Olympian banquet table, Tantalus was privy to the affairs and secrets of the immortals. He betrayed the trust of the gods, however, by revealing details of their hidden lives to the people of Earth. In further treachery, Tantalus smuggled the god's holy nectar out of Olympus and decanted it to his mortal friends. For committing these and other, darker sins, Tantalus was sentenced to an eternity of torture.

Shackled forever in the waves of Lake Tartarus in the Underworld, Tantalus was submerged to his neck. When he bent to quench his thirst, the waters rushed away from his parched lips. A fruit-laden tree, its branches suspended over the king, lifted its limbs just beyond his hungry grasp. The unfaithful Tantalus, thirsty and ravenous, was tortured for eternity by the nearness of water and fruit.

In the 16th century, English speakers took the name *Tantalus* and embraced it as a verb: *tantalize*. Those who are tantalized are tormented with desirable but unreachable hopes, as was the ancient, hapless king.

Tattoo

In 1768–71, Captain James Cook and his crew navigated the British ship *Endeavour* on a historic exploratory voyage throughout the South Seas. With a team of astronomers on board, Cook's mission was to record the movement of the planet Venus as viewed from the newly discovered island of Tahiti. Cook's botanists took note of the island's unique flora, while Cook himself recorded a custom practiced amongst the Tahitians:

> Men and women…inject a black color under their skin, leaving a permanent trace…. Some have…figures of men, birds or dogs; the women generally have the figure Z… on every joint of fingers and toes…or other figures such as circles, crescents, etc. which they have on their arms and legs.

Cook was probably the first European to describe the South Sea art of tattooing, which he spelled *tattowing*. The expedition found the Maoris of New Zealand a fantastically "tattowed" group as well. The elaborate designs of Maori body art have been preserved in the drawings of the *Endeavour*'s artists.

Cook introduced an ancient art and its accompanying terminology to the English-speaking world. His *tattow*, later *tattoo*, comes from the Polynesian verb *ta*, meaning "to strike," a reference to puncturing the skin with a serrated instrument.

TAWDRY

In the 7th century, a baby girl was born to the Anglo-Saxon king and queen of Northumbria, a region situated in what is now northern England. The sovereign pair named their daughter Etheldrida. When she reached adulthood, Etheldrida converted to Christianity and renounced her royal birthright. Instead, she founded an abbey where she devoted her life to good works.

When she became ill years later, Etheldrida attributed the tumor in her throat to the only vanity of her youth, a fondness for elaborate necklaces and beautiful scarves.

The good Etheldrida died in 679, and for hundreds of years thereafter her shrine was a favorite pilgrimage destination. She was ultimately canonized as St. Audrey, a Norman version of Etheldrida.

In tribute to her youthful passion for opulent neckwear, vendors fashioned lovely lace, jewelry, and scarves to sell at her feast day each October 17. Known as St. Audrey's lace (pronounced Sintawdry's lace), this neckwear was prized by the pilgrims.

As the centuries passed, however, the opulent St. Audrey's lace cheapened to gaudy souvenirs. The name of the abbess changed too, from St. Audrey (Sintawdry), ultimately to Tawdry, a word associated with the saint's showy mementos. The resulting word *tawdry* became common amongst English speakers in the 18th century, and we've been using it ever since as a synonym for poor quality or bad taste.

Theodore Roosevelt stands as a colossus amongst U.S. presidents. During his administration (1901–1909), Roosevelt fought for decent hours and fair wages for workers and championed the abolition of child labor. He negotiated the treaty for construction of the Panama Canal in 1903 and was instrumental in passing the Pure Food and Drug Act in 1906. Americans admired Roosevelt for his enthusiasm for adventure; he loved hunting, horseback riding, climbing, and hiking. Affectionately known as "Teddy," he popularized the expressions "Bully!" and "Speak softly and carry a big stick."

This president is responsible for another, perhaps lesser, known linguistic and cultural legacy. The story begins in 1902 when Roosevelt took a bear-hunting trip to Mississippi. Not wanting the president to return to the White House without a trophy, Roosevelt's hosts captured a brown bear cub for him to shoot, but the president couldn't bring himself to fire on the helpless creature.

That gesture impressed the reporters who were traveling with the hunting party. They filed the story, and the following day newspapers across the country were splashed with the account of Roosevelt's compassion toward the bear cub.

Inspired by this tale, a New York candy store owner named Morris Michtom fashioned a small, plush toy he called "Teddy's Bear" and displayed it in his window. This was the prototype of the enduringly popular *teddy bear*, the favorite toy for generations of children around the world.

English speakers on both sides of the Pond embrace the word teetotaler. Since the 1830s, Brits and Americans have been employing this term to refer to someone practicing total abstinence from alcohol. The origin of this expression is uncertain, but several theories have been suggested by word watchers both here and in Europe.

Perhaps the term arose during the many American temperance efforts when converts placed the letter *T* beside their rostered names to signify a pledge of "total" abstinence from spirits.

Another possibility is that teetotalers pledged to drink "tea totally" and nothing stronger. This theory, however convincing, does not explain why the tea in this word is spelled "tee" and not "tea."

The most plausible story about this word's genesis comes from England, where in 1833 temperance advocate Richard Turner is said to have first used this expression at a rally. Turner probably employed the *tee* as a reduplication or emphasis of the first letter in *total*, as in "I am tee-totally opposed to the consumption of spirits!" Indeed, the epitaph on his headstone reads: "Beneath this stone are deposited the remains of Richard Turner, author of the word Teetotal as applied to abstinence from all intoxicating liquors, who departed this life on the 27th day of October, 1846, aged 56 years."

The word *telescope* was invented in 1610 by Prince Cesi, head of the Italian Academy. The prince used his knowledge of Greek to couple the word *tele-*, "far off," and *skopien,* "to look." Galileo, adopting Prince Cesi's new word, was the first to record it in 1611.

Telescope was the prototype of several *tele-* words to come. In 1792, Frenchman Claude Chappe invented a long-distance communication device he called the *telegraph*. The word means literally "far-writing."

A device to transmit sound to a distant point is a *telephone*. This term was coined by Robert Hooke in 1667 and adopted in 1876 by Alexander Graham Bell to denominate his famous invention. *Telephone* means "sound from afar." The *phone* in this word also appears in *phonics* and *microphone*.

Television is the result of a Greek/Latin pairing. Adding the Greek *tele-* to a form of the Latin verb *videre,* "to see," produces a word meaning "far sight, vision." The word was coined in French and borrowed into English in 1907.

The psychologist Frederick Meyers invented the clever word *telepathy,* "far-feeling," in 1882. It refers to communication between minds without using the five recognized senses. The *pathy* element is identical to that in *sympathy, pathetic,* and *empathy*.

TERRA WORDS

The Latin term for "earth, land," *terra,* is the principal player in the formation of *terrain, territory, terra cotta, terrestrial, terra firma, terrier,* and *Mediterranean.*

Some of the world's oldest clay figurines, vases, tiles, and bricks are made of *terra cotta,* reddish or buff-colored fired earthenware. *Terra cotta* means "cooked earth."

Terrestrial pertains to planet Earth as distinct from other worlds; a *terrestrial* creature lives on land. *Extraterrestrial* means "beyond Earth."

Terrain is another term in this linguistic confederation. This word refers to the natural or topographical features of a given parcel of land.

Land under the jurisdiction of a particular nation is a *territory.* It can also be the "native earth" occupied by a specific group of humans or animals.

"Earthen" dishes made for cooking and serving food are *terrines* or *tureens.*

Terra firma is "firm land" and *terra incognito* is "unknown land"—figuratively, uncharted country or an unexamined object.

Terriers are dogs specially bred to tunnel the earth for such *subterranean* nesters as badgers, rats, and foxes. *Terrier* comes from the French *chien terrier,* "earth dog."

Terramycin is the trade name of an antibiotic that has been isolated from a soil mold.

The *Mediterranean* Sea is bound by Africa, Asia, and Europe; this body of water is both literally and etymologically "in the middle of land."

THERMOS

It was initially called a *Dewar's flask* after its inventor. In 1892, Sir James Dewar, a British physicist, constructed an insulated glass container for storing serums and vaccines at constant temperatures. The insulating properties of a Dewar's flask were enhanced by two walls of glass sealing an evacuated chamber. To prevent radiant heat loss, Dewar silvered the inner glass.

He then hired a German glassblower, Reinhold Burger, to fashion these insulated containers. While Dewar's intentions were scientific, Burger's were commercial. Envisioning a popular use for this technology, Burger devised a sturdy metal cylinder to house Dewar's glass container. Further modifications buttressed the flask and prepared it for portability.

In 1903, the glassblower patented this container. In a public contest, Burger offered a cash prize for a novel moniker for this invention. The winning suggestion? *Thermos,* the Greek word for "hot."

This ancient word with the modern application has a complement of linguistic relatives. *Thermostat* means literally "stationary heat," a *thermometer* is etymologically a "heat measure," and *thermodynamics* is the branch of physics dealing with the relationship between heat and other forms of energy.

Thomas

W hy does Tom wear so many hats? *Doubting Thomas; peeping Tom; tomboy; tomcat; Tom, Dick, and Harry.*

The first Tom on record was a doubter. This Thomas was one of the twelve New Testament apostles who refused to believe in the resurrected Christ. After he touched the wounds Christ had suffered on the cross, however, this *doubting Thomas* became a believer.

On the heels of the doubter is the peeper. The naughty tailor who espied the nude Lady Godiva on her Coventry ride, "Peeping Tom" was struck blind for his indiscretion. Today, a *peeping Tom* is a voyeur.

Tom also specifies gender: *tomcat, tom turkey.* Here it connotes maleness, like the word *jack,* a male mule. How, then, can a *tomboy* be a girl? *Tomboy* was once a moniker for a coarse, rude young man, a "boyish boy." The term was later applied, in a spirit of irony, to a boisterous, unfeminine girl.

The triad *Tom, Dick, and Harry* refers to a generic male population. The saying *every Tom, Dick, and Harry* comes from the early 19th century, when these were the most common masculine names.

When the names Thomas and Tom are used as synonyms for "Everyman," they are tinged with deprication. Thomas is the doubter, the peeper, the boyish girl, the fool in *tomfoolery*, and the *tomcatting* male who nightly prowls for action.

American English slang synonyms for "drunk" are too numerous to count. *Sloshed, wrecked, plastered, wasted, liquored up, pickled, embalmed, tanked.* Harold Wentworth and Stuart Flexner, editors of the marvelous *Dictionary of American Slang,* observed that Americans seem to be obsessed with talking about drinking. Each generation invents liquor lingo novelties, while at the same time retaining some of the old classics. One that has weathered quite well is the expression *three sheets to the wind.* Surprisingly, it has nothing to do with bed coverings.

Instead, the phrase comes from the nautical world, where a *sheet* is not a sail, as the landlocked might suppose. A sheet here is the rope or chain attached to the lower corner of a sail. The angle of the sail is determined by extending or shortening the sheet.

When the ropes of a three-sheeted craft are completely extended, the sails flap and flutter in the wind. The craft, out of control, reels like a drunkard, one who is lushed up, stewed, vulcanized, oiled, corked.

In his 1848 novel *Dombey and Son,* Charles Dickens wrote, "Captain Cuttle, looking...at Bunsby more attentively, perceived that he was three sheets in the wind, or in plain words, drunk."

THUG

The Hindi language has contributed a handsome collection of words to American English: *bungalow, bangle, shawl, shampoo, jungle*. These came to American shores with the British, who adopted many native terms during their two-hundred-year occupation of India.

The word *thug* is on the roster of Hindi-based English terms. In our parlance, a *thug* is a thief, ruffian, a beater-up, an assassin.

The Thugs of India were members of a religious sect who performed ritual murders in honor of Kali, the Hindu goddess of violence. Thugs moved in a tightly organized society and spoke in jargon comprehensible to members only. They also terrorized wealthy travelers in northern India for hundreds of years before British colonization. After following a traveling party for several days to evaluate the habits and status of the company, when the time was right, the Thugs moved in, strangled their victims, mutilated the bodies, and divided the spoils amongst themselves.

Flexing their 19th century colonial muscles, the British eliminated the Indian Thugs in the 1830s, hanging 412 of them and imprisoning another 3,000. Though the original Thugs are extinct, their title lives on to designate 21st century thieves and assassins.

The Titans of early Greek tradition were the twelve children of the world's first couple—Gaia the Earth Mother, and Uranus the Sky Father. A family of six sons and six daughters, the Titans were enormous, powerful gods, each personifying a force of nature. Oceanus was the sea god; from his name comes our word *ocean*. The sun god was Hyperion, and two of his Titan sisters, Themis and Rhea, were earth goddesses. Mnemosyne stood alone amongst her siblings as a goddess of a human attribute—memory. Her name is associated with the word *mnemonic,* a device for prompting the memory.

A second generation of Greek Titans included the mighty Atlas, who loaned his name to the *Atlantic* Ocean, the *Atlas* mountains in northern Africa, and the *atlas* as a collection of maps.

Collectively, the Titans symbolized powerful, elemental forces of nature. Their size and near invincibility inspired the adjective *titanic,* applied to anything large, durable, impressive. *Titanic* was, of course, the name given to the colossal, "unsinkable" ocean liner that capsized in the North Atlantic on April 15, 1912. A metallic element used to make light, strong alloys was named *titanium* by German chemist Martin Heinrich, in allusion to the power of the Titans of ancient Greece.

TORPID, TORPEDO

The Latin verb *torpere* means "be numb, stiff, inactive." Its etymological heirs are *torpid* and the *torpedo* that is both sea creature and explosive device.

Torpid is a neglected jewel in the crown of our vocabulary. An adjective, its denotation is "dull, sluggish." Samuel Johnson, 18th century English writer and dictionary editor, served this word well when he wrote, "It is a man's own fault, it is from want of use, if his mind grows torpid in old age."

Torpere gave us *torpedo,* the moniker of the electric ray. These creatures deliver electric charges from each pectoral fin to stun prey and repel predators. The ancients of the Mediterranean world used rays to alleviate the pain of headaches, gout, and tumors. The shocks delivered by the ray when applied to afflicted body parts either distracted the sufferer or cheated the malady by numbing its pain. The creatures' ability to stun and numb earned them the genus name *Torpedo* (family Torpedinidae).

Steamboat inventor Robert Fulton gave the name *torpedo* to the underwater explosive device in the mid-18th century. When detonated, the torpedo missile, like the ray, incapacitates, stuns, or kills its enemy. A slang use of the word glimmered briefly during the Second World War when a *torpedo body* was a woman with a slim, firm figure.

People are sometimes nicknamed for the remarkable color or texture of their hair: *Curly, Rusty, Whitey, Carrot Top.* In addition to the not-so-original *Blondie,* a flaxen-haired individual may be given the moniker *towhead.* But how many people who use the term know what it means?

The *tow* in *towhead* has been a part of the English word-scape since the late 14th century. Through the ages, the term was used by such literary icons as Chaucer, Arthur Conan Doyle, and Mark Twain.

Though it's a homonym and homograph of the *tow* that means "to pull along," it's not related to that verb at all. The "blonde" *tow* is a term from the textile industry. It refers to the stems of flax, jute, or hemp before they are combed and spun. These stems, especially flax, are golden in color; hence the comparison to blonde hair.

The word occasionally turns up in such combinations as *tow-yarn, tow-trousers,* and *tow-string.* What is called a gunny-sack in some regions is known in others as *tow sack.* The *yarn, trousers, string,* and *sack* in these terms indicate that the items are manufactured from fibers of jute, hemp, or flax.

Tractors and Contracts

The Latin term *tractus* is the antecedent of a score of modern English words. Tractus means "to pull." Perhaps the most familiar offspring of this ancient term is *tractor*. This word was put to use in the 18th century to denote a medical device that was "pulled" across the skin to relieve rheumatism. The agricultural motor vehicle was named tractor early in the 1900s.

Attract is etymologically to "draw toward." The *a* in *attract* is a variant of the prefix *ad-*, "to." To subtract is to take away by deducting a quantity. The literal meaning of the word *subtract* is "to draw under."

If your dog is *tractable*, he is docile, teachable, and compliant. This term means "easily drawn along."

Another term in this family is *contract*. This verb literally means "to draw together." It implies a shrinkage of surface parts resulting in a decrease in size. The noun form of *contract* carries a more figurative meaning. A contract draws two or more people together in a legal agreement.

Thanks to the remarkable geometry of the Latin language, the term *tractus*, when combined with still other prefixes, gives us the words *abstract*, *extract*, and *retract*.

TURQUOISE

The beautiful gemstone known to us as *turquoise* has been prized for its ornamental properties in both the ancient and modern worlds. The color of the stone ranges from sky blue to blue-green to green-gray, according to the varying amounts of copper present.

Chalchihuitl was the Aztec word for turquoise. The Aztec incorporated turquoise in their fine mosaics and jewelery. On the other side of the globe, in Egypt, turquoise neckwear and bracelets have been retrieved from the funeral goods of hundreds of tombs.

Egyptian turquoise was most likely imported from the Sinai Peninsula, where a hard-rock mining operation had been active since the 4th millennium B.C. Middle Eastern stone crafters coveted the vivid blue of the gems mined near Nishapur, Iran. In North America, turquoise is mined in New Mexico, California, Arizona, and Nevada.

This gemstone was first introduced into 13th century European markets by way of Turkey. Believing the stone was mined in Turkey, the French called this gem *pierre turqueise,* "Turkish stone," after its marketplace origin. *Turquoise* was first used as a "color adjective" in the 16th century.

TUXEDO

When tobacco baron Pierre Lorillard began construction of this opulent hunting resort in 1885, he named it Tuxedo Park, after the name of a nearby lake. Situated some forty miles north of New York City, Tuxedo Park was outfitted with tennis courts, stables, a fish hatchery, a boathouse, and elegant cottages in which the wealthy and titled might spend a rustic weekend.

In 1886, a young financier from the city named James Potter arrived at the Tuxedo Park dinner table wearing not the requisite swallow-tailed dinner coat, but a shockingly short, tailless jacket. Potter explained that he had seen the Prince of Wales wearing such a jacket in England just months earlier.

Following Potter's fashion example, all male dinner guests at Tuxedo Park soon began sporting copies of this short, informal jacket. It was eventually called the *tuxedo* or *tux* after its place of appearance; within decades, the jacket's popularity eclipsed that of the more formal swallow-tailed dinner coat.

Looking centuries behind the fashionable New York resort and its namesake jacket, etymologists have discovered the source of the word *tuxedo* in the language of the native Lenni-Lenape people, sometimes called the Delaware. In their tongue, the word *p'tuksit* meant "animal with the round foot" and probably insinuated the wolf. This native word, anglicized, became the familiar *tuxedo*.

The Germanic-based element *twi* means "two." It shows up in *twist, twine, twin, twice, twilight, twill, twain,* and *twig,* among others. Hidden in each of these is an etymological code that indicates a pair, or two, of something. *Twin* and *twice* are the most obvious examples.

Twine is *twin* with an *e.* The concept of "two, a pair" is embodied in the notion that joined and wrapped strings produce *twine,* etymologically the "double" string. To *twist* is to interlace two threads, filaments, or strands together. *Twill,* a type of fabric, is so named for the weft thread passing over one and under two threads of the warp, instead of the standard over one, under one.

The word meaning "small branch," *twig,* appears to have affiliation with the rest of the *twi* words. The word suggests a bifurcation, a joint between two branches.

The *twi* element is disguised in the word *between,* which represents an extinct Germanic phrase meaning "by two each." *Betwixt* means approximately the same thing.

The most graceful term of this etymological clan is *twilight,* or "two-light." Twilight occurs just before dawn or after sunset, when one light fades with the coming of another. It's a time when we see both sun and stars, the two sources of light in a liminal sky.

Sometimes word studies can lead us down unexpected pathways. Take, for example, the word *ukulele*. The instrument resembles a small, four-stringed guitar.

We associate ukuleles with Hawaiian music. And the word itself comes, of course, from the Hawaiian language. So far so good. What's odd in this equation, however, is that *ukulele* literally means "leaping flea." How so?

The ukulele was a musical import from Portugal, where the instrument was called the *machete*. Portuguese sailors brought machetes to Hawaii circa 1880.

Enter Englishman Edward Purvis, a British army officer living in Hawaii as a member of the royal Hawaiian court. Purvis took a shine to the Portuguese machete and quickly mastered it.

As the story goes, Purvis was a man of small and nimble stature who played the instrument with great showmanship and verve. Amused by the animated, diminutive Edward Purvis, the Hawaiians began calling him *Ukulele,* the Leaping Flea. The name was eventually transferrèd to the instrument itself. In the early years of the 20th century, when this little guitar made its debut on the American mainland, its new name, *ukulele,* was firmly established.

Umpty

Early in the 20th century, the curious term *umpty* arose, along with its variants *umpteen* and *umpty-umpth*—words to suggest large but indefinite quantities.

Umpteen stands for an unspecified cardinal number from 13 to 19. *Umpty* is any nonspecific number ending in *–ty* from 20 to 90. And *umpty-umpth* is any unspecified ordinal number from 24th to 99th.

But we know *umpty* and its cousins best as general numerical sarcasms, as in "He gave the same speech for the umpteenth time" or "Everyone's heard about Imelda Marcos's umpty-thousand shoes."

How did these curious number terms come to our slang vocabulary? The mighty *Oxford English Dictionary* explains that *umpty* arose in early 20th century British naval parlance; it's a fanciful verbal representation of the Morse code dash. In the 1919 *Sea Lawyer's Log*, we read, "Umpteen or 'umpty,' it should be explained, is to the Navy what x is to Euclid—the symbol of an unknown or unmentionable quality."

UPPER CRUST

People positioned at the apex of society, industry, or politics are the *upper crust* to those of us standing a few rungs below. Though etymologists are unsure of the exact origin of this expression, most concur that the crust in this phrase belongs to a loaf of bread.

The expression may come from earlier centuries in England, where commoners tore chunks of bread from a communal loaf. When dignitaries or nobles were at the dining table, the top of the loaf was carefully sliced off and presented to those of higher rank in a gesture of deference and respect.

Though this phrase may be of considerable antiquity, it was not captured in print in this country until 1835. Thomas Haliburton, in his Sam Slick tales, appears to be the first North American writer to use *upper crust* as a synonym for high society. James Fenimore Cooper used the expression in his 1850 *Ways of the Hour.* In America, the *upper crust* could have alluded to the top of a pie, that portion that advertises the quality of the food before it is bought or tasted.

Upper crust is typical of many references to high economic or social rank. *Upper class, upper circle, upper rank, hightoned, highfalutin,* and *high society* all imply "lofty" status.

VELCRO

Consider the usefulness of the hook-and-loop fastener commonly known as Velcro. It closes backpacks and briefcases, secures pockets, holds disposable diapers on babies, even anchors equipment on NASA's space shuttle. This simple hook-and-loop technology aids us in hundreds of daily tasks.

The product was invented n the 1940s by Swiss engineer George de Mestral, who was inspired by the hooked barbs of the burrs entangled in his dog's fur. Examining the spiny seeds through a microscope, de Mestral became convinced he could create a fastening device by artificially duplicating the burr's construction.

A decade of experimentation led the Swiss inventor to a two-sided fastener: one side covered with burrlike hooks, the other with soft loops to which the hooks adhered.

In 1951, de Mestral applied for a Swiss patent for the product that he christened *Velcro:* the *vel* for *velour,* the looped component of the fastener, and *cro* for *crochet,* French for "hook."

This term is doubly interesting. It is an example of a portmanteau word, a blending parts of two terms formed into one. (Other examples are *snort* and *chuckle* into *chortle,* and *motor* and *hotel* into motel.)

The second notable feature of the word is its sudden popularity. Not yet a century old, the word *Velcro* (which today is also the name of the company producing the fastener) is known around the globe.

Since first arriving on the American wordscape in the late 19th century, the expression *well-heeled* has meant "financially comfortable." Though lexicographers have been able to assign a date to its printed appearance, the origin of this cliché is uncertain. Two possiblities have been offered.

One has the expression coming from the cockfighting arenas of 18th and 19th century America, where artificial spurs were attached to the "heels" of the birds. The winner of the cockfight was declared to have been effectively outfitted, or *well-heeled*. This scenario provided the metaphor for a man who was amply equipped with protective weapons to assist him in a fight. By 1880, the expression referred to the cash that bought protection from the intangible adversaries of poverty or hunger.

Theory number two holds that the heels in this phrase belong to the shoes of a man who could afford the cobbler's maintenance bill. This explanation of *well-heeled* provides the antithesis of *down at the heels*, an expression of much older vintage. The latter, meaning "shabby, needy," refers to one who is unable to afford new or repaired shoes. *Down at the heels* appeared in print in England in the early 18th century.

Old-timers of every era shake their heads at the folly and irreverence of youth. They all have the same complaint: those young *whipper-snappers* don't show a lot of respect these days. But most old-timers were once considered whipper-snappers by the old-timers before them, and so it has been for generations.

The word *whipper-snapper,* meaning "young tough, hoodlum," has been around since the 17th century. A 1674 citation in the *Oxford English Dictionary* says, "Have a care of Marlbrough downs, there are a parcel of whipper Snappers have been very busie there of late." Another from 1827: "A whipper-snapper of an attorney's apprentice.... I'll teach him to speak with more reverence of the learned professions."

Whipper-snapper is probably based on the 16th century term *whipster,* a "cracker of whips," an animated, mischievous or violent person. The 1811 *Dictionary of the Vulgar Tongue* says a whipster is a "sharp or subtle fellow."

The formation *whipper-snapper,* in turn, was likely modeled after the earlier *snipper-snapper,* a term reserved for a small, self-important, conceited young man. John Ford, in his 1638 *The Fancies, Chast and Noble,* wrote, "Thou'rt a prick-eared foist...a knack, a snipper-snapper!"

Both *whipper-snapper* and *snipper-snapper* are examples of reduplications, pairs of words that rhyme or repeat a basic syllable or sound. Reduplication is a verbal attempt to deflate pomposity, often signifying contempt, mockery, or derision.

Attics, basements, closets, and storerooms across America are full of *white elephants*—possessions too unwieldy, too unpopular, too ugly to give away, but perhaps too valuable to sell. So we store them or move them with us, decade after decade. Why elephants? Why white?

The expression comes from a long-standing legend out of Siam, before that country was renamed Thailand. Siamese royalty demanded that all the rare albino elephants born in the kingdom were the sacred property of the king. Not one of these beasts could be ridden or destroyed without royal permission.

Occasionally, the king would bestow the gift of a white elephant upon one of his subjects or courtiers. Though the beast was sacred, the albino pachyderm was never received joyously. Its arrival meant the recipient had gravely displeased the king. Because the elephant could not be ridden, put to work, sold, or given away, the courtier was forced to stable the creature until its natural death. The feeding and care of the white elephant spelled financial ruin for its unhappy recipient.

By the 17th century the legend of the rare and ruinous albino became known in England, and by the 19th century the expression *white elephant* was extended metaphorically to any undesirable object.

In the beginning was the "length-of-fabric" theory. Next came the "cement-mixer truck" proposition. Then, behold, someone suggested the "yardarm" possibility. Meanwhile, the "machine gun ammunition belt" theory begged for attention.

These are suggested explanations for the origin of our expression *the whole nine yards.* Every native speaker knows this favorite American cliché but, ironically, no one has substantiated its birthplace. Since its initial printed appearance in the 1960s, word watchers everywhere have been seeking its source. Let's flesh out the theories mentioned above.

Some claim this cliché refers to the capacity of a cement truck—nine full cubic yards. Someone with a major construction project was said to have used that much material.

Others prefer the military version: machine-gun ammunition belts in fighter planes of the Second World War were nine yards long. Targets of these fighters were said to have gotten *the whole nine yards* of ammo.

The length-of-fabric theory suggests that a full nine yards of fabric was at one time the proper length out of which to construct a burial shroud, wedding dress, or three-piece suit.

Other wordsmiths claim the origin lies in the maritime trade, with the yards in this expression actually yardarms, spans that held a vessel's sails. Since each mast of a three-masted sailing ship carried three yardarms, a ship sailing with the whole nine yardarms, or yards, was fully operational.

Wimp, Sissy

American English is splendidly outfitted with slanderous terms for cowardly, indecisive weaklings: *wimp, sissy, namby-pamby, wussy,* and *milquetoast.* Let's examine the first two in this list of scurrilous insults—*wimp* and *sissy.*

Wimp is probably a truncation of *whimper,* a sound we consider cowardly. Amongst England's early 20th century undergrads at Cambridge and Oxford, a *wimp* was a very young woman, possibly because young men of that era considered girls weak and "whimpery."

The cartoon character Wimpy, Popeye's hamburger-loving friend, reinforced the term in the United States. *Wimp* and *wimpy* weathered the 20th century well, appearing in such mainstream publications as the *New York Times,* the *Boston Globe,* and the *New Yorker.* We've pressed this term into further service in the phrase *wimp out,* meaning to renege on a promise or to claim weakness as the reason for not completing a task.

Originally an affectionate nickname for a sister, *sissy* was an insult by the late 19th century. It became a mocking name for a boy who "acted like a girl" or who was considered a weakling or a coward. *Sissy* eventually lived long enough to serve as an insult for homosexual males, especially in the slightly altered form *sissy-boy.*

WINDFALL

For centuries, English speakers have used the term *windfall* in reference to unexpected good fortune or the sudden acquisition of a substantial sum of money. There is a literal "falling" behind this expression, but exactly what it is that falls depends upon the historical version of the story you prefer.

The *windfall* could refer generically to branches or trees blown down in a storm, yielding a ready source of firewood for a hearth or cooking stove.

It may be the fallen produce of a lord's fruit trees in the England of centuries past. The hanging fruit belonged to the estate, but peasants were allowed to gather and keep the wind-fallen produce for their own consumption.

According to another version, wealthy English landowners themselves gathered their own fortunate windfalls. Though English estates contained acres of forestland, the trees thereon were by law reserved for the Royal Navy for shipbuilding. Any oaks toppled by a storm, however, belonged to the manor lords to use at their own discretion.

For over a century now, Americans have been reciting *Don't take any wooden nickels* as an affectionate way of saying "Goodbye, and don't do anything stupid."

Since few are gullible enough to accept wooden currency, what generated this popular expression?

Several unsubstantiated theories surround the origin of this caveat. One suggests that the phrase may have arisen from wooden centennial tokens used as currency during a celebration, but which became worthless when the event was over.

Etymologist Stuart Berg Flexner, in his word book *Listening to America,* writes, "The wooden nickels in this expression are probably a humorous reference to the...counterfeit items said to have been sold to rustics by conniving Yankee peddlers [such as] wooden nutmegs, wooden cucumber seeds, and even wooden hams."

Some word watchers say that *Don't take any wooden nickels* replaced the earlier *Don't take any wooden nutmegs,* citing vignettes like this one from the 1850s: A Yankee trader salted bags of authentic nutmeg seeds with wooden imitations, each costing a penny to manufacture. Charging four cents for each seed in the bag, authentic or not, the unscrupulous trader made a handsome profit with the wooden nutmegs.

WORDS FROM THE SIXTIES

The decade of the 1960s set itself apart from its antecedents in scores of radical ways, marked as it was with lunar contact, student protests of war, sexual liberation, burgeoning television communication, and waxing and waning hemlines. American English enthusiastically rushed in to describe the new styles, attitudes, and technologies that hallmarked that decade.

The prefix *mini-* was wildly popular during the sixties. Abbreviated from *miniature,* a word of Latin origin, *mini-* was promiscuously attached to nouns of all types, giving us terms like *mini-budget, minibike,* and *miniskirt.* Later in the decade, the prefixes *midi-* and *maxi-* followed, reflecting falling hemlines.

In the late sixties, the prefix *eco-* became popular with the rise in concern over environmental issues. Some of the earliest recorded words containing this prefix were *eco-activist, ecocide,* and *ecofreak.*

By the sixties, baby boom children were experimenting with music and dance, both domestic and exotic. Some musical and dance terms introduced to American English in the sixties were *acid rock, reggae, ska, easy listening,* and *bossa nova,* the last being Portuguese slang for "new flair."

Though computer science was in its adolescence in the sixties, some of our most widely recognized computer terms were invented in that decade: *mouse, byte, cursor, software,* and the acronyms ASCII and BASIC.

In a darkened laboratory at the University of Würzburg, German physics professor Wilhelm Röntgen made some discoveries that would forever change the face of science and medicine. On November 8, 1895, the fifty-year old Röntgen was conducting experiments with the discharge of electrical current in vacuum tubes. When he observed that radiation from the tube penetrated the black cardboard that surrounded it, causing a nearby fluorescent screen to glow, the astonished Röntgen knew he had discovered something unusual.

In further experiments conducted throughout the next few days, Röntgen observed that this radiation passed through metal, wood, and even the flesh of his own hand, which created the outline of his bones on the fluorescent screen. In answer to a friend's query about the nature of his experiments, Röntgen said, "I have discovered something interesting, but I do not know whether or not my observations are correct." Because he did not understand the nature of this radiation, he called it *X-strahl,* which translates to the English *x-ray.*

In naming his discovery, the scientist Röntgen used the universal symbol for an unknown quantity, *x,* a tradition introduced by the 17th century mathematician Rene Descartes. X-rays are sometimes eponymously called *roentgen rays;* a *roentgen* is a unit of measurement of radiation.

The Greek-based prefix *xeno-* means "strange" or "foreign." This element engendered several engaging modern English words.

Perhaps the most familiar member in the *xeno* family is *xenophobia,* a fear of the cultures, customs, and languages of foreigners. Of recent vintage, *xenophobia* was recorded in print for the first time circa 1912.

Xenophobia has an antonym, *xenophilia.* A *xenophile* seeks out and embraces exotic foods and clothing and appreciates foreign languages.

The word *xenia* means "gifts for foreigners." *Xenia* were presents given to strangers and guests passing through Greek and Latin strongholds. In the England of the Middle Ages, xenia were delicacies from local kitchens given to traveling princes as they visited their far-flung estates.

The magical or unexplained acquisition and mastery of a foreign language is *xenoglossia.* A true *xenogloss* speaks a tongue he has never studied or even necessarily heard. (The *gloss* portion of this term comes from the Greek word for "tongue" and is related to *epiglottis* and *glossary.*)

A *xeno-* word adopted by geologists is *xenolith.* This means "foreign rock" and refers to a rock fragment or intrusion alien to the igneous mass in which it is found.

The Greek surname *Xenakis* was, in ancient times, bestowed upon a foreigner or a newcomer to a locality.

Dispute surrounds the origin of the word *Yankee.* For the past two centuries, writers, historians, and word scholars have proposed various etymologies for the word, but none of these has been authenticated.

The word was first recorded in a letter written by the British general James Wolfe in 1758. Commanding local soldiers during the French and Indian War, Wolfe called his American troops *Yankees,* adding, "They are the dirtiest, most contemptible cowardly dogs you can conceive." In 1775, British soldiers applied the word *Yankee,* as a term of insult, to the citizens of Boston.

By the late 18th century, Americans began proudly to call themselves Yankees; during the American Civil War, a Yankee was a northerner.

Some insist that the name arose from East Coast Indians' attempts to pronounce the word *English,* yielding such constructions as *Yengees* and *Yinglees.* Or, perhaps *Yankee* has its origins in Scotland, where a *yankie* was a sharp, clever, forward woman.

Since the Dutch were amongst the earliest settlers in the New World, some propose that *Yankee* comes from the nickname *Jantje,* a diminutive of the common Dutch name Jan. By far the most plausible assertion makes Yankee a variant of *Jan Kaas,* meaning "John Cheese," a disparaging nickname given to early Dutch immigrants.

Bibliography

Ammer, Christine

1989   *Fighting Words.* NTC Publishing Group, Chicago.
1993   *Have A Nice Day—No Problem!: A Dictionary of Clichés.* Plume Books, New York.

Ayto, John

1991   *Dictionary of Word Origins.* Arcade, New York.
1994   *A Gourmet's Guide: Food and Drink from A to Z.* Oxford University Press, Oxford.
1999   *20th Century Words.* Oxford University Press, Oxford.

Barnhart, Robert K., and Sol Steinmetz, editors

1988   *The Barnhart Dictionary of Etymology.* H.W. Wilson, New York.

Bryson, Bill

1995   *Made in America: An Informal History of the English Language in the United States,* Vol. 1. William Morrow, New York.

Byrne, Josefa Heifetz

1974   *Mrs. Byrne's Dictionary of Unusual, Obscure, and Preposterous Words.* University Books, Secaucus, NJ.

Cassidy, Frederick S., Joan H. Hall, et al., editors

1985–   *Dictionary of American Regional English.* 4 vols., continuing. Harvard University Press, Cambridge, MA.

Ciardi, John

1987   *Good Words to You: An All New Dictionary and Native's Guide to the Unknown.* HarperCollins, New York.

Claiborne, Robert

1983   *Our Marvelous Native Tongue: The Life and Times of the English Language.* Times Books, New York.
1989   *The Roots of English.* Crown Publishing, New York.

Collings, Rex

1993   *A Crash of Rhinoceroses: A Dictionary of Collective Nouns.*
        Asphodel Press, Kingston, RI.

Crystal, David

1995   *The Cambridge Encyclopedia of the English Language.*
        Cambridge University Press, Oxford.

1993   *An Encyclopedic Dictionary of Language and Languages.*
        Blackwell Publishers, Oxford.

Dalzell, Tom

1996   *Flappers 2 Rappers: American Youth Slang.* Merriam-
        Webster, Springfield, MA.

Davies, Peter, editor

1983   *Success with Words: A Guide to the American Language.*
        Random House, New York.

Dickson, Paul, with Paul McCarthy and Julie Rubenstein, editors

1994   *War Slang: American Fighting Words and Phrases from the
        Civil War to the Gulf War.* Simon and Schuster, New
        York.

Flavell, Linda and Roger

2000   *The Chronology of Words and Phrases: A Thousand Years in
        the History of English.* Kyle Cathie, London.

Flexner, Stuart Berg

1982   *Listening to America.* Simon and Schuster, New York.

Flexner, Stuart Berg, and Anne H. Soukhanov

1997   *Speaking Freely: A Guided Tour of American English from
        Plymouth Rock to Silicon Valley.* Oxford University Press,
        New York.

Freeman, Morton S., and Edwin Newman

1993   *Hue and Cry and Humble Pie: The Stories Behind the Words.*
        Plume Books, New York.

Funk, Charles Earle

1985   *A Hog on Ice and Other Curious Expressions.*
        HarperColllins, New York.

1985   *Thereby Hangs a Tale: Stories of Curious Word Origins.*
        HarperCollins, New York.

1986   *Heavens to Betsy! and Other Curious Sayings.* Perennial
         Library, New York.

Funk, Wilfred
1978   *Word Origins and Their Romantic Stories.* Bell Publishing,
         New York.

Gelbert, Doug
1996   *So Who the Heck Was Oscar Mayer? The Real People Behind
         Those Brand Names.* Barricade Books, New York.

Goldin, Hyman E., editor
1950   *Dictionary of American Underground Lingo.* Twayne, New
         York.

Grimal, Pierre, and Stephen Kershaw
1991   *The Penguin Dictionary of Classical Mythology.* Penguin
         Books, London.

Hanks, Patrick, and Flavia Hodges
1989   *A Dictionary of Surnames.* Oxford University Press,
         Oxford.

Hendrickson, Robert
1987   *The Facts on File Encyclopedia of Word and Phrase Origins.*
         Facts on File, New York. Republished as *Henry
         Encyclopedia of Word and Phrase Origins.* Holt, New York,
         1990.

Hirsch, E. D., Jr., Joseph F. Kett, and James Trefil
1988   *The Dictionary of Cultural Literacy.* Houghton Mifflin,
         Boston.

Jones, Harold W., editor
1949   *Blakiston's New Gould Medical Dictionary.* Blakiston, New
         York.

Kacirk, Jeffrey
2000   *The Word Museum: The Most Remarkable English Words
         Ever Forgotten.* Touchstone Books, New York.

Kohl, Herbert
1992   *From Archetype to Zeitgeist: An Essential Guide to Powerful
         Ideas.* Little, Brown, Boston.

Landau, Sidney I.
2001   *Dictionaries: The Art and Craft of Lexicography.* Cambridge
         University Press, New York.

Lighter, Jonathan E., J. Ball, J. O'Connor, and Jesse Sheidlower,
editors
1994-97 *Random House Historical Dictionary of American Slang.*
         2 vols. Random House, New York.

Mackay, Charles
1969   *The Lost Beauties of the English Language: An Appeal to
         Authors, Poets, Clergymen, and Public Speakers.* Arno Press,
         New York.

McCrum, Robert, Robert MacNeil, and William Cran
1986   *The Story of English.* Viking, New York.

McQuain, Jeffrey
1999   *Never Enough Words: How Americans Invented a Language as
         Ingenious, Ornery and Resourceful as Themselves.* Random
         House, New York.

Merriam-Webster
1989   *Webster's Word Histories.* Merriam-Webster, Springfield,
         MA.

Mills, Jane
1992   *Womanwords: A Dictionary of Words About Women.* Free
         Press, New York.

Morris, Evan
2000   *The Word Detective: Solving the Mysteries behind those Pesky
         Words and Phrases.* Algonquin Books. Chapel Hill, NC.

Morris, William, and Mary D. Morris
1988   *Morris Dictionary of Word and Phrase Origins,* 2d edition.
         HarperInformation, New York.

Palmatier, Robert A., and Harold L. Ray, editors
1989   *Sports Talk: A Dictionary of Sports Metaphors.* Greenwood,
         Westport, CT.

Panati, Charles
1989   *Panati's Extraordianry Origins of Everyday Things.*
         HarperCollins, New York.

Randall, Bernice
1991   *When Is a Pig a Hog? A Guide to Confoundingly Related English Words.* Prentice Hall, New York.

Rawson, Hugh
1981   *A Dictionary of Euphemisms and Other Double Talk.* Crown Publishing, New York.
1989   *Wicked Words.* Crown Publishing Group, New York.

Rees, Nigel
1999   *The Cassell Dictionary of Word and Phrase Origins.* Cassell, London.

Rheingold, Howard
1988   *They Have a Word for It: A Lighthearted Lexicon of Untranslatable Words and Phrases.* Jeremy P. Tarcher, Los Angeles.

Rogers, James
1985   *The Dictionary of Cliches.* Facts on File, New York.

Room, Adrian
1999   *The Cassell Dictionary of Word Histories.* Cassell, London.

Schwab, Gustav
1977   *Gods and Heroes: Myths and Epics of Ancient Greece.* Pantheon Books, New York.

Simpson, John, and Edmund Weiner, editors
1989   *The Oxford English Dictionary,* 2d edition. Oxford University Press, Oxford.

Sorel, Nancy Caldwell
1970   *Word People.* American Heritage Press, New York.

Soukhanov, Anne H.
1995   *Word Watch: The Stories Behind the Words of Our Lives.* Henry Holt, New York.

Sperling, Susan Kelz
1982   *Tenderfeet and Ladyfingers.* Penguin Books, New York.

Tannahill, Reay
1989   *Food in History.* Crown Publishing, New York.

Tuleja, Tad

1990   *Marvelous Monikers: The People Behind More Than 400 Words and Expressions.* Harmony Books, New York.

Urdang, Laurence

1989   *The Dictionary of Confusable Words.* Ballantine Books, New York.

Vanoni, Marvin

1990   *I've Got Goose Pimples: And Other Great Expressions.* William Morrow, New York.

Webber, Elizabeth, and Mike Feinsilber

1999   *Merriam-Webster's Dictionary of Allusions.* Merriam-Webster, Springfield, MA.

Wells, Diana

2001   *100 Birds and How They Got Their Names.* Algonquin Books, Chapel Hill, NC.

Wentworth, Harold, and S. B. Flexner, editors

1960   *Dictionary of American Slang.* Thomas Y. Crowell, New York.

White, Robert J.

1994   *An Avalanche of Anoraks: For People Who Speak Foreign Languages Every Day—Whether They Know It Or Not.* Crown Publishing, New York.

Winchester, Simon

1998   *The Professor and the Madman: A Tale of Murder, Insanity, and the Making of the Oxford English Dictionary.* HarperCollins, New York.

Index

f

fabulous 323
faggot 116
fallopian 114
fantastic 323
fascinate 204
fatuous 204
feckless 203
fefnicute 229
Fido 18
fin 225
flagrant 71
flapper 119
flash in the pan 120
flattery 121
flotsam and jetsam 122
fluent, fluid 124
fluke 125
fly off the handle 126
fornicate 129
foundations 14
frillies 14
frisbee 130
Frog 80
fudge 132
fuzz 91

g

gabo 90
gaderine haste 133
gadget 252
galvanize 202
gambol 134
gambrel 134
gams 134
Garlic Snapper 80
gauche 196
gee whiz, gee willikers 324
geranium 123
geyser 137
gimlet 138

gingham 212
glitch 135
go bananas 23
gobbledygook 139
God's in his heaven 140
golly 324
gomer 141
gong 212
goodbye 117
good egg 109
goody two shoes 142
Gorton 92
gosh 324
graham cracker 110
grapevine 143
green-apple quickstep 144
green-broke 144
greenhorn 144
greenies 144
greenware 144
green wood joint 144
groovy 145
grotesque 146
grotty 146
grub, grubby 147
guinea football 90
gum 148
gumshoe 148
gung-ho 64
gun moll 91
guppy 149
Gypsy 150

h

hack 151
halcyon days 152
hallmark 29
ham 153
hamfisted 153
have a nice day 154
haywire 155
heart of gold 156

Klempner 136
knock around broad 91
knock on wood 193
kowtow 64
Kraut 80

l

laconic 194
laurel 123
lay an egg, lay a duck's egg 109
learn by heart 156
left 196
left-handed 197
leg 14
lemon 198
let the cat out of the bag 199
Levi's 200
limb 14
Limey 80
Listerine 202
livid 73
loafer 135
loony 207
Luddite 205
ludicrous 206
lunatic 207
lush diver 90

m

mad hatter 213
magazine 208
magpie 210
main drag 102
make a kisser 91
malacocermous 230
malaria 211
mama bull 91
manuscript 304
march hare 213
margarine 214

marionette 284
maroon 215
Mary Magdalene 90
masochism 216
maudlin 217
mausoleum 218
maxi- 356
mediocre 219
Mediterranean Sea 333
melba toast 110
mellow 220
mentor 221
meteorite, meteoroid 72
microcosm 76
midi- 356
midwife 222
mini- 356
mint 224
mitt-glom 91
mnemonic 338
modesty 72
molar 15
moll whiz 91
money 224
money-grubber 147
moron 226
morphine 227
mortling 229
motel 20
Mount Rushmore 299
moxie 228
Ms. 231
mud in your eye 232
muggles 90
muscle 15
Muse, museum 233
music 233

n

nano- 234
nanoid, nanism 234

narcissism 235
Neanderthal 236
nebula, nebulous 237
nectar, nectarine 238
Necropolis 238
necrophilia, necrophobia 238
negligee 239
neo- 240
nerd 241
nether garment 14
Neubauer 136
Newcomb 92
newfangled 242
Newman 92
night on the rainbow 90
nimrod 243
noctivagation 230
nonplused 260
Novak 92
nylon 245

o

ob- 246
obstetric 222
odyssey 247
off the wall 248
OK 249
oligo- 250
on the Fritz 28
on the hypestick 91
on the light artillery 91
orangutan 212
ordinary 256
orient, Oriental 255
ornery 256
Oscar 257
oubliette 229
Ouija board 258
out of whack 259
overwhelm 260
owl 253

oxymoron 261

p

Pacific Ocean 209
pack horse 91
paint the town red 262
pajamas 165
paleomnesia 230
palilalia 229
palisade 30
pandemic 88
pan flute 263
panic 263
pan-pipe 325
pansey 123
pantry 44
para- 264
paradiastole 230
paradise 269
parasol 128
passion 204
pasteurize 202
Patagonia 209
patella 15
peanut 266
pedigree 77, 267
peeping Tom 335
peony 268
pettycoat's peeping 14
phalange 15
Philip 167
physique 14
pica 210
pictograph 270
pipe dream 254
pip-pip 117
pizzazz 271
plant 272
plantar 272
play possum 16
play with the squirrels 91